THE
SAINT

THE
SAINT

My Autobiography

IAN ST JOHN

with James Lawton

HODDER &
STOUGHTON

For Betsy, my greatest team-mate

CONTENTS

ACKNOWLEDGEMENTS

Thanks to my publisher Roddy Bloomfield, for insisting I still had a story to tell, and special thanks to James Lawton, who spent countless enjoyable hours with me recording my thoughts and then so expertly putting them down in good order. I'm also grateful to the patient, excellent editing of Marion Paull.

PHOTOGRAPHIC ACKNOWLEDGEMENTS

The author and publisher would like to thank the following for permission to reproduce photographs:

Colorsport/Andrew Cowie, Empics, L'Equipe/Offside, Ian Joy Photographic, LWT, Mirrorpix, Popperfoto.com, Radio Times, SNS Group/George Ashton.

All other photographs are from private collections.

PROLOGUE

A STATUE that you see often can blend into the background in the landscape of your life. Maybe you notice the bird droppings, or occasionally a touch of sunlight might bring the subject flickering back to life. Strange, then, that not so long ago I found myself standing alone behind the Kop at Liverpool's football ground, gazing intently at the bronze image of Bill Shankly, the legendary figure who for me will always be flesh and blood, always human to a fault.

Conflicting emotions rise to the surface when I think of him. I'm torn between love and hate, admiration and, sometimes, let me be honest, at least a little anger and disillusionment. That part of the account of my life is about me and my reactions as much as Shankly, and if you read my version of our relationship, it is for you to distribute blame wherever you might.

The point here is that on that day at the Kop I wasn't looking at *my* Shankly, *my* patron, the arbiter of all my hopes for ten years of the prime of my life, but the one who was imprinted so deeply on the wider consciousness of football and who was so adored by the people of Liverpool. I focused on the inscription – 'He made the people happy.'

'Aye, he did that,' I thought. The reflection was edged with more than a little bitterness because I had just seen my old team, his old team, play in a way that betrayed all the best of what Bill Shankly had stood for all those years. The Liverpool of Shankly played with passion, creativity and tremendous panache. The team of Gerard Houllier that I had just watched amounted to the very antithesis of that. I had looked at the terraces and, most keenly, the Kop. There was silence. It was as though Anfield was filled not with the most animated and humorous fans in football but zombies.

It might be said that I waged a vendetta against Houllier, at least as much as I could after the passing of those days when I appeared regularly on national television, and there is a degree of truth in that, but only in the sense that I believed Liverpool would never reclaim their place as a major force in football as long as he was in charge. Houllier hated the criticism from former Liverpool players, and he singled me out as one of his arch prosecutors, but that doesn't trouble me for a second. I knew my club and I knew what it should represent and now that Houllier is gone, with several millions of pounds of compensation, and Liverpool under the new man Rafael Benitez have won their fifth European Cup, I believe that a genuine linkage with the past has been recreated.

I do not say that Benitez, despite his extraordinary achievement in such a brief time at Anfield, is necessarily a messiah of Shankly's force, but I do see him as a genuine football man. He knows how to communicate with his players and the people, and heaven knows, he has pleased the fans. If it is true, as Benitez says, that the current Liverpool team is far from a finished product, it is certainly a side that is attempting to play football that I recognise, with commitment and flair. At its heart is Jamie Carragher, a local boy whom I believe represents all the best values of the club. For me, a part of my life, the core of my achievement as a football player, has been restored, if not wholly, if not as fresh and assured as it was when Shankly was roaring through the sixties, with genuine hope for the future.

Houllier killed such hope. He played doomsday football. At one point in our publicly conducted dispute, Houllier insulted me profoundly. He dismissed my views, sneered at my involvement in football after I was detached from the red shirt of Liverpool, and when he did this, he contributed to the mood that provoked me to write this book. I'm at least grateful to him for that because in the process I've been forced into reappraisals of my life and footballing experiences that in the normal way are, if not avoided, maybe in some subliminal way shelved.

One great benefit of such re-examination is that you are reminded of how many reasons you have for marvelling at your own good luck in doing something for a living that so many others see as a dream, a fantasy. Of course, you encounter some pain and disappointment, and you find reasons for reproach as well as celebration, but what you have in the end is bone-deep gratitude for all the experiences you have had and all the people who have helped you get through the days. Those who have helped me, and in some cases hindered, find their way on to the following pages and I can only say that I have tried to render an honest account of how it was to graduate from a tenement in Motherwell to a life that, in the end, was beyond the imaginings of a young boy who lost his father at a time when he needed him most and for whom, for quite some time, the borders of life threatened to be no wider than the shadows of a factory.

Betsy, whom I met when I was a teenager, has been at my side ever since we first danced to the music of Buddy Holly. We married early against pressure from my family and my football manager, but that was the best single decision of my life. She told me, when our first child, Elaine, was a babe in arms, that there was a great big world out there beyond the borders of Scotland and I owed it to myself to go out there and experience it. From that firm, unshakeable declaration everything else has flowed —

the Liverpool years under the spell of the man remembered in bronze beside the Kop, the flow and the ebbing of my managerial career, the time when 'The Saint and Greavsie' commanded a national television audience, and now the mature reflection that if there has been pain amid the joy, crushing disappointments to go along with all those moments of pure, adrenaline-soaked exhilaration, the journey has never lacked for riches, at least of a certain kind.

I have a good wife and children, Ian and Elaine, three grandsons, one of whom is named Alex James St John – no pressure there, then – a delightful granddaughter, more friends than I probably deserve, and a golf game that can still on the odd occasion stir some of the old competitive juice. It is also true that Liverpool are champions of Europe, so maybe this is not too bad a time to tell my story. Certain old truths are back in place, something I will no doubt remember the next time I pass the bronze figure that stands at the back of the Kop.

1
MOTHERWELL CHILDHOOD

THEY put my father Alex on a stretcher, wrapped him in a red blanket and carried him down the stairway of the tenement. It was quite awkward getting him into the hall. I was crying loudly and grabbing at him while my mother Helen, surrounded by my brother and sisters, wept silently. Then they took him off in the ambulance and I never saw him again. I was six years old.

Not until many years later, when one of my sisters produced a picture of him in his football gear, eyes bright and full of running, could I even look at a photograph. In those days you didn't see too many family albums lying around the tenements. You couldn't pop into the corner shop and say, 'Give us one of those wee photikits, hen.' By the time I got to see him in those unknown colours he had become a stranger; he was just that distant guy on the stretcher, coughing, beaten. I would never forget the blanket, though. It was such a vivid splash of colour in the gloomy old building and, who knows, that may have been the inspiration, buried deep in my memory, for my suggestion that my club, Liverpool, should adopt their famous all-red strip. I argued with great conviction that it would have tremendous impact.

The death certificate said pleurisy and pneumonia, but they weren't the only causes of my father's death. I may have been a distraught little kid but I knew that well enough. My father was thirty-six and worn out from the steelworks and the poor diet and the freezebox living quarters and one too many cruel winters when he was taken away from his wife and six children. Later, I wondered if he ever saw the irony that as a Scottish Protestant he had always voted Conservative, but then what had politics to do with anything?

He didn't go to the war, he was needed in the steelworks down the street. Most of the men worked there, or in the pits, and most of them had chest problems. It was simply that my father didn't have the strength to drag his into old age. It was bang – and he was gone. Another irony – football would give me my life but it also helped to take away my father. The day before he collapsed he had taken me up to Fir Park to watch Motherwell. We got soaked to hell. Even now, all these years later, I get a spurt of anger when I think of it. We had tried to shelter under some ramshackled steel erection, but the rain poured in. Why did football take nearly a hundred years, and all those massive gate receipts, before it considered building decent stadiums?

Of course, it took a lot of tragedy. You still have to shudder when you think of those old images of Ibrox Park, Parkhead and Hampden, the great crush of people standing in the open, in discomfort and danger. People died at Ibrox when Rangers scored a late goal and departing fans rushed back up the bank. Football said it was misadventure. It wasn't that. It was total neglect, and it would stretch out for so long, all the way to Heysel and Hillsborough.

No, I don't heap all the blame on football for the loss of my father; a lot more went into it than one cold, wet afternoon in Motherwell. A few steel barons and a lot of malignant social engineering have to be thrown in. It is no doubt also true that my father's generation of working men, like so many that went before them, made their own contribution to the hopelessness.

When he had a few coins in his pocket, my father would go to the pub with his mates at the end of his shift, and they would drink until they put the towels up at 9 p.m. which was the time that the pubs closed in those days. I have one little flashback of him coming home well bevvied around 9.30 and my kid brother Billy and me, in the bed whispering that it was a good job we didn't have more space in the flat because then he could really fall down. As it was he tripped up over a washing basket. He finished up in the basket with clothes and pegs all over the floor. Such an incident wasn't a common event in our house, as it undoubtedly was in many. My father was a hard-working man and he accepted his responsibilities, but occasionally he slipped. Looking back, it's not so hard to understand.

My father's death left me with a morbid fear that I might not live to the age of thirty-six. It never left me, even when I was brimming with health on the football field. However, it was something that could not be dwelt on in our new life as my mother, one of the latest members of that swelling band of Scottish widows as the Second World War drew to a close, fought to keep food on the table. I might not make it beyond my thirty-sixth year, but in the meantime what could I do? I had to get up in the morning, however tough a job it seemed on occasions, and I had to get through the day. I did what I could to help and I never felt harshly treated. Didn't everyone have to battle for their lives?

My mother certainly fought superbly in the great effort to keep us fed and clothed. In the dusk, as we played in the street, her cries for her brood to come up to supper were widely mimicked. In sing-song tones the other kids repeated her litany of 'Sheena . . . Wilma . . . Ian . . . Billy . . . May . . . Ellen.' Our building stood on the corner of Park and Scott Streets in Motherwell. Scott Street had a Catholic church, two Catholic schools and a non-sectarian Co-op. I got a job at the Co-op, riding the horse-drawn cart delivering the milk and bread rolls. On some mornings, as a great bonus, I was given some bread rolls to take home.

I remember those mornings as always being viciously cold. In winter, the cold took over. With no heating in the buildings, we had to scavenge for something to burn in the smoky fireplace – old shoes, rubbish, anything we could lay our hands on. Getting up in the morning was the recurring ordeal. You slid your clothes into the bed and dressed under the covers. Then you got up your nerve and jumped out of bed.

When I was old enough, I graduated to a paper round, read the sports pages and tipped up the money, giving it to my mother as soon as I had been paid. I did my best for my mother and the other kids but I do carry one twinge of guilt from those days. My mother went out cleaning. She did two houses, including a big one that belonged to a doctor, and when she'd finished those she came to our school to clean three classrooms. When school was over we went to help her. She worked so hard to eke out her widow's pension and now when I look back I'm astonished by her toughness and her lack of complaint. That's when I feel that little remorse. My mother did like a cigarette and several times I complained when she sent me to the shop to buy a packet of Woodbines or Capstan or Craven A. Sometimes she couldn't afford a whole packet and told me to buy two cigarettes. I grumbled that we could buy a little extra food with her fag money. I didn't see that it was her only indulgence, her one little luxury.

Sometimes I go over in my mind the difficulties of her life and recall our living conditions and the need for patience and care for each other if life was to be made to seem possible. The living room had a recess for a bed, a cold-water sink, a cooker and a door into the other room, another box, which had two beds and a wardrobe. That was our house. Occasionally, we escaped on the bus to Glasgow, where my mother had family. To us, they seemed amazingly grand. My mother's parents and brother and sister lived on the top floor of a big red-stone tenement building near Hampden Park. It was a place of astonishing luxury – a kitchen, a living room, three bedrooms and an indoor toilet. My grandfather sat in a big armchair and smoked a pipe. He was a master of the universe. He drove a tram.

Those visits were always enjoyable. There was warmth and plenty of food on the table, something to anticipate as I played football in the little yard at the back of the tenement. Naturally, they were a Rangers clan, except Uncle Charlie, who became the black sheep of the family when he announced his support for Celtic. Uncle Charlie introduced me to a revolutionary concept. You could follow a team because they touched you in some way, you liked their style and some of the characters in the team, and none of this had to have anything to do with whether you were a Prod or a Fenian bastard. This was a great surprise to me because although we lived together, Protestants and Catholics, shared the ghetto and had so much in common as we faced our daily lives, in some ways we were also aliens to each other.

No family were more alien, or at times menacing, than the O'Hanlons who lived in the next block. For a while, Billy and I co-existed with the O'Hanlon boys but problems often arose, and when things went wrong we were threatened with serious violence . . . and the Paper Lady. The Paper Lady was the Virgin Mary and the O'Hanlons knew how to terrify us most truly. They would whisper, 'The Paper Lady is coming.' Initially, we said, 'Who the hell is the Paper Lady?' When we knew, she haunted us, day in day out.

Once we were in the O'Hanlon flat when they were having their Sunday dinner. They were all at the table, the mother and the kids – old man O'Hanlon had been killed in a pub brawl – helping themselves from a bowl of potatoes, which were still in their skins. That was their dinner. Billy and I agreed that maybe they were the only family in the world who could make us feel quite posh.

In the summer when I was nine, I entered a state of war with the O'Hanlons. They announced they were going to do me. It was official. Whenever I saw any of them, maybe when I was playing footie in the backyard where the women hung up the washing, I had to race up the stairs for safety. I became a prisoner of my own stairway. My mother would go chasing down the stairs but they just ran away and hid – and waited. I was terrified of them. I woke up in a sweat, crying out that a whole posse of O'Hanlons was coming for me, along with the Paper Lady. My mother said that as the police were no use we would go along to see the parish priest. Father Flynn was a huge, imposing man. When he walked down the street with his cassock flying in the wind, people made way, even Prods, and when we knocked at the presbytery door, my mother and I agreed we had never been so scared. He came to the door and said, 'Come in, daughter.' My mother announced in a small voice, 'Father, the O'Hanlons are terrifying my boy and making his life a misery.' He sighed and said, 'Everything will be fine, daughter, leave it to me.' That was it – all sorted, in a flash, by the power of the church. That power has gone today. No one has it, not the church, the police or anyone who tries to bring a little bit of order to the streets.

In the peace, the middle O'Hanlon brother, Joey, who was a useful fighter, took me to the boxing club. I have often wondered what became of him. He definitely had some talent. He moved well and had nice co-ordination when he threw a punch. Then suddenly the O'Hanlons were no longer around. No one knew what happened to them. Maybe they went back to Ireland. The eldest boy, Raymond, was a little bit puddled, not quite right in the head, and so was his mother. No doubt they had had a lot to put up with, but then so many people did. Hardship was the norm. You shrugged it away and got on with your life, but from time to time a very strong anger indeed welled up. A woman like Mrs O'Hanlon could go crazy with all that pressure, but who really cared?

Certainly not the police. I still feel anger when I think of the time I was taken to court by a big copper who caught me playing football in the street. It was not as though Scott Street was a raging thoroughfare – seeing a car was an event. Horses and carts for the milk and the rags and bones were more usual. The copper didn't care about that. He had me in the court, standing in front of my mother. Some crime, I thought, playing footie, and the magistrate looked over his spectacles and fined me, or rather my mother, ten shillings. She had to do a lot of cleaning for that. Even today, I think, 'You bastards, what were you thinking about?' There was never any traffic, never any danger. When I saw the expression on my mother's face, which said more eloquently than words, 'Where am I going to get an extra ten shillings?', I looked at the copper who had given his evidence, and I wanted to say, 'Couldn't you have just kicked me up the arse, you big useless bastard?'

When I think of incidents like that, the lack of bitterness in people whose lives were so tough amazes me all over again. So little help was forthcoming from those whose job it was supposed to be – the puffed-up councillors who came around at election time and then disappeared from your lives, and the coppers who hauled kids off to the nick rather than spend a few minutes of their time explaining a different way. They could have shown that the authority they represented was fair and just not out to crush folk.

There was my mother, withered by the effort to keep herself and her kids alive, untouched in herself by the harshness all round her and scrubbing us up for church on a Sunday. On our side of the divide, we also had quite a strong religious upbringing. We went to the Sunday morning service, then Boys' Brigade and youth fellowship, where we had an organist and were taught all the hymns. Quite a bit of gorging on religion went on whether you were Catholic or Protestant, but it didn't always seem to have any effect on the way people treated each other. It didn't deter the police from dragging me into court, no more than it persuaded my mother and my father's sister, Minnie Corner, a pair of widows, to speak to each other even though they lived next door on the tenement landing.

My father never had much to do with his own family once he married, and that was probably the result of some big fight causing hurt that could never be healed. This was a pity because, to an extent, the St John family were achievers. None of them could claim to have driven a tram, but one cousin, John, owned a tobacconist-newsagent's shop. He went on to become quite a prominent businessman in the town. Even more spectacularly, one of my father's sisters became the world highland dancing champion – Isobel St John, world champ, had a good ring to it, I always thought.

Helen St John's clan battled on together, a small alliance helping each other as best we could. Tuesday, when the pension came, was our big day. It was great because it was the one day when we were always guaranteed a good breakfast. One of my older sisters or I would go up to the post office, collect the £5 pension and pick up bread rolls and butter on the way back. All of this had to be compressed into the half hour between the post office opening and the start of school. If you were late for school, they just pulled you to one side and gave you the belt. Even when you had a good breakfast inside you the belt was hard, but you learned to take it in your stride soon enough, as you did most other things that befell you; you shrugged your shoulders and did what you had to do.

From some old, faded school pictures, it seems that my mother did quite a good job of feeding and dressing her children. We look reasonably well nourished and certainly we weren't in rags. What the pictures do not show, though, is whether or not we had holes in our shoes. That was just about the worst thing that could happen. You looked at the soles of your shoes every night and if you saw the beginnings of a hole you thought, 'Oh, Christ, here we go.' Shoes were the big item in the family economy. The hole in your shoe would make a hole in your sock. So you would double your sock down, fold it over so that everything was okay for a little while, but gradually the sock got lower and the heel of the sock slipped under the back of the shoe and then when you came into school on a wet morning, and you were walking down the corridor, you would be leaving a footprint with a big hole in it. That was embarrassing. It told the world that you were really poor. As a stopgap measure you could put a bit of cardboard or linoleum in the shoe but that would wear through too. I have never forgotten the misery of having a hole in your shoe. It was one consequence of losing your father. The kids who still had fathers generally didn't have holes in their shoes.

One great consolation of winter was that the council issued free boots. We called them tackity boots because of the big tacks, steel studs, they had on the bottom, which made them brilliant for Motherwell's version of winter sports. The boots also had three holes punched in the side to identify them as council issue. This meant you couldn't take them to the pawn shop – but who would want to pawn them during the Scott Street Olympics?

Scott Street had a superb long slope, perfect for toboggan races, but most thrilling were the slides, with the tacks on your boots biting in. In the snow and the frost, you wouldn't call the king your cousin but you were the future Franz Klammer. The thrill of the race took away the stigma of those punched holes because the tackity boot kids were always the champions. Suddenly everyone envied you because your big clogs gave you such an edge, helped to make you a brilliant slider. Sliding in the hard winters of Scotland was always popular, hence the remark, 'That bastard is so mean if he was the King of Switzerland he wouldna' give you a slide.'

I will never forget the empowering feeling that came at the top of Scott Street when you were ready to go. When you flew down that street no one could give you the belt or order you into a corner. No one could touch you – and when you tired of Scott Street, there was Hamilton Street, where you asked the kids, 'Can we have a go on your slide?' We were ingenious in devising fresh games and dares, coming up with new challenges, new thrills. Nobody wanted to be at home in front of the fire, which was just as well because more often than not there wasn't one – who mooches for fuel for the fire in the middle of the Olympics?

We also had summer Olympic Games along Scott Street. Some of the events took a little planning. We had to produce piles of grass to provide soft landings for the high jump, and grass wasn't the most accessible commodity in the neighbourhood. The big event, the 800 yards around the block, attracted a vast entry.

A version of these Olympics was staged most days. We never stopped running, climbing or jumping, and when we weren't athletes we were quick, daring thieves raiding orchards and allotments. Often we were chased, but rarely caught. We were as fit as butchers' dogs. We took most of the food home – potatoes, carrots, turnips, rhubarb – but sometimes some of the boys would make a camp fire and throw some of the tatties into it. After breaking the black skins, we would eat them so hot they burned our lips. Our most daring raids were on the Catholic church allotment because these missions were always conducted in a state of deep terror. If Father Flynn in his big black coat or cassock didn't get us, maybe the Paper Lady would.

The record shows that I was possibly one of the quickest because I was never caught, although on one occasion I did fear for my life. It happened not during an allotment raid but a snowball fight. A kid had landed a big hit on me and I scooped up a lump of ice and snow – these could be bitter, unscrupulous battles – and took aim. Unfortunately, he ducked and the missile sailed past him and struck a big man, who was walking down the street, right in his face. He screamed out and immediately charged at me. I took to my heels but he was running hard and uttering terrible cries about what he was going to do to me when he caught me. Racing down an alleyway, I came to a wall. I should have remembered the terrain better than that, but there it was – a wall to be cleared or, at best, a very bad beating. Climbing walls was a local speciality, as I reminded myself as I ran towards this division between life and death. I remember thinking that if I didn't get over it, I would be dead. He was grabbing at me and had half a hold on my ankles as I slid over the wall and kept running.

Suddenly, miraculously it seemed, our snowball fights, food raids and Olympics were floodlit. The street lights came on again with the end of the war and we could slide and play football in the streets bathed in council light. We had lived in darkness for so long that even today, when I think of those times, I find myself humming the song, 'When the lights came on again all over the world . . .'

Street lights were not the only sensational development.

When I was twelve, I came home one day to find my mother glowing. 'We've got the radio in,' she announced with tremendous pride and excitement, pointing to a small box with knobs marked 'Home' and 'Light', screwed to the wall. It would be hard today for a young boy or girl to understand the magic of that frail-looking contraption. My mother switched it on and what I heard was indescribably thrilling – commentary on Scotland against Wales at Hampden Park. It was as though those great remote heroes George Young, wee Jimmy Mason, Willie Waddle and Lawrie Reilly were coming into our little flat. They were becoming part of me in a way I could never have imagined before my mother turned on the radio.

The radio brought an entire new world of excitement and terror. 'The Man in Black, Valentine Dyall' was compulsive, terrifying, and then there was 'Dick Barton, Special Agent' and his sidekicks Jock and Snowy. By then I was playing for the Boys' Brigade team and the only time I got in trouble with them was when we had a 7 p.m. kick-off. Dick Barton came on at 6.45, and there was one episode I just couldn't miss. Jock was in the deepest trouble in the previous instalment and I had to know his fate. My mother told me I was going to be late for the football and when I arrived at the ground the man in charge said, 'I don't see why I should let you play.' The game had been going for a few minutes, but I was a good player and they needed me, so the manager reluctantly sent me on to the field.

The magic box on the wall also made heroes of two West Indian cricketers, Sonny Ramadhin and Alf Valentine. I read in a comic about the technique of spinning the ball and devoted one whole summer to working on the art. It was the most wonderful thing to see the ball I had thrown down a patch of grass or concrete, often in the washing area with the women trying to shoo me away, spinning in exactly the way I wanted it to spin.

Cricket for boys in a raggedy Motherwell school might seem unlikely but it happened suddenly, magically, when an Englishman joined the teaching staff. He brought the gift of cricket. We were fascinated when a concrete strip was laid between two ash football pitches and our new cricket master announced that matting was to be put down 'as they do it in India, lads'. Unfortunately, the matting never arrived.

Now we were playing with a hard red ball and one of the boys fancied himself as Scotland's answer to Freddie Trueman. The ball flew off the concrete and we dived in the cinders. One day a fantasy came true — we went up to Hamilton to play a private school on a beautiful grass field. The Hamilton boys came out in their pristine whites. We looked like liquorice all-sorts. One of the great treats of the day was diving for a catch. What a feeling it was to take the ball and then roll on the soft green turf. We didn't win, but we gave them a game, and I proved I could spin the ball on a proper pitch.

That thrill came again many years later when I was playing in a celebrity match for London Weekend Television on a fine ground in Dulwich, one of the posher corners of south-east London. One of the opposition batsmen was Michael Grade, ex public schoolboy and now chairman of the BBC. He came to the wicket in his immaculate whites and hooped cap and took guard. He went to stroke my delivery through the covers but the ball moved, beautifully, and he was gone.

It wasn't Valentine against Hutton, or some dramatic night at Anfield or the San Siro, so why do I tuck it away with some of my fondest sporting memories? It brought back a warm waft of how it was when you were a kid with everything before you, when playing on cinders for a raggedy school in the shadow of a steelworks was easily mistaken for a joy rather than a hardship. Batting was, however, more of an ordeal than a pleasure. Once I played against Fred Rumsey, the former Somerset and England paceman. Fred had grown to a formidable size since his playing days, when he wasn't exactly slender, but he could still whip down the ball. One flew past my nose and earned the heart-felt tribute, 'Jesus Christ.'

It may seem odd to read about the cricket reflections of a boy from Motherwell, but a strange pull was exerted by the game of the British empire. Indeed, if you ask me to speak of one of the most memorable collisions I have ever had in sport, I'd cite the day in Barbados when I met Sir Garfield Sobers, the author of those astonishing six sixes off six balls. I saw that amazing passage of play live on black and white television, and the thrill it provoked has never left me. His movement was lithe and graceful, and even with his knees shot he still had the physical aura of one of the greatest sportsmen the world has ever seen. I suppose the great appeal for me was that sport was always an available means of expression, an area where I was sure that I had some talent, whether it was a footballer, a boxer, even a trainee offspinner. It gave me confidence, a feeling of self-worth.

On Saturday mornings, another new wonder soon came into our lives at the picture house – Dick Barton on film, and Flash Gordon and Emperor Ming. As well as films, there were competitions, including a skipping contest. All the girls lined up and I joined them with some confidence. I had learned to skip at the boxing club and I won the prize, which was two tickets for the Saturday night show. Proudly, I gave them to my mother.

I loved the boxing club, even though it was mostly full of old pugs and there was a distinct lack of glamour. The club was housed in a tilting old hut and the moment you walked in you were hit with the smell of stale sweat. A rickety ring, a few punchbags and the odd skipping rope made up the equipment, but the atmosphere was full of life and character. No one likes getting that first serious belt in the face, especially without the headgear, but I came to terms with that quickly enough and boxing gave me a lot of confidence. I gained a strong belief in my ability to handle myself, both on the football field and in the street. This was particularly useful when my brother Billy, bad Billy, got into scrapes and I was obliged to sort things out.

We had our own local boxing hero, Chick Calderwood, Olympic medallist, and for a while it was difficult to know who to follow most passionately, the fighters or the footballers. Chick's father coached him and it was plain he was going to be good. He moved so well and he had great timing. My mentor was an old guy we called Leachy Port. On Sunday mornings he took us into the woods where we ran and skipped and sparred. Leachy would stick his face in front of you and say, 'Hit me, hit me anywhere,' and you were expected to give him your best shot.

I was fourteen when I fought, officially, for the first time and I'll never forget the sensation, the edge that came to me. I won my early fights and one night I went home, clutching my first prize with immense pride – a sugar bowl with a silver base and a spoon.

The circumstances that pushed me away from boxing and towards football occurred in Beath in Ayrshire, an area renowned for the quality of its fighters. The kid I was due to fight was pointed out to me, and when I looked him over I felt no apprehension. 'Yes,' I thought, 'I can take this boy.' He looked a little soft to me. Unfortunately, one or two lads had cried off and, shortly before I was to go into the ring, the guy who was running the show told me that he'd had to rearrange the fights. I had a new opponent, who turned out to be the top kid in the show, and naturally that gave me a little bit of concern. Even at that level, you didn't want to be pitched in over your head, and this boy was a champion. He came at me very hard and in front of that crowd, which was very lively indeed, I'd never felt under such pressure in all my life.

Fortunately, I settled down and gave a good account of myself. I knew I could fight and after taking a couple of heavy shots I began to give some back. He got the decision, but everyone said I had done well, and old Leachy said he was proud of the way I had come through it. I had a black eye but then so had the champion. We went to his house for tea and biscuits and pies, and it was clear he was a bit of a local celebrity, but he avoided me – I was told it was the first time he had collected a black eye – and I thought it would be interesting to get into the ring with him again. I saw this night as something of a rite of passage, a hard fight to give me a better idea of what I had inside me. In fact, it wasn't the arrival I had imagined it to be. It was the beginning of the end of my boxing career.

My mother was appalled by the state of my face. I remember her crying, and saying, 'Oh, just go and look at yourself, son. You've had a battering and you'll get more before you're through. Stick to the football, boy, you're good and they don't smash in your face on the football field . . .'

Her opposition was a big factor. I didn't want to give her more worries than she already had. It also happened that around about that time, Leachy just disappeared, like the O'Hanlons. I never quite got to know what became of him. I asked around, but no one seemed quite sure. With my mother opposed and Leachy gone, my time as a fighter just petered out. It is still a regret, even though I knew back then that sooner or later I would have to make a decision between the football field and the ring. I couldn't do both, and nobody needed to tell me that I stood out a little bit on the football field, or that it was a much less hazardous place than the ring. The truth is that whatever success I had as a football player, I always knew that it would never take away, at least not completely, that hankering for the fight game. For me, the boxing champion has always occupied a special place, carried a unique aura. When I told my mother that the boxing was over, and her relief was so obvious, I still told her, 'Mammy, I would have loved nothing more than to be a champion.' Then, I could imagine no higher status in life.

Fancy, for example, being able to say, as Mike Tyson used to do so often, 'I'm the champion of the world, the best guy on the planet.' You cannot say that in football, unless you're indisputably the best, as Pele and Diego Maradona were, because football, at least in theory, is a team game. Everybody is working together and your efforts, or lack of them, merge with the team's so you can get away with carrying an injury, for instance. In boxing, you're alone. It's just you against the world – your conditioning, your work, your investment in yourself. You can lose everything if you are just a little easy on yourself. So many tests of will have to be faced, from running on cold mornings to getting up from the floor when you have been stunned by a punch you might not even have seen coming, and then going again.

I've never kidded myself that I was guaranteed any success in boxing. If I had taken it up seriously, it could have ended anywhere. I could have had some success, even become a champion, but just as easily, I could have been washed up, badly hurt, long before the age when I became familiar with the great football stadiums of the world and for a little while had the sense that, like my tram-driving grandpa in Glasgow, I ruled quite a bit of the universe. Boxing was perilously uncertain in almost every way, but that didn't take away any of my love for it or touch the exhilaration I felt when I knew I had done my work and was ready to step between the ropes and give a good account of myself. Looking back, I suppose it was the training I loved most of all. No doubt that would have changed and on this I have the best possible witness, Muhammad Ali, who said that in the end it was not the fighting that he couldn't stand any more but the idea of going back to training camp.

Boxing's decline has been more or less relentless since those days when the sport took hold of my boyhood imagination and spirit, but the essence of its appeal remains as strong as ever. What maybe drew me most to the ring was the idea that two men could fight each other with everything they had and then, when it was over, embrace with the deepest of respect. The game I eventually chose could follow that example with great benefit, perhaps never more so than today.

So football, the national passion, would be my true calling, but even this was in some jeopardy, despite the enjoyment I had on the field and the encouragement I received while playing in the company of many excellent young players, notably the future England international Joe Baker. It is impossible to calculate the wastage of talent caused by Scottish working-class life, especially the casualties of the pubs. My sporting future, for a little while at least, became questionable when I started my working life as a fifteen-year-old. First I went to the Taggart and Wilson coach works, then moved on to the Colville steelmill before finishing up at the Motherwell Bridge Engineering Company. I loathed that last place, which claimed five years of my life. The company, quite fairly, might also say that my departure did not fill them with despair.

Beer and women are two elements classically opposed to great football careers. I shall never forget the taste of my initial encounter with the first of these hazards. I was a small, very young-looking teenager and the guys who had taken me into the pub said, 'You just sit there in the corner and we'll bring you a pint.' So here was the big world, the big destiny – the smoky pub with drink flowing, transporting you to apparently sweet oblivion. One of my older friends planted the pint of beer in my hand. I sipped it, tentatively. As I go back to that moment, the taste of the cold, strong black beer is in my mouth.

It could, I suppose, have been a pivotal moment, a crossroads of sorts, but of course it wasn't. Life at the Bridge Works was full of tedium and often terrible frustration, but I wanted a lot more than the brackish taste of beer in my mouth to alleviate the daily trial of misery. It was my good luck that someone recognised in me the ability to do a lot more. His name was Pat McCourt and his son worked in the factory. Pat knew about football and, soon enough, he became, at least in his knowledge of the game and the interest he showed in me, the first father I had known since my own was taken from our building wrapped in the red blanket.

2

'COME OVER AND TRAIN'

P AT MCCOURT was a pinnacle in my life, a decisive, timely influence in a way that Leachy putting his gnarled old face in the path of my punches could never be. Pat ran North Motherwell Football Club, which comprised a little field across the road from the factory, another old hut and a set of superb values.

At North Motherwell you learned that mere ability was just the beginning of any success you might have. A bit of talent was a visiting card. You put it down when you first kicked a ball under Pat's gaze and he would find out quickly enough whether you had the temperament and the character for serious business. You had to learn to compete truly, to handle yourself under all kinds of provocation. If you couldn't do that, if you gave way at the first hint of pressure, you were a goner. Under Pat's guidance I had my rite of passage in football, as did my contemporary John McPhee, who went on to play for Blackpool.

As well as being a wise old football coach, Pat McCourt was a good man. When he looked at the youngsters who came to his team, he didn't see Catholics or Protestants but boys of varying degrees of potential. He made such a difference to my future, stretching my horizons way beyond those of most of the kids I had grown up with in the streets of Motherwell. Most important, I have to believe, was the fact that probably, deep down, I had been crying out for a father figure, someone to say with a little firmness, 'This is the way to go, son,' and who would take the trouble to make sense of it. Until Pat arrived in my life, I had made almost all of those decisions for myself. I suppose it was out of a combination of survival instinct and good luck that I had probably got the majority of them right.

Pat was in the sharpest contrast to one primary schoolteacher, a big guy who taught maths and seemed to draw pleasure from making me cry. He didn't do it with a belt but with constant references to the fact that I didn't have a father. 'Do you miss your father, laddie?' he would ask, looking at me intently as though willing my tears to form. Today I would dismiss him as a sadistic bastard, but back then I was one of his prey. In fact, I wasn't tortured by the loss of my father, at least not unless I was forced to think about it. Mostly, I pushed it to the corner of my mind. Occasionally it might come to me that if I'd had a father I wouldn't have needed to work so hard to help the family win a crust. I might not have had to help deliver milk and rolls or do the paper round or shove a piece of cardboard into my shoe, but these were things that I didn't dwell on. If you don't have something, you try not to think about it. However, looking back, I see how eagerly I responded to anyone who gave me a little encouragement or the odd pat on the back.

Pat got hold of me at a most crucial time. I was playing with his son in the Bridge Works team but there was no training, no edge and no pride. Most of the lads were more interested in the pubs and the dance halls than putting any effort into improving their game. Pat's son put in a word for me, said that I was a talented kid but it was all wasting away in the factory team. The coach sent the message that changed my life — come over and train.

One of my first games for North Motherwell was against the Bridge Works. The factory lads treated me as a traitor and tried to do me at every opportunity. Three of them, older, bigger boys who had taken me to the pub, seemed particularly intent on kicking me out of the game, and I realised that this was a test similar to the one I had faced in the boxing ring a few years earlier. I could either submit to the pressure or make a stand. It was my first and most basic lesson in the game that would shape my life. I sorted out the big boys. I said, 'Okay, you want to give some, how about taking a little back.' We won the game and I played well. The exhilaration I felt coming off the field was so strong I recall it as freshly as though it was yesterday. Later, after I came out of the communal cold-water bath and got dressed, Pat put his arm around my shoulder and said, 'Well done, son, you did the business today.'

When Pat said that, he was ushering me back into a world that I thought had gone with the best of my boyhood, the Scott Street Olympics, the boxing and, later, gymnastics and athletics – even cricket on a strip of concrete laid on a field of cinders, when I reported for duty at the Taggart and Wilson coachworks. I hadn't been driven by the idea that I would be a professional or maybe one day play for Scotland at Hampden Park. Sport had just been part of life, but Pat gave me the idea that sometimes you do get back what you put in. Under his guidance, all the running, climbing, fighting and training seemed to come welling out in my performances. I was quick and hard, and I had been given some talent, and gradually it came to me – maybe one day I could be a player.

Before then, though, the factories of Motherwell claimed my time and, dominating everything, was the terrible fear that I might have to spend the rest of my life clocking on and off and going back to the tenement, usually via the pub.

I got the job at Taggart's when an employment guy came to the school, asked me to fill in a form and assessed my potential in life in about two and half seconds. He told me to go down to the coachworks. My weekly pay would be twenty-one shillings, less tax. I hadn't been bad at school, but I was no academic, not under the pressure of pulling off all those Olympic medal-winning performances, and I suppose my assignment to Taggart's was no better or worse than I could have expected.

It was different, and much harder, for my sister Wilma when she went off to work at fifteen. As a schoolgirl, she worked every night at her books in the gaslight and beside the smoky fire. She was good and she won the medal for the top student at secondary school. In a different, more just world, somebody would have picked her out and said 'This girl deserves a better future'. She had worked for it and she had the talent to make a great success of her life but for Wilma, further education was just a fantasy. She went off to the offices of the steel company to help the family as soon as she could. She married and had kids and when the children grew up a bit, she went back to her books. She enrolled in the Open University and achieved an honours degree. When she did that, I felt as much pride in her, and for her, as I ever felt for myself when I walked out on to Hampden Park for Scotland.

Sadly, I cannot speak of my brother Billy in the same terms; quite the opposite in fact. I hope that he made something of his life but I just don't know if he ever sat down to think about the need for some changes in how he treated people. I haven't spoken to him for forty years. The odd scrap of information has filtered through – I know he married and had a son who has made a name for himself as a chef, and I was very glad to hear that – but otherwise, nothing. I last saw him when he went back to Scotland after coming down to stay at my house after I moved to Liverpool in 1961. We had one final row in a series of them that erupted during the time he was with me and my young family after I had got him a job with the help of a neighbour, George

Hansen, who worked for the local electricity company. I loved my brother and I wanted to protect him, put him right, but it was never easy. I happened to have a work ethic, at least when I was doing something I wanted, and made quick progress in football, and sometimes I wondered if he resented that. It is not, I imagine, the most unusual development in the lives of brothers.

I never made any attempt to pursue him after his departure from my life. I felt I had done all I could for him, and that the time had come when I had enough to do making my career and trying to do the best for my wife and kids while still keeping an eye out for my mother. The truth is a lot of bitterness entered our relationship when I was first playing for Motherwell and able to put some money my mother's way. I would leave cash under the linoleum, and say, 'Look, here's a little hideaway for you to go to when you need it,' but on several occasions, Billy pinched the money. I found that unforgivable. When he came in from work on a Friday, my mother would say, 'Well, where's your pay packet?' More often than not it was gone, spent in the pubs and the bookies. I realised that if I didn't do something to help my mother and my sisters, there would be none forthcoming, certainly not from Billy.

He abused the job I got him in Liverpool and he was fired soon enough. Another problem was that he hadn't lost the argumentative streak he had shown as a young boy. Once, in a nightclub, he got involved in a row with an Everton player, and there was talk of them going outside to settle it. Johnny Morrissey, the talented and notably hard Everton winger, was in the club at the time. He threatened to get involved, and I had to say, 'Stay out of this, Johnny, it's between the two of them.' No dire consequences resulted from that incident, but a pattern had been formed and, inevitably, it ended with bad feelings. After more pinching of money in the house, finally I said, 'That's it, that's you finished as far as I'm concerned.' It was always hard when my mother asked, 'How's Billy?' because I wanted so much to give her a positive answer but it was impossible.

When he got back to Scotland it was disturbing to hear that he had taken up with many of his old crowd – lads who had no ambition beyond getting through the day as best they could. In the way of mothers, mine couldn't make a stand against her black sheep son. I suggested that maybe she could shock him into taking a good look at himself by saying that he was no longer welcome in his old home until he did something to reshape his life. Such a gesture was beyond her, though, however many times I said that everything possible had been done for him and now it was for him to do something about his fate.

For a long time after he left Liverpool, the roughest characters would come up to me to ask, 'How's your kid?' It is said that blood is thicker than water but after those patience-draining years the theory was for me extremely diluted. Yes, I loved Billy as a brother, someone I slept beside and with whom I shared all my first secrets, fears and hopes, and I wanted to be a good brother, but it is an old truth that you can't choose your relatives. You choose your friends, people to whom you draw close because they have touched your life with honesty and have never been looking for anything beyond your friendship. In the end, I decided that with Billy I had tried my best but had reached a point where I couldn't go on with him.

Maybe the lack of a father hurt him more than me, maybe he too had a great need for someone like Pat McCourt, but had such a person arrived, would Billy have recognised him? I doubt it. Billy's big problem was that he didn't have any discipline and maybe a Pat figure might just have had some influence. A good mentor might have used an approach that wasn't necessary with me. In my case, Pat simply brought me back to a point of conviction that had, mostly because of new influences, been briefly lost. Billy didn't seem to have that starting point; he didn't grasp that in our circumstances everything came down to our own efforts. We didn't have a father to say, 'Get your gear and go training, do this, do that.' If it was going to happen, if you were going to do anything, you had to do it yourself. I would fight the battle with myself and go and do it and, except for that little time immediately before I played for North Motherwell, I would never dodge anything. I never missed a day's training in my life.

Billy just didn't have a self-starting mechanism. He seemed to be drawn to the layabouts, the corner boys, and when something better was on offer, he never reached out. When Billy slammed the door of my house, I realised that it might well be for the last time and all those stored-up feelings of anger came welling up in me. For many years after that, I said that I never wanted to see or speak to my brother ever again; he had just slipped off my radar. But as you get older, and maybe a little more sentimental, you wonder what happened to someone to whom you were once so closely attached. The odds are that I would open the door if he ever happened to knock on it again. One thing is certain – he will always be part of my life.

At Taggart's I went from one disaster to another. An early one was forgetting to make the tea for the men when they came for their break and one of them chased me around the factory. He swore he would kill me, and he seemed to mean it. I found one of the hiding places I had already established in case of emergencies such as this one, and spent most of the afternoon peeking out to see if he had calmed down sufficiently for me to return to my duties safely. I hated all of my tasks, most intensely the need to lie under a car or a van amid bolts and wrenches while fitting replacement parts.

There was just one job I fancied – driving around the yard in one of the ambulances we serviced for the local hospital. Some of the older boys were given the privilege but for various reasons, possibly including the fact that I could hardly see over the steering wheel, it was denied me. However, one morning an ambulance needed to be moved and before anyone could stop me I was in the driving seat and putting it into gear. Unfortunately, the gear I found was reverse. A terrible crashing noise indicated that I had smashed in the back doors. The foreman explained, quite patiently, all the work that had been done on the ambulance, all the skill and man hours that had gone into making it as good as new. Then, before I could say anything, he told me I was sacked.

My duties were heavier at the Colville steelmill, where I worked under Tam Pettigrew, a wiry, craggy old Scot who chewed a toothpick and was always covered in sweat. For me, he was the stoic face of the Scottish working man – tough, philosophical in a rough way, utterly attuned to the hardness of the life he faced. He directed me in operations that, even now, tend to make my blood run cold. The big job was to open the furnace and inject into it room-long billets of steel, great joists that arrived on a conveyor belt and were rolled, after being roasted in the fire, into various shapes and lengths. My responsibility, for which I was paid the staggering amount of four pounds a week, was to make sure the joists came rolling along the belt, which I controlled with a shunting switch. If things went wrong, if not one but two joists came off the belt at the same time, the job was stopped amid terrible recriminations. The men would come at me as fiercely as the flames emerging from the furnace. So I sat there, my eyes glued to the switch, in a state of more or less permanent terror.

The horror was not just in my head. I saw some bad things in the steel mill. The worst was when a guy was killed. He was a good-looking, blond-haired man who worked in a big leather jacket to protect against the sparks. His job was torch burning. His burner nicked a barrel that contained some flammable material. There was a shocking whoosh and it turned out that the torch had gone through his head. Bad accidents were routine.

For me, the steel mill was a dead end. It brought in extra money but sometimes it seemed like a version of hell and I was very happy to escape, with all my limbs intact, to an apprenticeship at the Motherwell Bridge and Engineering Works, even though it was quickly apparent that the whole business would be a desperately extended, five-year joke. At the Bridge Works I acquired a major reputation for skiving, which just goes to show how important it is to do something in life that you enjoy, not that this particular option was available to too many of the lads.

I had the release of football and by the time I left, at the age of twenty-one, I was playing for an excellent Motherwell team and Scotland. Looking back from the perspective of today's game, it all seems so bizarre now. In the evening I might be playing alongside Denis Law and Dave Mackay for Scotland. In the morning I would be clocking on at the mill and somebody would be bellowing in my ear, 'Jesus Christ, St John, how could you miss that fucking goal?' One benefit was that it was quite hard to acquire a big head. One minute I was someone who in those days passed for a superstar, the next I was bang in the middle of a crowd of punters.

Shift work could have been a problem. It didn't help the rhythm of a football career any more than it did a decent social life. The favourite shift was 6 a.m. to 2 p.m. It meant an early start, but after a siesta you could go to the pictures with your girlfriend. Between the other two stints, you would always choose 10 p.m. to 6 a.m. because that didn't destroy the day. You could sleep in the morning and still have a bit of free time before you clocked on again. Two to ten was the killer, the dead zone. One guy had done twenty years on the night shift. I never chose to speculate on the nature of his life and was happy enough to have been offered the apprenticeship, which meant day work.

In theory, I was learning to be a fitter. In practice, I was acquiring the skills of a world-class skiver. It was five years of ducking and diving and when finally I left the factory, I knew roughly as much as when I had walked through the gates for the first time. Along the way, my work ethic, for want of a better term, became so notorious none of the tradesmen would have anything to do with me. When my services were offered by the foreman, the classic response was, 'Not that little bastard.'

I was more relieved than upset. It meant that I could stay fresh for football. I also became quite well read, easing my way through working days, mostly reading novels in one of my hideaways, and then emerging at break time to have a cup of tea and sandwiches with the rest of the workforce. I enjoyed that. It was nice to have a bit of company for a little part of the day, although the most I would get out of the tradesmen, certainly before I began to make my name as a footballer, was a grunt of contempt. I got on well enough with the other lads, though, and sometimes one of them would join me on factory 'break-outs'. We would sneak into the back of a lorry in the yard and then sail through the gates, jumping off at traffic lights and seeking the matinee darkness of the cinema. Then, when the big picture was over, we would go back to the works and climb over the wall just in time to clock off.

By age the age of eighteen I was established in the Motherwell first team, which of course brought me a little recognition, a development that proved costly one afternoon when I didn't have the money for the cinema. I was loitering in the big park when a gang of schoolkids started to play football and I joined in. The following day – it must have been break time because I was visible – one of the top foremen marched up to me and said, 'What was the score, you skiving little bastard?' Indignantly, I asked him, 'What do you mean, what was the score?' He said, 'My lad was playing against you in the park – if you do that again, you're sacked.'

The worst scrape was when six of us apprentices were sitting in a factory hut, chatting happily in front of a coke fire. Suddenly someone said to be quiet; he had looked out of the window and seen a foreman marching angrily towards the hut. We locked the door and lay flat, trying to suppress our giggles. The gaffer hammered on the door, then yelled, 'Look, I know you're in there. Get out right now.' We didn't move until we heard him giving instructions to the crane driver – 'Left, lower, left, a little more.'

'Christ,' said one of the lads. 'They're going to lift us into the sky.' Terrified, we rushed out into the open, where the foreman was standing with a fierce look on his face.

'That's it,' he said. 'You've done it now. You're all sacked.'

I thought that now, as a player of some reputation for both Motherwell and Scotland, was probably as good a time as any to end my career in industry. The following day, a huge picture of the lads and me walking down the street adorned the newspaper. The headline announced: 'Scotland's centre-forward is sacked'.

For me, it might have all ended there but for a tough little trade unionist named Willie Smith. He had the reputation of being to the left of Khruschev. 'Right,' he said. 'All the apprentices are coming out on strike until you lads are reinstated.'

It was absurd, really. We were a bunch of epic skivers and the factory was up to its neck in foreign orders, including pipelines for Kuwait that had been rolled in the mills and come to the works to be welded and finished. With the oil and atomic energy market booming, the factory had never been doing so well, but Willie was adamant. The job would be stopped. The apprentices were important for all the little jobs they did to keep the tradesmen going. One of my jobs, when I happened to be working, was to fix a card to the orders, saying whether they were going to Kuwait or Saudi Arabia, but there was more vital work for an apprentice and it was decided that, in view of the pressure to get out the work, we would all be reinstated. So I hung on, earning a fiver as an apprentice — and £6 as a football star.

Apart from the money, another incentive to finish my apprenticeship was that I wanted to avoid national service. I thought conscription would be over by the time I reached twenty, but when I got my fitter's qualification a year later, I was still liable to be called up to the army. The papers came through the front door with a sickening thud. I had to go to Glasgow on the bus and sit a bizarre entrance exam. The questions were so easy I thought there was a catch. One of them was, '2,4,6, what's the next number?' and I'm thinking, 'That can't be it.' It seemed that it didn't matter how thick you were, you could still get in the army.

However, I believed I had an ace in the hole. I could tell the examining doctors about my wrist, how it hadn't properly healed after I'd fallen badly on the track that runs beside the pitch. The ground was frozen hard and I'd broken a little bone. They put me in plaster, which meant I could train but not play. The frustration was terrible. I was in plaster for six weeks, doing all my training but being forced to sit on the sidelines for games. Eventually, I was so desperate to play, I cracked and tore off the plaster. I announced I was ready for a Cup-tie against Airdrie, which was no exaggeration as it turned out. I scored four goals, maybe five but I generously accepted the claims of a team-mate that he had got a touch on what would have been the fifth.

I told the army doctors the story, how my impatience had prevented a complete healing of my injured wrist. They listened impassively, then announced, 'You're passed for the army – grade one, you can take John White's job.' John White, who would so beautifully illuminate the world of football with his brilliant play for Spurs and Scotland before being tragically struck down in 1964 by a flash of lightning, was in charge of the game at the big camp in Berwick. He had done his time and I was to be his replacement. As I was coming out of the office, another lad came up to me and said that he had been posted to the same camp. He seemed quite pleased, and suggested we go off for a bevvy. My reply was not sociable. I got on a bus back to Motherwell and went straight to Fir Park, where I told the manager about the disaster. He asked me if I'd told them about the wrist. I said I had but it had had no effect. He said he would get a specialist to write a full report. It didn't seem to strike either of us as odd that a footballer playing for his club and his country should be excluded from military service on medical grounds. Still, however outrageous, it worked. I was called back to Glasgow for a recall medical, then told, 'You're free to go.'

Later, a Colonel Mitchell, who was in charge of the British Army team and for so long had the pick of the nation's emerging talent, saw me after an international at Hampden Park and barked, 'St John, you're the one that got away.' Behind the bluster, though, he seemed an amiable guy and I was told that for me, a man who had shown such skiving talent all those years at the Bridge Works, the army would have been something of a home from home. Still, I had my wife Betsy and already we had a child and it seemed so much better that I stayed with them and the football. It was clear enough now that whatever I achieved in life, including a decent standard of living, would flow from the game in which I already made such striking progress.

Pat McCourt had so influenced my development because he was a great teacher of basic strengths, and he performed the same service for Gary McAllister and Joe Jordan. Joe came to him as a big ungainly lad, brave-hearted but raw, and in the briefest of time, he signed for Morton, and then the giants Leeds United, Manchester United and Milan — and went on to play in three World Cups for Scotland, scoring, uniquely, in all of them. McCourt shaped the boys who brought their talent from some quite unpromising beginnings. He made sense of the game.

That so many boys survived their original exposure to football, and came to love it so deeply, was, when you thought about it, something of a miracle. My own experience at Calder primary school was less than ideal. The janitor was in charge of a team that played on an ash pitch, which made it tough when you went down hard on your knees or your hips. Sliding tackles were attempted only in the most desperate circumstances. There was also the lunacy of playing on full-sized pitches, with goalkeepers standing under crossbars they could touch only if they climbed up on to a team-mate's shoulders. No one seemed to think that surely there was a better way for boys to learn the game and develop their skills. Later, coaching would be done on smaller pitches and with smaller goals, but by then so many generations of potentially great players had passed by. It's amazing when you think how many adults must have watched little kids playing with those big, leather, laced-up balls. When mud and water had gathered on their skins, they might have been something you fired out of cannon. Sometimes a kid could play at full-back and never touch the ball. A game could end prematurely because someone humped the ball over the wire fence separating us from the River Calder. In secondary schools, ash pitches were the norm, but always for me, and so many others, the sheer love of sport triumphed.

I went to gymnastics at night school, vaulting over the horse, working the beam and somersaulting and, as the little guy, climbing to the top of the pyramid to show my strength. I also enjoyed athletics and was quite a useful hurdler. For a while, I was a member of the Motherwell Harriers club, and I loved every minute I spent in my wee running vest. Now, I know that everything you do as a kid has a knock-on effect, which is something that was confirmed for me recently when someone showed me a picture of an old Liverpool–Everton derby. It shows me climbing above the Everton and England centre-half Brian Labone, a fine player who stood at around 6ft 2in, a good six inches taller than me.

Grainy pictures of my sporting youth remind me that in amid the pain and the difficulties, the cold mornings when the belt of a master cut into you with particular force, I had a great boyhood. Yes, of course, I missed having a father, a big protector, but then Leachy and Pat McCourt came along, and there was always the running, jumping and vaulting, and the sense that you were alive. I didn't have my father but I had a body that worked pretty well and enough of a brain to know that without anyone at home driving me on, I had to make something of myself.

There was also Motherwell Football Club, the heroes of my youth, the men who coloured my dreams. I saw them for the first time with my father, and twelve years later, I was a first teamer, a coming boy, and it is amazing to me that I went so far so quickly. As a child, on Sundays I would climb over the Fir Park wall with my mates and we would have a kick-about. Then, as an eleven-year-old, I played for Calder in a schools' final on the field of my heroes. It was a wet, miserable night but I was filled with such excitement going out to the pitch I could hardly catch my breath. We lost and everyone agreed it had to be put down to the fact that our big centre-half was playing in new boots. His proud father had bought them a few days before the big game. They were yellow with big toe-caps but unfortunately they were so unfamiliar to the boy that they destroyed his game. He couldn't kick the ball properly; almost invariably when he made contact it went spinning somewhere behind him, creating all sorts of problems. Joe Baker's brother, Gerry, who later went to Ipswich Town, was playing against us that night and he was able to do some damage. Back in the dressing room we cursed the new boots. Maybe we resented someone else having the shiny new gear but if you did have that astonishing luxury, you had a duty to break it in. That was the angry consensus and it was one I was bound to go along with. I never had new boots until I started working. Before that it was hand-me-downs. You had to stick newspaper into the toes to fill them up and, on the ash pitches, often the nails would come through the studs, so when you took off your boots your socks were soaked with blood. You put the boots in the last and banged the nails flat, as carefully as you could.

Your boots were your badge of honour. You would tie them together and put them around your neck, and you would go down the street feeling like a gunfighter. Everyone in the street knew you were a player. You were a serious man. You were going down to the park. You were going to play.

3

LEAVING SCOTLAND

M Y WIFE Betsy was still not twenty but she was strong and
feisty – and right. When English football came calling, she
said it was time to move on. If she hadn't been at my side, maybe I
would have settled for being a star of Motherwell. It did, after all,
seem as if my world had been filled to the point of overflowing.

I was on £16 a week and I no longer had to skulk around a
factory for most of my working life. I was living the dream that
showed on the face of a kid in the crowd at Motherwell Cross
when the heroes of my boyhood came back from Hampden Park
after winning the Scottish Cup in 1952. The kid is at the centre of
the celebrating crowd, pictured in an old copy of the local
newspaper. His smile glows from the fading page. His Motherwell
scarf, folded into a hat, is perched on his head.

The kid is me, and the feelings I had that day will never be
extinguished. I can still get inside the head of the kid at the Cross.
I remember stepping back in awe and shock one day when the
late Queen Mother and her lady-in-waiting cruised by the Cross
in their open-topped limousine on a royal visit. In their finery
and heavy make-up – it was the make-up that caused the impact
– they might have been visiting from another planet. It was
different when the boys came home from Hampden. They too
operated in another dimension, but you felt they were part of
you, that somehow the glory that trailed behind them was
shared by everyone who pressed down on the street.

Ever since I joined my father on his last, fatal visit to Fir Park the men in claret and amber had been huge players in my life. Deep in one winter, the club appealed for volunteers to help clear the pitch and I joined an army of kids working with shovels and barrels to clear the snow. There was a great feeling of pride when the job was done and the manager, George Stevenson, a fine inside-forward and winner of twelve Scottish caps in his time, came out to address the troops. He said we had done a fine job and he led us into a room where tea and pies were laid out. After that, we were shown to our seats in the stand. It was the first time I had watched a game while shielded from the worst that the weather could bring.

Sometimes my role at Motherwell games was less honourable. At half-time the club would send round a fund-raising blanket and the fans who could afford it would toss down coins. When the blanket reached my section I would hop over the wall and help retrieve the coins that missed the blanket. I used to go to the games in wellies with this chore in mind. I would return one coin to the blanket, and send another down a wellie. This worked flawlessly until one day a big policeman grabbed hold of me and threw me back over the wall. 'Get in there, you thieving little bastard,' he said.

When Celtic or Rangers came down to Motherwell, the ground and the streets were littered with bottles. Between Fir Park and the station were twelve pubs, and after filling a sack with the empties we would go to each of them to get tuppence on the returns. Invariably, it provided Saturday night fish and chip money.

The football always mattered most, though — heroic and skilful football that brought the Scottish Cup and the League Cup to Fir Park, and was always such a vibrant part of our lives. My special hero was Johnny Aitkenhead, a little left winger filled with craft and guile. He came from Hibs with an injury that had

left him with a limp but that didn't prevent him from perform-
ing all kinds of trickery. He would nudge the ball through the
legs of an opponent and the crowd would give a great roar
because they knew 'Wee Johnny' was off on one of his torment-
ing runs. Motherwell knew they had damaged goods when they
signed him, but they recognised that along with the gimpy gait
he still had great talent.

Wilson Humphries, a big man who would today be described
as a grafting midfielder, was not in Johnny's league in the creative
department but he too filled me with pride. He was my Boys'
Brigade officer, a teacher at Wilma's school. I could name the
team in my dream-filled sleep – in goal, big John Johnson, full-
backs Willie Kilmarnock and Archibald 'Baldy' Shaw, half-back
line Charlie Cox, Andy Paton, Willie Redpath, forwards Tommy
Sloan, Humphries, Archie Kelly, Jimmy Watson, Aitkenhead.

Johnson was big, straight-backed, immaculately dressed. I
thought of him as a great goalkeeper, and so was he was in
his time, but in today's game he would have had to do a lot of
work to get by. He was a line keeper, a shot-stopper, and when I
think of his game it reminds me of how much the position has
been developed down the years, not least by my friend and team-
mate at Anfield, Tommy Lawrence. Tommy was christened the
'flying pig' and he was a revolutionary – one of the first
goalkeeper-sweepers in British football.

Kilmarnock was the captain and he lived the part. Like
Johnson, he was tidy, his clothes and his hair were always in
place and so was his game. He read a match extremely well and
was one of those defenders who enjoyed a sixth sense about the
break of the ball and the flow of the play. He was always tight on
the ball, smooth and accurate.

Archie Shaw was more than a player. He was a force of Scottish
nature, a character who was both loved and respected. Fierce in the

tackle, he caused apprehension among the biggest named opponents. Once, in a match against Celtic, one home fan bellowed to the celebrated winger Charlie Tully, 'Baldy's going to break your fucking leg.' Tully, a little shocked, said to Baldy, 'Did you hear that?' Baldy replied, 'Aye, and he's right.' Baldy was still around when I joined the club and the youngsters used to flock around him. On one occasion we were in a hotel in Aberdeen and the manager, Bobby Ancell, said, 'Archie, I want you to look after these young boys tonight.' Baldy said, 'Aye, Boss, I'll show them the way,' which was precisely what he did. It was straight to the bar where he ordered in the drinks. His was a large Scotch.

Charlie Cox came down to us from Hearts. He didn't have a spectacular touch, but he would run up and down his side of the field all day, a traditional, hard-working half-back. The fireworks came along the rest of the middle line. Centre-half Andy Paton was a huge and enigmatic character. There were two ways of assessing the way he played. You might say he had a fine touch and nerves of steel. On the other hand, you might conclude that he was simply crazy. There was widespread sympathy for Johnson the goalkeeper. 'How does he ever know what Paton's going to do next?' was the question. Johnson never knew when and how he was going to get a backpass; it could be a flick, a backheel, a tap-up and a header. On one legendary occasion, Andy played a one-two with the goalpost. The crowd was stunned, then burst into wild applause. Paton would never shake hands with an opponent. He entered his own little world of competition. He never played for Scotland, never got a look in against the big guns – Tommy Docherty of Arsenal and Bobby Evans of Celtic – but in Motherwell, Paton was the king, the big item, and he was several times voted player of the year. Once, when I won that award, he gave me the trophy. It was a moment of vast pride.

Beside Paton, Willie Redpath at left-half was a ball artist. The ball was his prisoner. His skill did earn him a place in the Scottish team – also a few stage appearances as the master of 'keepy-uppy'. Like almost all Motherwell players of those days, Willie didn't own a car, so you would frequently see him walking down the street. He was always willing to sign an autograph and have a little chat. You remember such things when you hear of fans baiting today's superstars in nightclubs and see the resulting publicity, which is so often poisonous. It makes you realise how profoundly both the game and society have changed.

Tommy Sloan came in a job-lot from Hearts with Cox. He provided an excellent counter point to the wiles of Aitkenhead on the left. Sloan, quick and straightforward, would get to the line and cross with great consistency. In the centre, Archie Kelly was small, lively and good in the air. I was able to follow his style naturally when I made my way into the team. Jimmy Watson played next to Kelly and was particularly effective in the air. He was the first Motherwell player to go to England, taken there by Bill Shankly, who installed him at Huddersfield Town alongside a puny young Scottish refugee named Denis Law.

My love affair with these demi-gods was interrupted twice, but never broken; first by the glitter of Glasgow of a night-time when, as the Kilmarnock-reared novelist Willie McIlvanney once observed, the city could create a rodeo in your head, and then by Betsy. Before I met Betsy, when I was sixteen and seventeen years old, with greased hair and the misguided belief that I could travel up from Motherwell and bend Glasgow to my will, I walked the terrain made famous by comedian Billy Connolly – the Saracen's Head pub with beer at six pennies a glass, and then on to the great dancing palace, Barrowlands. According to Connolly, you drank in the Saracen's Head in a plastic mac, then took it off to show your sartorial splendour once you got into the dancehall. Plastic mac or not, we arrived at Barrowlands strutting like peacocks.

Those were the days of the razor gangs and the teddy boys and we all knew we had to be careful when we got off the bus in Glasgow. Everyone stressed the need to stay mob-handed because if you were stranded on your own, you could find yourself in desperate trouble. Some of us took the extra precaution of fashioning knuckle-dusters when we should have been labelling the pipeline for Kuwait.

'Grab-night' at Barrowlands was one of the pivotal social occasions. Grab-night was when the girls had about ten 'ladies' choices' and as we sat in front of the coke fire at the factory, we would make the odds on the guy who would enjoy the most 'grabs'. It was quite a cruel process. The good-looking boys would go into the arena at evens or 2–1 and a 'homely' lad might enter the fray as long as 100–1.

The girls would have tickets and when the music stopped, a number would be called out. The girl with that number would go up to the stage with the chance of winning a jackpot. This of course created a frenzy of dancing as the girl would have to be on the dancefloor with a boy in order to win, so the girls would come at the boys in great waves. If you didn't get snaffled up in the first charge, there was a temptation to panic and sneak away to the toilet for fear that suddenly a big fat girl would lay hold of you. One of our lads was dancing with a girl when she won the jackpot. He said, 'Oh, yes,' and she replied, 'What do you mean, "Oh yes?"' He said, 'Well, don't I get half?' She said, 'Fuck off.' No one ever mistook grab-night for 'Come Dancing'.

It was not the most promising time for me, what with the drinking and the knuckle-dusters in my pocket, and when I look back I see that Betsy, two years younger than I am but strong-willed and sure of herself, didn't come into my life a moment too soon. There was no strong presence in Motherwell to say to me, 'Hey, what the hell do you think you're up to?' until Pat McCourt got hold of me and John McPhee. Under his influence, we stopped going to the Saracen's Head and Barrowlands, and soon after that I saw Betsy at the Miners' Institute in Bellshill, a mile or two up the road from Motherwell and the home town of Sir Matt Busby. Betsy was fifteen and I admired her from a distance for a couple of nights – I wasn't the bravest in the romantic stakes – before getting up the nerve to ask her for a dance, and that night I walked her home. That was me, or, I should say, us.

Our courtship lasted just two years but some of that time was extremely hazardous for me. After seeing her home to her mother's house – like me, she had lost her father, killed while going to work when a bus knocked him off his bike – I had to dodge and duck my way back to Motherwell because the road home passed through housing estates that were rife with gang life. There was only one road to Motherwell and the last stretch of it ran uphill. I used to gather my strength for that last dash from danger.

Eventually, I earned safe passage with the help of one of the lads at the Bridge Works, Willie Calhoun. He was from Bellshill and was widely considered the king of the teddy boys, not because of any ferocious reputation but because he looked so fabulous with his thick Presley sideburns, his long jacket and tight trousers and his blue suede shoes. Willie was more a model than a fighter – someone once said he had decided he could never risk his beautiful, shining white teeth in any kind of rowdiness – but his aura was such that he didn't have to fight. He seemed to look down on everybody and the more arrogant he was, the more the guys loved him. Fortunately, he took a liking to me and made it clear to everyone that, as far he was concerned, I could walk the streets of Bellshill without fear.

Many years later, when I was playing for Liverpool and had a tour match at Randall's Island in New York City, I met my protector again. He was living in Queen's and insisted on taking

Ronnie Yeats and me back to his house, where we had a few drinks, which were very welcome. It had been a draining hot day in New York and Bill Shankly and Bob Paisley had denied us any liberal use of the water bottles, even when we complained that we were in danger of dying of dehydration. Shanks just said, as he would, that we should get on with the game. Willie was sympathetic and after plying us with drinks, he took us off to Greenwich Village. He had finished his time at the Bridge Works and gone to live in America after marrying a girl from Brooklyn. He had been away from Bellshill for just three or four years but had acquired the purest American accent. I strained my ears but I couldn't detect even a hint of Lanarkshire. This was not a total surprise because the consensus back home was that he had always thought he was starring in a movie.

Willie's protection had meant that I could conduct a normal courtship without feeling like a hero out of 'West Side Story'. Betsy's mother thought we were a bit young when we announced our engagement, but she said she could see how we felt about each other and she had no serious objection. The strong opposition came from my mother. She formed an alliance with her brother James, son of the Glasgow tram driver, and my Motherwell manager, Bobby Ancell.

One night, after I'd played for Scotland at Hampden, my Uncle James was waiting for me outside the ground. He got hold of me and said, 'You've got everything before you, laddie, you're too young to get married. Take your time. Concentrate on the football.' Ancell gave me the same treatment. He said I had enough to do getting to the top in football. A young wife and bairns, well, that would drag me back. No one could shake me, though. I said it was a simple matter. I wanted to be with Betsy. At the same time, I could understand my mother's position. She had had such a hard time and now, when things were getting a little easier, she saw my money going out of the house. I had looked after her as well as I could and I told her that I wouldn't abandon her now, but it was also true that I had to live my life. I loved my mother, of course, but I was also locked into first love, true love, all those sentiments that Matt Monro and Pat Boone sang about so relentlessly. 'Think of your career, laddie,' said Ancell and Uncle James, and my mother wore a hurt and troubled look, but I was beyond any argument.

Betsy's mother had married again, but there had been no more children and she said I could move into Betsy's room. After six months, the club provided us with a flat. It had only one room, but there was an indoor toilet.

For a little while the marriage did create a problem with my mother, and that was hard, but I never believed that any bad feelings would be permanent. We had been through too much together, fought too many battles, to be separated for any length of time and soon enough I was calling at her flat and leaving a few bob.

In the circumstances, organising Motherwell's wedding of the year proved a little difficult and, in the end, just six of us gathered together in the church in Bellshill – Betsy and me, my best man John McPhee, Betsy's best friend Ann Simpson and another friend, Willie Watson, from the Bridge Works, and his girlfriend. They decided they would get married at the same time as us and that was the wedding party, two married couples, John McPhee and Ann Simpson. We told John and Ann they shouldn't wear themselves out with the confetti.

The wedding night was spent in Glasgow but unfortunately the taxi taking us to the hotel broke down. For a while McPhee and I helped the driver push the taxi along the street in Glasgow but it was all very embarrassing. Guys recognising me as a Scottish international came out of the pubs saying, 'All right, wee man, are you needing some help there? Can't you afford the petrol?'

We had a meal in the hotel and then went along to the 'Five-Past-Eight Show' starring Stanley Baxter and Jimmy Logan. The following day was sweltering when Betsy and I loaded our cases into a crowded train, heading to the exotic honeymoon resort of Birmingham, where we stayed for two weeks with one of Betsy's aunts. The bridal suite was the spare room.

We had married on 18 July, which meant that a new season was looming. I took my training kit and every day worked out on a nearby school field. In the evenings Betsy's uncle took me to the local pub, where I learned that Celtic and Rangers fans were not the only ones to draw so much warmth from hating the other team across the city. Most of the banter was about Villa or City. Strangely, in this alien place, and at the age of twenty, I was discovering that football passion stretched a lot further than my own streets, and I began to realise that my own place in the game had, if I wanted to claim it, been a lot more secure and for a longer time than I had imagined.

My first significant breakthrough came when I played for the Scottish Association of Boys' Clubs at the age of sixteen. I was an emerging star for North Motherwell when Motherwell sent a message that they wanted two youngsters to report for training at Fir Park. I was sent along with Eddie Boyle, a classy little player who had, in the eyes of the manager, one serious drawback – he was an out and out teddy boy, a trainee Willie Calhoun. He had it all, the greased hair, the sideburns, the long jacket and the tight-bottom trousers. I was a much more modest version of the phenomenon, with semi-tight trousers and just a hint of a Tony Curtis hairstyle. Ancell was not impressed with either of us. He said to me, 'The next time you come here I don't want to see those trousers.' The order to Eddie was much more drastic. 'You,' he said, 'have to get rid of the lot, the haircut, the clothes, everything.'

As we walked away, Eddie said, 'He can fuck off.'

'Eddie, you can't say that. You have to come back. This is a pro club, this is your chance, you can be a great player, you can make your life here,' but I could see that I was wasting my breath. Eddie's face said no. Nothing would persuade him to put away the gear.

I went to get a new haircut and a pair of trousers that weren't too tight at the bottoms. I hoped Eddie would change his mind but he was quite emphatic. Later, whenever he came into my mind, I said to myself, 'Christ, Eddie, you will never know which way it might have gone. They said come and train with the pros and you turned it down.' Of course, the teddy boy craze passed out of fashion soon enough, as did the special talent of Eddie Boyle.

Motherwell signed me as a provisional player and paid me £2 a week. For this I had to thank one of the top local scouts, Peter Keachie. Not much local talent passed him by, and he had been instrumental in getting some of us started in Boys' Club football. His recommendation was that I should spend some time in Junior football with Douglas Water Thistle, a club based in the village of Rigside, which is ten miles outside Motherwell and most notable to the outside football world as the home of Bill Shankly's sister.

Rigside was a mining community. The pitch, located at the bottom of a big hill that, on match days, was always dotted with fans, was huge and lovely. It seemed to be on another more luxurious, picturesque planet than the one that required you to play on cinders and ash. I signed for Douglas Water Thistle, which made me twelve shillings and sixpence a week richer on top of Motherwell's £2 and my pay at the Bridge Works. Another advantage was an excellent bus service from Motherwell.

It was a sharp step up from the well-taught but amateur

football of North Motherwell to the rigours of Scottish Junior football in the Lanarkshire League, but I handled it well and scored regularly. Junior football implies another intermediate stage of the game, but the reality was that you found yourself up against a mixture of seasoned pros on the way down and some of the brightest young talents in the country. Suddenly you were in a man's world and some of the implications went way beyond the simple matter of how you played the game. You had to have your wits about you both on and off the ball. If you were playing against some old sweat who was beginning to struggle, you were still entitled to play the best you could – you had, after all, your future to make – but the wise kid didn't take liberties.

You played hard but with a degree of respect, and if you were slow to reach this sound approach, there was no shortage of incentives. I certainly heard more than one echo of Baldy Shaw's menacing approach to his duel with Charlie Tully. 'If you go by me again, I'll break your leg, you little bastard,' was one caution I received, but ultimately you had to have the nerve to do it again, and whenever it was necessary. The trick was to do your job but without too much showy provocation to the heart of a fading old pro.

Half a season was enough for me to establish my credentials for the big league and no one was surprised when I got the call-up to Fir Park. Playing for Thistle was certainly a formative stage of my career, although on one occasion I did wonder whether I was going to survive physically. It was during an away game in some remote corner of Lanarkshire. There were times when you got the idea that most of the county was nothing but barren hills and sub-zero temperatures. The rain was tipped with ice and wherever you looked, someone seemed to be on the point of freezing to death. Eventually, the referee called it off because of the extreme conditions. We all rushed to a hot communal bath and club officials came into the dressing room with reviving whisky. I'd become convinced that if they hadn't abandoned the game, someone was going to die of hypothermia, and I was the prime candidate.

After the Saturday afternoon battles for survival, there was the night training with the pros. The Motherwell trainer Tommy McKenzie, who had been a fine player, believed in the value of consistent habits and good basic fitness. His opening instruction was invariably, 'Assemble on the track.' Then he would say, 'Ten laps,' and when we had finished he would usually say, 'Right, let's have four more.'

The pitch was alien ground during a training session. We pined for the ball but the best we could hope for was a bit of a kick-around on the cinders of the car park, and maybe a brief five-a-side game. After about eight weeks of this routine, Tommy surprised us one night when he declared, 'I'm going to change the training tonight.' I murmured, not quite under my breath, 'Thank God,' and I fancied he was looking at me hard when he added, 'I want you to run the other way around.'

When I returned to Motherwell as manager fourteen years later, I discovered little had changed. I arrived to supervise my first training session to be told, 'You can't go on the pitch.' I told them to switch on the floodlights. I was going on the field to work the goalkeepers. Astonishingly, I had discovered that the keepers never handled the ball between games.

Even more remarkably, I can say that when I played for Motherwell it was in some ways the best football I would ever know, and of course that includes the high tide of Bill Shankly's Liverpool. It was wonderfully sharp football – we interchanged positions, we ran behind defences, we were tight on the ball and we passed it fluently. It was proper football of bite and imagination. I benefited particularly from the brilliant wing play of Billy (better known as Willie) Hunter, who was quick and had the killingly effective knack of swerving without touching the ball.

I went straight into the Motherwell team after my call-up from Thistle, which was the result of Peter Keachie's close monitoring of my progress. They stuck me on the right wing for a game against Queen of the South in Dumfries in the border country. I told the lads at the Bridge Works that I was heading for England, which was just a little bit premature. In those days, they also put me on the left wing because of my speed, but that was never going to work too well because my left leg was a swinger. However, I made the best of it and it helped that I was good at cutting in to the centre. It was there, it was clear enough, that I would make my mark.

When I signed as a part-time professional, my wages were bumped up to £6 a week and I received a £20 signing-on bonus. I shared it with my mother. It is laughable now when you remember what you could buy with a tenner. I bought myself a new suit and a fine sweater. I didn't spend all my new wealth quite so wisely. On Saturday mornings I would go up to Glasgow to a little barber's shop, Fusco's, that had pictures on the wall and fancy prices. I would have my hair trimmed, shampooed and blow-dried and then get the bus back to play for Motherwell, where, of course, it was often raining. Naive behaviour, no doubt, but then they were naive days for most professional footballers. We played because we loved the game. It was an attractive, even glamorous, alternative to the pit and the steelworks, which had, one way or another, claimed the lives of so many of our relatives.

Motherwell Football Club had become my life and they had four highly productive years out of me before selling me off for £37,500 in 1961, and when that happened they didn't give me a penny. No one said, 'Well done, lad, you've been great for the club, here's a few hundred quid as a parting gift.' If agents had been around, no doubt I would have had one and done rather better for myself, but a player of course had no rights, no freedom of action, and if an agent had shown up at Fir Park, he would have been ushered to the door with some force. In those circumstances, I didn't have the nerve to say anything. In fact, if it hadn't been for Betsy, I would probably have accepted my fate, played down the years as most other favourite sons of Mother-well had done, a Willie Redpath or an Andy Paton, a character in the street, a man to be honoured as he faded away with a store of memories and a lean bank account.

As it was, when the choice came, when I had to decide between two offers from England or the maintenance of my celebrity status in Scotland, I was lucky to have the strong presence of Betsy at my side. Her voice was insistent. She said, 'You are the centre-forward of Scotland. You deserve more. You deserve sixty pounds a week.'

One repercussion of a move to English football, I knew well enough, would be a weakening of my position in the national team. It was an inevitable consequence of a move south. The Scottish press tended to take their collective eye off you when you crossed the border, and I was reminded of this only recently when I saw that David Mackay – rated by Jimmy Greaves as the best player with whom he ever shared a dressing room – acquired the grand total of twenty-two caps. That is just one of the many travesties thrown up by that old prejudice against the 'Anglo' Scots who, throughout the sixties and seventies, were such a huge presence in the top flight of English football. Denis Law, Paddy Crerand and I also suffered to some degree, but the case of Mackay stands out as a crowning scandal. Mackay was a supreme example of the best that Scottish football could produce; he had both iron and a silky skill.

No doubt Betsy was right in her instincts, as I was right to

Cast in bronze, Bill Shankly's constant demand – 'make the people happy'.

Above An outbreak of peace as I stroll with the O'Hanlon boys, Raymond (*left*) and Jimmy – and no sign of the terrifying Paper Lady.

Below The man I knew so briefly, my father Alex (*far left, middle row*).

Above Big sister Wilma, a star influence, and brother Billy, who did not always follow the lead. Our kilts were hand-me-downs from Glasgow relatives.

Above Motherwell's player of the year in 1958, I was given an expensive radio as a prize. Clearly, I was beginning to enjoy the attention.

Below 'Be first,' a striker always tells himself, and on this occasion my reward is a headed goal against Djurgaarden of Sweden in the Fairs Cup in 1958.

Above The wedding taxi Betsy and I shared with my best man John McPhee and Betsy's best friend Ann Simpson looks grand enough, but the glamour dwindled when we had to get out and push.

Below As Scotland's current centre-forward, I received most of the headlines when I was sacked from Motherwell Bridge Engineering Company along with five other apprentices – the charge, 'bone idleness'.

Above In 1977 Tom Watson and Jack Nicklaus fought out one of the most memorable Open finishes at Turnberry. Twenty years earlier, four other hopefuls – (*left to right*) John McPhee, me, Pat Quinn and Willie Hunter – stepped out on to the great course. Reaction to our play was less reverent.

Below 'So tell us how it was back in those days, Señor…' I lead the questioning of Real Madrid's famous president Santiago Bernabeu as he watches his team train before their epic European Cup final with Eintracht Frankfurt at Hampden Park in 1960. Bernabeu had played for Real against Motherwell in 1923.

dismiss with contempt some criticism of her that she was a go-getter who had attached herself to a famous Scottish footballer. That was nonsense. When we met, I was still a warrior of the Boys' Club. I had yet to make my reputation and send signals to some of the big clubs beyond the border.

However, none of this is to say that I left Scotland with the easiest of hearts. Certainly, I would never forget the excitement of growing up as a professional with Motherwell, the sense of achievement as we punched our weight in a Scottish League, where the powerhouses of Rangers and Celtic were obliged to fight off our serious challenge and those from Aberdeen and Dundee.

One key stage of our development was a visit to watch Real Madrid preparing for their famous European Cup final with Eintracht Frankfurt. That was the match in which Alfredo di Stefano and his team-mates enshrined their brilliance in a 7–3 victory, and is regarded as the climactic performance in their dominance of European club football.

Going up to see Real was a voyage of discovery. Malcolm Allison, who did such superb work at Manchester City in the late sixties and was such a big influence on coaching methods, reported a similar sensation when he watched the Red Army team Dynamo training in the Viennese woods while he was on national service in the late forties. So much of our training had been by rote. Now we realised, as Allison had done when he was a player at Charlton and West Ham, that players could teach and improve themselves. The game was wide open for improvisation and intelligent experiment.

As we developed as a team, we became more ingenious in the matter of taking free kicks. Few other teams in Scotland considered them and it gave us a big edge. In this process, Pat Quinn became the quintessential Scottish inside-forward – small, tough and creative. He won a few caps for Scotland but it always seemed to me that he was worth more. He was hugely popular in the dressing room, no doubt for several reasons but the overwhelming one was that he was the only one of us to own a car. It was a big old Ford Zephyr into which most of the team crowded from time to time. How was it that a young professional footballer enjoyed the extraordinary luxury of a car? His father was a bookie.

Quinn set the tone of our team with his intelligence, and around him a bunch of small, quick fellows, including Billy Hunter, Andy Weir, Sandy Reid and me, darted forward and interchanged positions. On Quinn's best days it must have appeared that we were operating at the end of his string. However, it has to be said that we were not always best served by our goalkeeper, Hastie Weir. Once he conceded a goal against Dunfermline from a free kick taken from the other side of the halfway line. 'Christ,' said one of the lads, 'we'll have to score three if we want a draw.' Often when we kicked off, we would all take a look back at the goalie and he would shout something comradely, like, 'Get on with the game, you cheeky swine.'

Eventually, Ancell realised that he had to find a stronger goalkeeper and brought in Alan Wyllie, a big lad from Edinburgh. Some years later he was killed in a car crash. Wyllie brought us more security at the back and, having finally identified the problem, the manager took two further steps to stiffen the last line of defence, signing Joe Mackin, a classic goalkeeping type who refused to see anything but the funny side of life, and Johnny Duncan. They were all good pros, but the problem was solved just a little too late. The team was on the point of breaking up and the great chance of adding a little silverware to that won by boyhood heroes had come and gone.

In many ways, Ancell was a lucky manager. Good players fell

into place largely as the result of the excellent work of the scout Peter Keachie. Billy Hunter, Charlie Aitken and Bobby Roberts came down from Edinburgh, and good local blood included John Martis, who was a rougher version of Andy Paton but still an extremely accomplished centre-half. Big John was a Motherwell boy and played for the team with great passion and determination. Indeed, he was so determined he never smiled, not in any circumstances.

If Ancell had some good fortune, he was certainly not without vision. He had seen the impact of Wolves' trail-blazing in England when they played floodlit games against Spartak of Moscow and Honved of Budapest. Ancell imported teams from Europe after Preston North End came up for the opening game under flood-lights, with Tom Finney, Tommy Docherty and Willie Cunning-ham. I was quite dazzled that first night under the lights, standing in the band box and feeling something of that great sensation when the street lights came on so brightly at the end of the war.

Athletic Bilbao were important visitors and then came the greatest thrill of all — Brazilian opposition in the lithe shape of Flamenco. They had two little black wingers and for a while they made it seem just possible that we might never the touch the ball. They scored quickly, and then added another, but we forced our way into the game and showed that Scotland too had a number of snappy little fellas up front. I was one of them and I managed to score — six times. It was argued later that this was maybe the most thrilling game ever played at Fir Park. Certainly, I knew when I came off the field that I would always have this match with me as a reminder of how the game is played at its best — full of wit, fluency and sheer cleverness on the ball.

Another rite of passage came when Leeds United arrived for a floodlit game. I was playing against Jack Charlton, and although Leeds hadn't at that point acquired the formidable reputation that would come soon enough, they still represented a severe test for a Scottish side that was beginning to make its mark with the quality of its football. We put seven goals past Leeds and by the end of the game Jack's mood was not good, especially when I nipped by him to score the second of two goals. After the game, the Leeds winger George Meek, a Lanarkshire lad, said to me, 'I told them on the way up that you boys were a little bit useful but they didn't seem to want to know. So I said, "Okay, boys, I'll leave it to you to find out."' He seemed quite pleased that we had murdered his team, perhaps because it might just have worked against more than a touch of arrogance.

At that point you wouldn't have picked out Jack Charlton as a future pillar of England's 1966 World Cup triumph. He was a big, raw-boned character but his game was far from complete. Many years later I talked to Don Revie, the man who shaped Jack's career at Leeds, and he shook his head when he went back to those first months after he took over at Elland Road.

'When I first arrived,' said Revie, 'Jack made it clear that it was his way or no way, and the trouble was that his way was the wrong way.'

When I put this to Jack he admitted it was true. 'Eventually, I suppose the penny dropped,' he drawled.

It certainly had at Fir Park; we had a tremendous unity and enthusiasm for developing our game. Pat Delaney came in at left-back and did a fine job. He was the son of Jimmy Delaney, Cup-winning hero of Celtic and Manchester United and a star of Scotland. A fine, hard defender, his Motherwell days reached an early peak when he scored against Rangers at Ibrox, in a 5–2 win. We had ambition and a fine assembly of talent. We also had a player who seemed to me at the time – and that image has never dwindled down the years – to represent the best that a professional could be. He was Charlie Aitken.

In England, there are regular claimants to the title of the best player who never won an international cap. In the case of Scotland, Charlie would always be my choice. He had been in the army when Motherwell reached the Cup final in 1952, but the club had successfully argued for his release. He had a wonderful touch and calmness on the field, and his heading was especially fine. He had the knack of rising high and perfectly directing the ball to a team-mate. He was also a gentleman.

History wasn't kind to Charlie, no more than it was to Norman Hunter, a tremendous defender, physically and technically, who was condemned to occasional appearances for England under the awesome shadow of Bobby Moore. Charlie's misfortune was to operate in the era of Dave Mackay. Other rivals, such as Bobby Evans of Celtic and Ian McColl of Rangers, had an immediate edge because they played for those more prestigious clubs. Charlie's reputation was built not in the eyes of the selectors but in those of the more discerning fans.

Our most flamboyant half-back was Bert McCann. He loved to dash forward and play one-twos. McCann was a university graduate, which separated him a little from the rest of us. He didn't come off the streets and we believed there would be a touch of the amateur about him, but there was never any question about the fact that he could play. Sometimes he lacked a certain edge, probably because he never saw football as his entire life, but that didn't stop him being popular and, unlike Charlie, he did win a Scottish cap.

In front of players of such good quality we had 'Ancell's Babes' – five little wizard boys all in a row: Billy Hunter, Sammy Reid, me, Pat Quinn and Andy Weir. Wee Sammy Reid could have had the most sensational career. In fact, he did well enough to attract the attention of Bill Shankly at Liverpool, but after a year he returned. Like his brother, Billy, who played for us at full-back,

Sammy never grew. He had been brilliant as a boy in Motherwell and was chosen to play for the Scotland schoolboys team, but apart from his lack of growth, he had another serious problem – he just couldn't finish off a move. He could get in some remarkable positions but when the time came to apply the killing stroke, he became over-excited. Fortunately, though, he created as many chances for others as he squandered himself, and I benefited particularly. Reid was a vital part of our team.

I was convinced we would finish up with a major trophy and that belief was strong right up to the moment we lost the last Cup-tie I played for Motherwell. It was against Airdrie in 1961, when we were strongly fancied to win the Scottish Cup. We battered Airdie. Charlie Aitken leapt in his classic way to send the ball crashing against the crossbar. Lawrie Leslie, who would go on to play for West Ham United and Scotland, was a giant in the Airdie goal. Long before the end, and even while we were still completely outplaying them, we became convinced that the ball just wouldn't go in. I don't know whether something snapped inside me that day, or whether there was a dawning sense that, for all our talent and teamwork, we were not destined to go all the way to a piece of silver.

Whatever the reason, my time in Scotland was fast ebbing away. So much had been achieved in the way we played. We had given pleasure and received it in the response of the crowd and our own exhilaration in the quality of the football we had produced – but inevitably I felt a tug of desire for something more. Soon enough a combination of Bill Shankly and Betsy provided the impetus for a new stage for football – and life. First, though, the old one had to be dismantled in my brain and my heart. It would prove a painful and quite complicated business.

4

THANKS TO
HASTIE WEIR

B ILL SHANKLY swept into my life, talked me out of signing for
Newcastle United and, within a matter of hours, Betsy and I
had been bundled into a Rolls-Royce and were being driven to
Anfield. Shankly, ferret-like, darted from one dream of a dazzling
future to another, but as the miles ticked by, I found myself to
some extent still locked in the past.

There was, after all, a lot of baggage to contend with – so
much fear and laughter, crisis and hope. Even now, when I could
see the value of Betsy's strength and the dynamism of a football
manager who was plainly on the way to making a great name, I
felt apprehension about what the future might bring. I was a big
name in Scotland, a king in my little empire, and now I had to
prove myself all over again.

I thought of the hard days in Scotland – and the great ones. I
thought of how it was, getting the first call to the Scottish colours
and running out at Hampden Park in the company of Dave Mackay
and John White. I recalled scoring a hat-trick against Hibernian at
Easter Road in just two and a half minutes, and then there was that
other one against Third Lanark at Fir Park. That was the one I
scored in a fever of guilt and then much relief. Behind it was the
most difficult and maybe outrageous story I have to tell of my days
in the Scottish game. The hat-trick came on the day Motherwell, a
team beloved of their fans, a team of the brightest football and the
biggest hopes, were supposed to throw a game.

Instead of losing and causing one of the biggest upsets in the Scottish League programme, we scored seven goals. No team ever played with such intensity. It was as though we had helped let loose the hounds of hell and were running for our lives – or at least our respectability and a place in the game that, as we would tell anybody who asked, we loved so deeply. Undoubtedly, a betting culture was working its way into the game. Later in England, newspaper revelations exposed the terrible scandal of the betting coups that eventually led to the imprisonment of three stars of Sheffield Wednesday, Tony Kay, Peter Swan and David 'Bronco' Layne. That this activity had reached Scotland became clear when the Motherwell players received a message about a meeting of 'interested parties' in Glasgow. Some of the people involved are now dead, some are not, but because in the end no crime was committed I feel entitled to tell the story strictly from my own perspective, and how it affected me and some of my closest friends in the Motherwell dressing room.

The proposal was based on the need to back two outsiders away from home from a list of ten matches issued by William Hill. It was a standard 10–1 bet. We were confidently expected to beat Third Lanark. Our representatives in Glasgow were told that if we managed to lose, each player involved in the 'fix' would be paid £100. It may seem like a piffling amount to receive in exchange for your football soul but it was the equivalent of ten weeks' wages. Perhaps it was not surprising that the criminal end of the betting fraternity had begun to infiltrate the game, playing on the weaknesses of 'star' players who were paid so poorly they couldn't afford even the most modest car. The temptation for lads gleaning such meagre rewards, who despite drawing huge crowds had no security, no chance of buying a house, was maybe stronger than it should have been. I could see that easily enough, and it probably didn't help in the moral dilemma that some big names attended the meeting with the betting crowd. We can moralise at any length we choose on what is right and wrong, and those who were most interested in accepting the deal were no doubt aware of the terrible potential to bring shame on the team and all our families. On the other hand, did one match matter against the chance of having a little money in the bank, the possibility of putting something down on a small car or taking a holiday in the sun, something beyond any of our dreams as we were growing up? All we had to do was throw a game, but when you got down to the nitty gritty of it, there was another big question – how do you do it? One point was obvious. It was no good ten outfield players conspiring to lose if the goalkeeper wasn't in on the arrangement. We had all played games in which one team had been utterly outplayed but their goalkeeper had produced one of the performances of his life.

At the meeting in Glasgow our team representatives and some players from Third Lanark were told we would be informed later about the other match that had been fixed. This was part of the deal – we got the £100 plus the chance to bet at long odds on two 'certain' results. Of course, there would be danger in placing the bet if you were involved in either of the games. You would have to get a friend, someone you felt you could entrust with the quality of your life, to put the bet on.

It was obvious to us that the betting guys had done this before. We were not, it seemed to us, their first targets – they had everything worked out. One startling, telling fact was that at the Glasgow meeting there were some famous names of the Scottish game, older players who no doubt were in some agony over the fact that, as their physical resources were beginning to run out, they faced a return to the crowd, maybe even the factory or pit from which they had imagined, like me, they had escaped forever.

A few years after the Rolls-Royce drive to England the

Sheffield story broke and Shankly went mad, marching around the dressing room declaring, 'Anyone who bets against his own team should go to fucking jail . . . they should throw away the key,' and while he ranted my blood ran cold. I could only be grateful that the disaster hadn't happened because by then I didn't have to hear Shankly to know that for a professional to throw a game was the worst thing he could do. I thought then that if I'd been playing on a team when some of the others were not trying to win, but instead were actively attempting to lose, I too would have gone mad, but that was, relatively speaking, in my maturity. Back in Motherwell, as a teenager, I hadn't seen the issue quite so clearly. Deep down, I probably knew it would be wrong, deeply wrong, but because of the state of football then, the absolute refusal to give a player anything more than was considered his due – and that was so very little – the moral dilemma didn't hit me so hard. This isn't so much a confession, although maybe you think it should be, as a statement of reality.

What would a professional at the top of his game but with no prospect of the good life have been giving up, in practical terms, if he took the betting money, which with a successful wager could have added up to a stunning amount, as much as £1,000? A £2 win bonus. Yes, it was wrong that the possibility of taking a dive had lodged so dangerously in our minds, but what do we say about the attitude of the clubs, and their failure to reward young men of talent properly? In so many cases in those days, players displayed terrific dedication and became great heroes of their community.

Another problem was that in the planning stage, no one seriously entertained the possibility of being caught. How could you prove someone had thrown a game? Already I had played in games when I had missed unbelievably easy chances, toeing shots over the bar while facing an open goal. On several occasions anyone looking for the 'fix' might have nominated me as a citizen weighed down with suspicion but, of course, such missed chances are part of the game. Who could prove that a mistake was deliberate? When the Bruce Grobbelaar affair exploded across football a few years ago, a witness as experienced as Sir Bobby Robson went into court to declare that, in his professional opinion, Grobbelaar had done nothing wrong.

So the strategy was quite straightforward after the Glasgow meeting. The forwards, Ancell's wee wizards, would have an afternoon of bewildering inefficiency. They would shoot not for the goals but the stars, and the profit – but the other, burning question was the goalkeeper, Hastie Weir. As I've already mentioned, Hastie was not one of the great keepers; nor was he one of us. He had a good job as a works manager and when he joined us from the amateur club Queen's Park, he reputedly signed for £10,000, which was rather more generous than the bonus received by the rest of the dressing room with the exception of the other former amateur player of note, McCann. The pros joined for a mere £20 and the discrepancy lodged in the craw, most violently when Hastie made one of his more spectacular errors.

However, there was always the possibility that he would have one of his great games, as even the most erratic goalkeepers do from time to time, against Third Lanark. The big question was how to handle Hastie. Should we leave it to chance, play in the outfield in a way that gave Third Lanark every opportunity of winning the game and hope that the goalkeeper provided some inadvertent help? In the end, the decision was to compromise. At Thursday-night training Hastie was given an inkling that something was afoot, but nothing was spelled out. Then in the dressing room before the start of the game he was cornered, told what was about to happen and asked quite bluntly, 'Do you want in?'

Hastie Weir went berserk. He stormed off to the manager's office and re-appeared almost immediately with Ancell. Weir was raging and ranting like some fire-and-brimstone preacher. Ancell was cold and hard-eyed. Eventually, he said, 'Right, what's going on here can't happen. There will be no such thing.' He said that throwing a football match was an unspeakable crime. A terrible price would be paid by anyone proved to be involved. Naturally, we stood there open-mouthed and with innocent expressions fixed on our faces. Just a few minutes before kick-off, everyone in that dressing room knew that the great betting coup was dead in the water, but there was no time to get the word out to the betting boys.

Strangely enough in those hard days, when the razor gangs were rampant on the streets of Glasgow, there were no repercussions. I suppose the betting fraternity fell back on the old philosophical point that sometimes you win, sometimes you lose. From the moment Hastie exploded with that great force of moral indignation, losing was simply not an option. No combination of circumstances could have dislodged our fight for redemption. We played quite brilliantly, scored seven goals and my hat-trick was the centrepiece of a performance that earned rave headlines.

So we saved both our reputations and our future in the game. There it was, a pivotal moment in my life, when circumstances could have pushed me down the wrong way at the crossroads. We were rescued from the folly of youth, and, in a way, I suppose the game also had a reprieve. From what, though? Maybe the consequences of meanness and a total failure to understand that football couldn't forever be corralled as just another enclave of working-class life. Whatever an old pro feels about players' progress to today's astonishing wealth, however he reacts to such news as Rio Ferdinand, the England centre-half, demanding a weekly wage of up to £120,000 a week from his club, he is bound to utter at least a small chuckle when he thinks of how such developments would have been greeted in those old boardrooms.

The directors — local businessmen and councillors — who gathered to pronounce on the fate of some ageing player who had given the club the best years of his life, would have been stunned at the new deal, nonplussed to hear that an obscure Belgian footballer had won the right of every player to further his career prospects in the way of any other member of a free society.

Many times, when reflecting on those old days, I have thought that if I could stand the pain of it, and do all the necessary research, I would write another kind of football book — not one of personal reminiscence but a detailed account of the way the game had treated some of its greatest performers. It would be a story filled with regret and sadness, about how so much glory was turned into bitterness, how men who knew the constant sound of cheering soon enough had to deal with the hollow rattle of ingratitude along with the creaking of their bones. Where would I start? Probably with Andy Weir, our brilliant little winger.

Andy escaped, as I did, the nightmare possibilities of the Third Lanark 'fix' but he was less fortunate when we went to play against the same team in an away game. I loved the way Andy played. He could cross the ball on the run as well as any player I've ever seen. He had two great feet, which meant that he could come inside at will.

Third Lanark's ground was near Hampden Park but they are now just an item of Scottish football history, all their efforts ending in liquidation. In the first half Andy was involved in a clash of heads with an opposing defender. He was knocked out and had to be stretchered off. When we went into the dressing room at half-time, Andy was lying on a table. He had come round but he was terribly white and was waiting for an ambulance. We were all a bit shaken and didn't want to crowd him in that pokey little dressing room, so we went straight back out on to the field. The crowd were shouting, 'What's going on, boys?'

Andy lived in a corner flat in the tenement building into which the club had also moved Betsy and me. The following morning the club doctor knocked on our door and told us he had just visited Andy's wife and kids. Andy was still in hospital. The doctor told us, 'I want you to be strong for his wife,' which didn't sound too good. It wasn't good at all. The doctor said that Andy had about twenty-four hours to live. He had cracked a bone in his head and had developed meningitis. We went over to the flat and tried to console his wife. We didn't tell her anything of what the doctor had said but it was clear enough that she knew her man was fighting for his life. In fact, after months in hospital, Andy pulled through. He had lost his hearing on one side and, understandably enough, was never the same player, or the same man, again. He struggled on for a little while, going to training, hoping to find the old speed and confidence, but it was clear it was never going to happen.

That was one of the greatest tragedies I ever saw in the game. Andy had fought his way out of a very bad slum area in Paisley. Football was his one chance of making something of himself, although, initially, even this was something of a long shot because, in all honesty, he wasn't anybody's idea of a dedicated athlete. Andy always had a fag on and his wife was also a heavy smoker. They always seemed to be besieged by their kids, and Andy's habit was to retreat to the betting shop. He seemed to be a lost soul in those weeks after he came out of hospital. The purpose of his life, playing football with great talent and spirit, was seriously threatened, if not ripped right away. I remember saying to Betsy, 'This is ridiculous, you know, the club should be looking after him. They should send him and his wife and kids to get some sunshine in Majorca or somewhere. They should be trying to build him up. He's done a lot for Motherwell.'

I was dreaming, of course, as was confirmed to me when I talked about the possibilities of helping Andy at the club. That's when I felt my first real wave of bitterness about the way players were treated. We might be heroes to the crowd, but for the club we were just cheap and disposable labour. There would always be more of us coming along, nursing our dreams. The pattern would be played out many times in the course of my career as a player and a manager and, after a while, you get used to the way it is. The rage dwindles in the face of a familiar story, but in the case of Andy Weir my feelings were still raw. I hadn't reached the point of swapping too many experiences with old pros, and hearing them say, 'And you think it was bad at your place, listen to this story . . .' That business could remind you of the bleak Monty Python sketch dealing with the deprivations of working-class life, when one character talks about the 'pure luxury' of licking the road for sustenance.

There wasn't much humour, black or otherwise, in watching Andy, a kid in his early twenties, wasting away. He was in a wheelchair soon enough and he died young. He could have achieved much in a football world that nurtured its best talent, but he had certain handicaps. One was his own modest nature, and that of his wife. While Betsy said that we had the world at our feet and we had to go and find it, Andy and his wife couldn't see beyond what they had; they were at the mercy of fate much more than most of us. I don't blame them for that; it was the way they were, or maybe the way they were conditioned to be.

Andy did have one supreme moment, though, and I was glad to be there to share in it. It was my first appearance for Scotland, against West Germany, at Hampden Park in 1959. We won 3–2 and Andy scored. While I didn't score, I had an excellent game, partly because of the wonderful subtlety of the great playmaker John White, who was, like Andy, marked down for tragedy. He was struck by lightning and killed on a golf course. After the Scotland v. West Germany game, one headline proclaimed, 'St John and White make the future bright . . .' Andy should have been part of that future, and he too played in my thoughts as the Roller bore us down to the new world of Merseyside.

Another reflection on the journey was that instead of embarking on this great adventure with my young wife, I might have been on the football scrapheap. The cause would have been, not a chance collision, but quite shocking neglect.

The crisis came early in the 1958–59 season, when my career was just flying along. I had passed quickly through the Under-23 and League teams and established myself with Scotland. I was playing at Fir Park when suddenly I went down and found that my knee was locked. I was in great pain and couldn't straighten the knee. They took me straight to the Law Hospital, which wasn't promising. At that time, the Law Hospital was notorious for its low success rate. It was said that if you weren't seriously ill when you went to the Law, you would be soon enough. The specialist who eventually saw me was not encouraging. He said that the cartilage would have to be removed. So I had the cartilage taken out and was in plaster for several weeks. When the plaster was removed, it was clear that I had suffered considerable muscle wastage.

Motherwell didn't have a scrap of rehabilitation equipment, unless you counted an old medicine ball that was left in the visitors' dressing room, where we went for some basic exercise if the weather was too hard for outside work. The producers of medicine balls must have done very well in those days. No club was too proud or too humble to have one lying around. The lack of anything resembling a treatment room meant that I had to take the bus up to the hospital every day. There, I worked on every available machine in an effort to get the strength back in my knee. Working next to me one day was a guy who didn't seem to be putting his heart into it. I was pushing as hard as I could and when a doctor appeared, I went over to him and said, 'This fella is never going to get his muscles back, look at him.' He was lifting one small bar very slowly. The doctor said, 'Don't worry about him, he's from the nuthouse and he's worried about you. He thinks you're the nutter.'

There was no doubt I was working like a beast. Rivulets of sweat ran down me in the hospital sessions and it was the same at Fir Park, where I continued to push myself at every opportunity, working with the medicine ball, running up and down the terrace and setting myself the target of a record return just six weeks after the cartilage operation. I was told that nobody had ever done that before. Naturally, I congratulated myself as I ran out on the field again in the first-team colours. However, the celebrations were painfully shortlived. In the early minutes of the game, in the first little tackle I received, I was hit on the knee. I went down and, as I lay there looking anxiously at my knee, a lump came up the size of a goose egg. I felt empty inside as they loaded me on to a stretcher and carried me away.

The treatment at the club was primitive. The knee was wrapped in bandages to reduce the swelling and in a few days I returned to training. This was the start of the bleakest period of my playing career, filled with pain and great fear about my future. On the Friday before the next match, they sent me back to the Law Hospital to have the fluid drained. The specialist gave me a small jab to numb the feeling, and then produced a monster phial. A bright light was shining down the table and in the chrome I could the reflection of what he was doing. After the fluid was drained, they put some strapping on my knee and told me I could play the following day. I got through the game but by Monday morning the knee was up like a balloon. I wasn't able to train during the week and then it was the same routine – up to the dreaded Law Hospital, more draining and back in the traces for the Saturday game.

This went on for several more weeks and, not surprisingly, my form was going through the floor. I had started the season as one of Scotland's hottest young players. The press were building me up and I was desperate to add to my reputation with a run of goals but this was difficult as I hobbled around like a one-legged man. Finally, when I presented myself for still another draining session, the specialist said, 'I just can't do this any more. You're knee is being ruined. You have to go away and rest and let the fluid drain away naturally.' When I told Ancell, he shrugged and said, 'Okay then, that's what you'd better do.'

It struck me then that it was a quite hopeless way to run a football club. I was making my mark in the game and, as things operated then, I was a valuable piece of football flesh. Not only were Motherwell putting my career at great risk, they were also endangering one of their prime financial assets. Everyone was in danger of losing.

It took three weeks for the knee to drain naturally. More than ten years later at Liverpool, this was the knee that brought about the beginning of the end of my career. I began to suffer nagging pain and eventually Shankly sent me to the Broad Green Hospital for a cortisone jab. In those days, cortisone was the footballers' wonder drug. Later, it was proved that, in the long term, it did a lot more harm than good. After the jab I returned to training feeling wonderful. I jogged around the training pitch on a tremendous high. 'This is fantastic,' I kept telling myself. It was as though the joint had been given new hinges and thoroughly oiled. I was okay. It was a miracle. 'That's me back,' I thought as I joked with the guys in the shower.

The knee was fine for a month before all the old problems

came back – pain, stiffness, swelling. I went back for more cortisone. I was like a junkie in need of a fix, but eventually I was told once again that I could no longer receive treatment. The jabs were getting me by but sooner or later they would turn me into a cripple. Later, Bob Paisley told me that Shankly had reported the doctor's verdict to him – I had the knees of a sixty year old.

So what could I do? Struggle on towards the end of the road, fighting the pain, trying to make something of my last years as a player? It was only after I finished that I went to Manchester and saw a specialist recommended by the Professional Footballers' Association. I was told that many former players were suffering as I was. I needed an operation and when it was over I asked the surgeon, 'Now, can you tell me what the problem was?' He said that the original operation, all those years ago back in Mother-well, had been a botched job. The Law Hospital had lived up to its deadly reputation. The Manchester doctor explained that a piece of cartilage had been left in the joint and had been floating around, causing trouble. My past – and football's – had simply caught up with me.

Unfortunately, as for so many old professionals, it seriously affected the quality of the rest of my life. Eventually, I spent some time in South Africa, where I did a lot of swimming in the ocean and got as much sunshine as I could. That seemed to help matters for a while but never to the point when I could forget I had a problem. Over the years I've had to make regular hospital visits to have my knee cleaned up. It's what the medical profession calls 'hoovering out'. The pain is more or less constant but you learn that there is no point in carrying any bitterness because almost all old professional players are, to some extent, victims. In so many areas of fitness, the game simply didn't know what it was doing.

Vital work was left in the hands of old players who, mostly, didn't have any medical training. They had survived even more brutal times and if a kid complained, he would be told it was the way it had always been, and would always be. You played hurt, you dragged yourself through a game, you took painkillers, had jabs, were strapped up. It was the way of the beautiful game and you were told you were privileged to be part of it.

All of this came to me in that spring of 1961 as Betsy nestled against my shoulder and the words and dreams of Bill Shankly flowed over our heads and the Rolls purred through the border country, carrying us to our new life. Some positive thoughts rose to the surface, too – the excitement of a new challenge, the wonderment that comes when you realise you are extending your experience and chances of success. Shankly filling the great car with his passion and wit, and some extraordinary insights into how a football team should be run, gave us enough reasons to believe that we had made the right decision.

Another encouragement was the fact that a strong link existed between the football of my past and the future in the shape of Reuben Bennett. In time, Reuben would become a key influence in the legendary Anfield Boot Room, where Shankly would retire at day's end to ruminate with his advisers and friends about the quality of his players, and those he might sign, and where the team was strong and where it was weak.

Reuben came from the old school and few in the game had ever been harder, but he had wit and kindness, too. He never asked a young player to do anything beyond his ability. I first met Reuben when I went up to Motherwell to train with John McPhee while we were playing for Pat McCourt's team. His official title was trainer but he was a lot more than that. He was a mentor, a guide. When we trained, Reuben was always in the front of the running pack. He always gave me a bit of encour-

agement and, as I travelled to Anfield, I thought of him —
accurately — as a warming presence. He had served in the army
through the Second World War and was, I'm sure, a physical
training instructor of formidable toughness. He had played as a
goalkeeper in Aberdeen and Dundee and, after his stint at
Motherwell, took the manager's job at Third Lanark. He didn't
last long there and moved to the coaching staff of Liverpool,
where Shankly very happily inherited him.

As people, they were completely different. Shankly was the
extrovert, the activator; Reuben kept in the shadows but he saw
all that was happening. When it was time to relax, no one knew
how to do it better. He delighted the Liverpool players with
stories of the old days in Scotland. One of his favourites
concerned the time he was playing with his junior team up
in the Highlands. In those days, he insisted, the team would take
a pigeon with them in order to get the score home to the club's
most devoted supporters. On this occasion, the chairman of the
club told a particularly faithful travelling fan, whose name was
Willie, that he was going to be honoured with the job of sending
the pigeon off on its homeward journey. According to Reuben,
Willie was so excited he grabbed hold of the pigeon, shouted in its
ear, 'We won 2–1,' and threw it to the heavens.

Reuben, who was an Aberdeen fisherman's son, also told of
how, when he was playing for Dundee, he got injured and had to
come off the field. They looked at his injury and said he couldn't
go back on. Reuben insisted that he was fit enough to play but
they held him back. He appeared to accept the decision and said
he was going back to the dressing room. Instead, he slipped out of
the front door of the stadium, raced to the first turnstile, leaped
over, made his way through the fans down the terracing, jumped
over the fence and ran back on to the field. Not surprisingly, said
Reuben, by this time crowd and players were falling about

laughing. Whether or not the story was precisely true was not so important as the fact that knowing Reuben made it seem feasible enough.

He was immensely proud of his fitness and, back in Mother-well, he had impressed deeply on McPhee and me the value of going on to the field feeling strong. 'Nothing is better for your confidence, laddies, than going out there knowing that you could run all day and stand up to any challenge.' He would take us to the crush barriers on the terraces at Fir Park and have us work on our strength, saying how important it was to develop the abdominals. 'That's your engine,' he would declare. Many years later at Anfield, he told me how he had gone to Ancell and said, 'Come and look at these boys. They are so strong and fit they are models for everybody at the club.' He told the story with great and touching pride.

Reuben was part of the old football culture but he knew how to connect with a new generation and, given all the limitations of a club such as Motherwell, he did a magnificent job in explaining, and working on, the need for good basic fitness. It certainly served me well when I scored a record hat-trick against Hibs at their ground, Easter Road. We played up the notorious sloping pitch in the second half and were losing 1–0 when I broke loose. I scored three times in less than three minutes.

One of the Scottish papers nominated my effort as 'Feat of the Week'. Those words were engraved on a Ronson lighter that was presented to me, and that was one of the few trophies I ever won with Motherwell. Although I had no use for a swanky Ronson, I valued it as a memento of one of those days that are the best a player can ever experience – a day when no doubt enters your mind and your body feels as strong as it could be.

5

FIGHTING MY CORNER

WHEN I went to Goodison Park to play my first game for Liverpool against Everton in the final of the Liverpool Senior Cup in the spring of 1961, the guy at the gate didn't want to let me in. He didn't know of any Ian St John of Liverpool and it took a little bit of negotiation to get me into the ground. Everton knew me soon enough – I scored three goals in front of the 70,000 crowd.

For me, it was hard to imagine a gathering that size for a game that mattered only in the streets, factories and pubs of one city, a match that in the purest sense offered just a passing edge in bragging rights. That phenomenon had long fired the spirit of Bill Shankly and made him feel that he had finally collided with his true destiny.

I was twenty-two, Scotland's centre-forward, and had kept company on the field with Mackay, White and Law. I was surely permitted, I thought, a little bit of swagger before this new, huge audience. In this, I suppose, Shankly and I had something in common. His whole life seemed to be a gesture of aggression and ambition. Like me, his emotions were never far from the surface. He had hired me to be his hitman in the drive out of the Second Division and the supplanting of Everton as Merseyside's top club. We lost that first match against the big guns, 4–3, but everyone agreed that Shankly and his new man had issued a serious warning.

Over the years I would see so many sides of his nature – his strength, crazy humour, sadness and passion. Although our relationship did not finish in a way that I, and on reflection maybe he, would have hoped, I will always say that behind the bluster, the exaggeration and the bizarre capacity to believe that he was involved in one of the greatest missions the world had ever known, lay a superbly original football mind.

Of course, I could confirm a thousand times the Shankly caricature. I was around, for example, one day when he took a bemused reporter into a toilet cubicle in the new dressing room at Anfield, pulled the chain, and said, 'You know it refills in fifteen seconds . . . it's a world record.' Once, when Italian opponents came to town, he urged them down to the training ground and claimed, 'It's the greenest grass you'll ever see.'

His sayings and his style have burrowed far into the folklore of the game, but this is surely one case where legend has needed little or no invention. I was there, for example, when he delivered his classic, side-splitting team-talk before a game with Manchester United. If my memory holds half decently, this is what he said, just about word for word. He stood by a table, moving about and removing a set of markers one by one. 'They've got Alex Stepney in goal – Christ, he couldn't catch a cold – and Shay Brennan at right-back . . . now I'll tell you something serious, they say Matt Busby has got a bad back but it's not true, he's got two, because the other one can't play either. Then there's wee Nobby Stiles . . . I've got a gnome in my garden bigger than Nobby, and he's blind as well . . . Crerand is assertive but he's even slower than you think . . . [then, after picking up a marker and turning to me] here's Bill Foulkes. You, laddie, can get a hat-trick against him . . . I've seen a juggernaut move more quickly.' When three United markers were left, representing Denis Law, Bobby Charlton and George Best, Shankly's gaze swept around the room. He paused and then he said, 'Now boys, don't tell me you can't beat three men . . .'

When you scrape away the outrageous froth, you come to the real football man. He was the first one I ever met who really got into talking the game, training for it, living it and, in effect, bringing it back to those days when we were kids. After the clockwork running around Fir Park, training under Shankly was an escape, a joy, everything you wanted. As soon as you came out on the training field he was there with bags of balls. After a brief warm-up, the balls would be rolled in your direction as though they were an astonishing treat. 'There you are, boys,' he would say, 'let's go to work.'

He brought in shooting boards, which were great. You worked in pairs, one shooting, one laying it off, and all the time you were turning and hitting the boards. Then you would be crossing and heading, and playing two-a-side games. You would be doing all the things you had done in a Scottish street or tenement backyard, where for so long the nation's best talent had first flowered. Everything he asked us to do came from his experience as a boy back in Ayrshire and with Preston North End and Scotland. As a young manager at Carlisle, Workington, Grimsby and Huddersfield, he had come to see English football as essentially amateur in its failure to understand what best developed a team and individual gifts − familiarity with the ball, playing the game at every opportunity. Every skill was polished on the training field and in the gym, where we battered the ball against walls, playing head tennis and football squash. More sophisticated and officially qualified football theorists may have followed Shankly, but he was the first to realise that for the highest possible performance you had to take the players back to their roots, back to that time when they most enjoyed playing the game.

Shankly's fundamental point was quite simple. He said, 'If you can't pass the ball and you can't control it when it is passed to you, well, you can't play.' He hammered that home relentlessly, and much time was spent passing and receiving the ball in many ways. It meant that if I pick up the ball and pass it to you, it doesn't matter whether it comes to your chest, thigh, foot of anywhere else, you have to take it. If you don't control the ball, or I mis-direct it, the effect is the same – the opposition have the ball and we have failed in the most basic task of keeping possession. I thought of Shankly when I watched Manchester City in 2005 in the last days of the managership of Kevin Keegan, who as a player responded so brilliantly to the promptings of the old master of Anfield. The passing was quite wretched. At one point, a City player hit the ball into a void. No one was these to receive it and thus the pass had no purpose. I could almost hear one of Shankly's blood-curdling cries of frustration. Another Shanklyism – 'Look at a great player, boys, and see how he brings the ball under control, see how he always knows where to go, and where to make the pass or the run.'

Nowadays, it is often painful to watch a game when you imagine you are seeing it through Shankly's eyes. You have to suppress the urge to try to get hold of the manager or coach and ask, 'Have you looked at the film yet? Have you grasped how many times you lost possession in the most unprofessional way?'

Much of the work at set-pieces and throw-ins at Liverpool during Gerard Houllier's time there would have dismayed Shankly. Generally, it is shocking to see how many times the ball is surrendered at a throw-in. You find yourself screaming out for the receiver just to head back to the thrower; he is at least in a little bit of space. Shankly drummed it into us that when the ball is dead, it is a professional duty to come alive. After one match I remember my Scottish compatriot Billy (usually known as

Willie) Stevenson, an excellent ball player, saying, 'One thing you have to say about our team, we all know how to pass the ball – and receive it.' For the boss, such proficiency was not an ambition but an article of faith.

He arrived for me in Motherwell just in time, although later he said that he had been monitoring my position. When Motherwell, after denying my first transfer request, said that I could go, he came to Fir Park on the same day with that record offer of £37,500, but if I was Liverpool's as far as the board was concerned, Shankly had to fight off the challenge of Newcastle's manager Charlie Mitten. The former Manchester United star had paid a heavy price for his rebellion at Old Trafford when he was suspended after flying off to Colombia to play for Bogota without the permission of his club or the world governing body, Fifa. When he knocked on our tenement door, he made a very persuasive case. Most tempting was a £1,000 illegal signing-on bonus, but when I spoke to Ancell about the possibility, he said, 'I'll tell you one thing, you will not be going to Newcastle.'

In the discussion that followed, he made no attempt to talk me out of a move, something he later described in a book as 'my greatest mistake in the game'. His sense of resignation convinced me, along with Betsy's enthusiasm for a new adventure, that I had to head south. Mitten was a suave and impressive fellow, reminding me a little of George Raft, the Hollywood star of gangster movies, and his offer of a grand might have been the clinching factor until Shankly broke off briefly from his speech about the unlimited future of Liverpool Football Club. 'By the way,' he said, 'what's Mitten offering you?' I told him and he said, matter of factly, 'Don't worry about that, son, it will be covered.'

He had apparently swept the move through a questioning boardroom with the help of Eric Sawyer, a director appointed to the board by John Moores when the pools millionaire took a big shareholding in the club. The board had set the limit on how much Shankly could spend on a single player at a mere £12,000, but after listening to his passionate arguments on my behalf, the board wavered and Sawyer made his decisive contribution. 'Listening to the manager,' he said, 'I'm convinced that we should do the deal. In fact, I don't see, if we have real ambition, how we can afford not to do it.'

Shankly at once summoned director Sid Reakes and his Rolls for the drive to Scotland, sweeping into Fir Park like a one-man boarding party. I had never met him before but I was immediately impressed. Like Mitten, he was a sharp dresser – he explained to me that his father was a tailor and he got his ties, which invariably had the colour red as a significant element, from Germany. He was filled with a quite amazing urgency. When he came to our flat, Betsy, like me, was a little overwhelmed – especially when he said we had to go straight down to Liverpool. She said, 'Mr Shankly, you know we have a baby . . .' He brushed aside the problem. 'Take the baby to your mother's,' he ordered. 'We have important business here.'

When we arrived at Anfield we were taken into the boardroom, where a fire glowed and soup and sandwiches were served. That was an early indicator of another staple of Shankly thinking – at all times his players should eat 'wholesome' food. After the intensity of the journey, and the speed of the transfer deal, it was a relief to see old Reuben Bennett sitting in a corner of the room, nodding and smiling and smoking a cigarette.

On the following morning, Shankly took us to Shangri-la. In fact, it was the Liverpool suburb of Maghull, which might not have been mistaken for paradise too many times before, but it certainly looked good to Betsy and me. We were pleased enough with our flat in Motherwell – it did, after all, have an indoor toilet – but the little club house we were now being shown might have been built in dreamland in the eyes of a young Scottish couple bringing up a child in what did, once you got over the luxury of the loo and the running water, still remain a big, gaunt tenement building.

The little house was just being completed. Staggeringly, there was a patch of grass in the front and one at the back. An even more dramatic hint of upward mobility for the St Johns was a car port, a slight, spindly erection for sure, but a sign of impending wealth and new status. Heaven knows, it was a modest enough place but we loved it. The kitchen was big enough to swing any number of cats and eat our wholesome meals, and the living room – or 'lounge' – was separated by glass sliding doors. Betsy was happy, vindicated and triumphant and I was both pleased and proud. The running and the battling and the refusal to settle into the streets of Motherwell had brought some tangible reward. We were in a new world, surrounded by other members of my suddenly prospering profession. Alex Young, Everton's 'golden vision' striker, Alex Parker, an international full-back also of Everton, and his compatriot team-mate Sandy Brown all lived nearby. Soon enough my own team-mate and great friend Ronnie Yeats, the slaughterman from Aberdeen, would come bounding into this Scottish football enclave.

We were proved right to believe in our future happiness in this shining new house and new life. Of course, you cannot trust happiness entirely, and we would soon enough know some of the pain that comes to most lives. Betsy lost two babies, and I will never forget the bleakness of the day when, with Betsy still in hospital, I went along to the church alone with the little coffin of the one who lived for three days. I didn't know you could suddenly plunge into such sadness. The fact that Liverpool were playing Preston in an important game later that day slipped far down in my priorities as I stood mourning the wee boy I would never get to know. You heal in time and we are grateful for the happiness of a good family life, which Betsy and I have always enjoyed with our two children, but that Saturday morning lay heavily on me, more than anything I had ever known.

On the other hand, there was another side to that pain, which Betsy and I have always cherished. It was the relief that came when our son Ian, who had given us some worries when he was born prematurely and had to be placed in an incubator for the first days of his life, survived falling into a neighbour's pond. He toddled through the fence of our back garden and into the fish pond of our great friends, the Hansens. I was sleeping on after playing the night before and Betsy had left the boy with her mother. In the flash of time it takes for a small child to step out of your gaze, Ian had tumbled into the water. I awoke to my mother-in-law's screams. Ian had turned blue but, quite miraculously, the Hansens' son Colin had been doing life-saving in school and he knew what to do. Colin gave the kiss of life while I called for an ambulance. After a few days in hospital, Ian was fine, but it was another reminder that, in life, it is too easy to take the good things you have for granted.

Other less piercing regrets and less dramatic mishaps peppered our time in Maghull. One of them was that we spent the £1,000 signing-on bonus entirely on a new car – a smart Vauxhall – and some furniture. It would have been much wiser to have paid a lump off the cost of a house and taken a mortgage. Instead, we paid rent for our clubhouse. That conclusion came with more mature reflection, however. For quite a while we were immersed in the excitement of our new lives.

One treat provided by the club was a visit to the 1961 FA Cup final. Tottenham Hotspur, the great double-winning team, beat Leicester City 2–0. After the game, which was disappointing considering the quality of the Spurs team – they had Mackay,

White, Danny Blanchflower and Cliff Jones on show – Shankly came up to me in the hotel where we were staying and said, 'Come with me, son, I'm going to see somebody.' He took me to another hotel, where Leicester were having their banquet, and got hold of team captain Frank McLintock, the fine Scottish player who would eventually play such a key role in the Arsenal double-winning team. Shanks yanked Frank out of the dinner and said to him, 'Now, how would you like to join us, son?' He painted an astonishing picture of the future. Liverpool were going to march through England and Europe. His team were going to go off like a bomb in the sky. Here, he said pointing to me, was the best young striker Scotland had produced for many a year, and he had signed up for the big adventure.

Frank seemed quite impressed by the impassioned sales talk but the flagrant 'tap-up' failed when he finally decided to sign for Arsenal. A little later, Bob McNab, the Huddersfield and England full-back, decided the same thing after receiving Shankly's blandishments. When McNab called Anfield to tell Shankly his decision, he was met only with growls and contempt. There were no good wishes for the future. Instead, Shankly said, 'Don't worry about it, laddie – I won't because you cannae play.'

Another, much more tragic, reason to remember that trip to London says a lot about how football lurched towards a new age of big exposure and dramatically increased pressure. I was put in the care of the club secretary, Jimmy McInnes, a small and kindly man who had played for Liverpool. McInnes handled the work-load presented by the Second Division comfortably enough, but later, despite the rush of success in the Shankly revolution, promotion to the top flight, two title wins and a place in Europe, the club saw no need to provide him with more assistance. His world had suddenly changed but he was given no chance to adapt to the new demands. The consequences could not have been more terrible. One day this nice wee man, overwhelmed by the volume of mail, contracts and telephone calls, got up from his desk, walked behind the Kop and hung himself above a turnstile.

It seemed such an unnecessary waste of a good life, but I also have to say that it underlined some of those raw feelings I had about how the game handled itself. Why couldn't the club have seen that the demands on Jimmy McInnes were too great? When you stepped beyond the former players such as Shankly and, in his much more modest and desperate way, McInnes, who really cared? It was not something that did you much good to dwell on as you went about the business of helping to create Bill Shankly's dream, the one that back in the office, well away from the spotlight, had become an unshakeable nightmare.

The dream had taken on a force of its own, a surging power generated by Shankly's obsessive need to win. Later he told me that it just happened to be Liverpool that bore the ripe fruit of his ambition. His extraordinary identification with the city, his embrace of the people, his capacity to turn a victory parade into something much more emotional by waving a red hand-kerchief from the balcony of the city hall – football's equivalent of President Jack Kennedy announcing he was a Berliner – might just as easily have occurred in Huddersfield. He left there in frustration because the potential of the club, he claimed, was never recognised by the directors.

'Aye, I had the basis of a real team there,' said Shankly. He had breathtaking talent in the bespectacled, puny frame of Denis Law. The emerging Mike O'Grady was a future England international winger. 'If they had given me a few quid, they could have been the Liverpool today,' added Shankly, 'but this lot beat them to the punch. They said I could sign a few players and that's what every manager needs – the chance to back his judgement. It was

The greatest of days — my first game for Scotland, against Germany at Hampden Park in 1959, was also a proud day for Motherwell with three players in the national team. I'm pictured with Bert McCann (*left*) and Andy Weir.

Above A proud moment – Sir Matt Busby puts a hand on my shoulder as I report for
Scotland Under-23 duty.

Below Piling the pressure on West Germany in my Scotland debut – the reviews were
good for me and the tragic John White.

Above Wembley, 15 April 1961, was one of the bleakest days for Scottish football. The ball eludes both England goalkeeper Ron Springett and me. We did have some success in front of goal, scoring three. Unfortunately, England scored nine.

Below Jimmy Greaves became my partner in 'The Saint and Greavsie Show' but first he tortured Scotland. This was the goal that brought his hat-trick in the 9–3 victory.

Above Preparing to meet Northern Ireland at Hampden Park in 1962 – Pat Crerand (*fourth from left*) always swore we had the talent to beat the world, an argument supported by the presence in this line-up of Jim Baxter (*sixth from left*), Denis Law (*fourth from right*) and Dave Mackay (*second from right*). I'm standing next to Denis Law.

Below Gordon Banks, England's great goalkeeper, cuts off my header as Bobby Moore and Denis Law move to cover the ground.

Above Scotland had a forward line of some menace in 1965, when England were the opposition. *Left to right:* Willie Henderson, Bobby Collins, Denis Law, Davie Wilson and me.

Above Jimmy Greaves and John White embrace in triumph after Tottenham's second successive FA Cup victory in 1962. For England and Scotland, they worked against each other with brilliant talent. Together at Spurs, they were a defender's nightmare.

Right Goals, the lifeblood of football, don't always come prettily but they all have the same value. I hustled this one in against England at Wembley in 1965.

Left The big move to Liverpool in April 1961 – Bill Shankly and chairman T.V. Williams look on as I sign.

Below Back in the big-time, Liverpool return to the first division in 1962. *Back row, left to right:* Gordon Milne, Ron Yeats, Jim Furnell, Ronnie Moran, Gerry Byrne, Tommy Leishman. *Front row, left to right:* Ian Callaghan, Roger Hunt, me, Jimmy Melia, Alan A'Court.

Above The man who denied us the Cup – Gordon Banks. The world's best goalkeeper punches the ball off my toes.

Below The first title is gathered in by Shankly's team and the champagne flows.

Above In another fierce battle with Leicester City, Richie Norman is the man causing frustration.

Below Tension rises in the battle of Vancouver against Meidericher – I try negotiation, but my German isn't so good.

the chance I had been looking for. I got the opportunity to show I knew something about football – and about the people who play the game, really play.'

At Anfield, Shankly quickly showed that he had both the drive and the vision. When he looked at a player, he was plainly examining more than mere talent. He wanted to see confidence, an aggressive approach to the challenge of football and life in all of his players. In those early days, he said that he thought if I'd been a fighter, I would have made a good middleweight, fast and hard. I don't think he ever gave me a more deeply felt compliment.

Promotion came in a whirl in 1961–62, followed by the league title in 1964 and 1966 with the FA Cup in between. The foundation of all that was to follow at Liverpool over the decades had been laid. Shankly created more than a winning team. He instilled a spirit, a sense of how the game should be played, and in the process he dragged out feelings and perceptions that some players never realised they had – not until he set their blood flowing and gave them a glimpse of the stars.

Shankly's first serious investment at Anfield was Gordon Milne of Preston North End. He paid £16,000 for the small, clever midfielder who had a nice creative touch and would go on to win England caps. Shankly felt he knew all about Gordon. He had played with his father, Jimmy, at Preston and naturally, given his enthusiasm, with Gordon in the cobbled streets. When I arrived, Johnny Wheeler was already there. Wheeler, another wing-half, had played for Bolton in the legendary Stanley Matthews final of 1953. The breakthrough into the top flight was still a year away but I realised immediately that I had already encountered the big time.

Although I went to that first game, against Everton, with Betsy and a friend from Scotland, joining the other lads in the corridor at Goodison – after my discussion at the gate – I had already met the team. Shankly had introduced me and, despite a few dressing-room problems, I had a good feeling about what lay ahead. The atmosphere that night crackled as we went up to the ground from the fine hotel where we had been lodged, just behind Lime Street station. The hotel is gone now and I forget its name, but Betsy and I will always remember it for what it represented – our first days in a new and thrilling life. When I got to Goodison on that spring night, I thought, 'Yes, this will do for me, very well indeed.'

Liverpool didn't care much about Everton winning. They'd got a new guy who looked as if he could score in any company and as Betsy and I celebrated the hat-trick later in our luxurious quarters, we agreed we couldn't have written a better script for my debut on Merseyside. After just a couple of days training with my team-mates, I had gone out and scored three good goals against the club's most bitter rivals, the millionaires of Everton, the team of such fabled players as Dixie Dean, Tommy Lawton and Joe Mercer.

It wasn't all glamorous, though. The other players had been measured for suits for a close-season tour of Czechoslovakia and I had to have an express service job done by Lou Glanz. The Liverpool tailor didn't inspire great confidence in me – a veteran of the Barrowlands dancehall peacock parade – when he confessed he could no longer bend down with his tape measure and had to guess trouser lengths. Some events in eastern Europe were just as hazardous. We played three games and in one of them I was sent off for the first time in my career – the result of a brief altercation after I was on the receiving end of a tackle that I thought just a little reckless, if not sinister.

Another problem came on the flight home from Prague, which we made in the company of fellow tourists Nottingham

Forest. Someone had forgotten to lock the rear door of the plane and there was a tremendous thump as we climbed into the sky. The cabin staff all threw themselves at the door, finally wrestling it closed. This was just a few years after the Munich tragedy of Manchester United in 1958. More than a few scares occurred in the early years of mass air travel and all through the sixties, many relieved footballers applauded the pilot when he made a success-ful landing. After a European tie in Budapest, we sat in the plane on the apron of the runway with the door wide open and the snow swirling in. The stewards said that they couldn't close the door until 'de-icing' was completed. The general consensus was, 'Oh, how great – maybe you would kindly open the bar.' When they did, the brandy flowed to a degree that didn't entirely impress Bill Shankly, Bob Paisley or Reuben.

By the start of the 1961–62 season we were in very good shape, winning our first game at Bristol Rovers and going undefeated for another ten games. One of the early matches was against Sunderland, where Brian Clough lay in wait. The lads were saying to me, 'This guy Clough is some striker, he always scores against us,' but he didn't get one that day. I did, helping along the team's sense of momentum, as well as my own in England. We won the prize of top-division football, the vital first stage of Shankly's revolution, with a clutch of games still to go.

We didn't know how permanent our stay in the top flight was going to be, but we certainly believed, after a season of playing together and more than a little brainwashing from Shankly, that we had reasons for optimism. This wasn't the case with our promotion companions, Leyton Orient. They suffered a bad case of vertigo when they collided with Manchester United, Arsenal and Tottenham. Each day, Shankly told us, the press and himself, Liverpool would continue soaring upwards. One reason for his confidence was the arrival, a few months after me, of Ron Yeats.

If I was Shankly's prize middleweight, Ron was his 'colossus'. He said he was going to organise tours around Ron Yeats, a true 'phenomenon' among human beings.

Ron and I had played together with the Scottish Boys' Clubs team and, as new boys, we formed a natural alliance. We had a great friendship and roomed together for ten years. In all that time, we had just one fight. It was quite a serious one, however. A little tension came to our friendship when he joined the commercial venture of somebody he had got to know in Liverpool. The guy was, in my opinion, a typical businessman and I couldn't warm to him. Apart from football, Ron's experience of life didn't stretch much farther than the abattoir where he had worked as a boy in Aberdeen — maybe not the best grounding for business.

This fellow, John Mansley, persuaded Ron to invest some money, as well as putting his name to the venture, and the trouble was that Yeats, like any footballer of that time, didn't have too much spare income. We used to go out together most Saturday nights and Mansley was often in the company. Sometimes it became a little tense because, as I said, I was suspicious of the guy. I thought he might be taking the big man for a ride. Ronnie was a superb character and player but if it ever came down to business instincts, he was never going to make it into the Forbes top 100.

One morning at the training ground, Ron seemed to be seriously down, morose. I had the suspicion that he had been hit with some bills and might be feeling that possibly I had been right in my advice. During a five-a-side game he took a heavy kick at me, and I responded with some feeling. A little later he did it again and it was all bets off at Wincanton. We were dragged apart but later, when the players gathered to have the traditional cup of tea, it started up again. Up at Anfield, Shankly summoned us to his office under the main stand.

'Now, boys,' he said, 'you've been the best of pals. Don't spoil it all. You've got to let this rest, put it behind you.' Then he got down to what to him was, no doubt, the main priority. 'We've got a big game in a couple of days' time.'

Some years later, in an echo of that remark, a young player who was just making his way into the team knocked on the manager's door on the Thursday before a game with Everton two days later. The boy, who when he signed didn't have a scrap of meat on his bones and was put on a special diet of prime beef by Shankly, reported that his girlfriend had become pregnant and both sets of parents had got together and arranged the wedding for when he was supposed to be playing against Everton.

'Jesus Christ, laddie,' said Shankly, 'we're fighting for our lives and you come to me with this.' When the chastened boy left the office, Shankly raced down the corridor to pass on the news to his confidant, Bennett. 'Reuben,' he said, 'something terrible has happened. It seems we've bred a monster.'

In the end, Shankly persuaded Ron and me to make peace. Yeats put his hand out and said, 'I'm sorry about that . . . it shouldn't have happened.' It hadn't been my instinct to say sorry but when Ronnie broke the tension I went along with it. On that Saturday night we went out with our wives and we never had another cross word — Ronnie and me, that is. His first wife Margaret and Betsy, who had also been very close, were never the same again. During the evening, Margaret and Betsy agreed that the whole affair had been quite ridiculous. How could such good friends fight each other like that? Unfortunately, Margaret added, 'I just couldn't believe my Ronnie would hit a man half his size.' Betsy reacted so ferociously that suddenly it was Ronnie and me doing the separating. 'Ian's dealt with better men than your precious Ronnie,' said Betsy.

It was sad that the girls' friendship crashed like that. Ronnie's marriage dwindled even more sharply and ended in divorce a few years later. It cannot have helped that I had been proved right in my assessment of Mr Mansley. The car business, which he told Ronnie would carry them to untold riches, fell apart very quickly but by then Ronnie had shared the expenses of a holiday in Bermuda, limousines and white tuxedos. It was, as I had suspected, all an expensive illusion. When the bills started coming in, and without any balancing revenue, the bailiffs followed soon after. Ron was forced to declare bankruptcy after trying to meet the debts in an honourable way. Mansley? He did a runner, disappearing permanently from Ron's sight.

Some fights carried a lot more significance than a brief falling out between good friends. The most serious one I had at Liverpool occurred on the beach at Southport, and I like to think it was instrumental in breaking what I had come see as the Anfield 'mafia'. It took the best part of two years to build into a real fight, but long before it happened I knew that I was on a collision course with Jimmy Melia, the midfielder and former lord of the dressing room, and his mates Johnny Morrissey and Ronnie Moran.

They were local lads who had come up through the city's schoolboy football system, and they didn't like their Scottish manager showing such a preference for the products of his home country. His move for me and then Ronnie Yeats suggested strongly to them that the old order was changing rapidly and on that early trip to Czechoslovakia I felt the first negative vibrations. I caught the full-back Moran referring to 'Scottish bastards'.

The violent climax to that resentment came when Shankly, driven almost to distraction by the effects of the heavy winter of 1962–63 on his training programme, announced that we would have a day out by the sea. What he had in mind was the perfect surface of the beach when the tide went out. That was a typical Shankly solution. All through that difficult time he was looking for ways to keep us sharp and give us an edge when the game was resumed. Earlier he had taken over some tennis courts, pointing out that beneath the packed snow, the surface was sure to be flat. The sand was wonderfully level and Shankly was so happy he might have been Lawrence of Arabia catching his first sight of Damascus.

His mood changed quickly, though, when Melia took a snide kick at me and I went straight for him, with the lads trying to cling on to both of us and break us apart. The manager always liked to think he was in charge of a fiercely united family, and that this fondness for each other would be shot through our performances on the field. Now he was seeing his midfield general and his striker trying to land the big knock-out punch. Shankly bellowed, 'Fucking hell, stop,' and eventually we were separated. On the bus back to Anfield, I bombarded Melia with threats, one of the milder ones being, 'When we reach the ground, I'm going to get you.' There was a little gym down the corridor from the dressing room, and I said to Melia, 'I'll see you there — right now,' but he refused to come. That signalled the end of the Liverpool mafia. In a way, I could understand how the bad feelings developed. If a crowd of Englishmen had invaded Fir Park, I might have reacted in the same way as Melia and the others did.

The pity was that Melia was a good player, a terrific passer of the ball, who might have had a run with England but for the competition of Johnny Haynes and Bobby Charlton. He didn't make the Cup final team of 1965 and that seemed to be the end of his highest ambitions. He moved to Wolves and after that he didn't have much of a career as a player — although, as a manager, he came close to glory when his Brighton team lost the 'Smith must score' Cup final against Manchester United in 1983. Looking back, I wonder if I could have made more of an effort with Melia but, in the end, you are who you are and there's not a lot you can do to change your nature. As with any group of men operating under the pressure of needing to win and to be seen as competitive, a football team is subject to the usual battles for territorial rights within the dressing room. There is also much insecurity; you are at the mercy of form and injury and the judgement of the man who picks the team.

For Shankly, the good news was that he would never lack for skill and courage in his dressing room. Englishmen, including Milne, Roger Hunt, Ian Callaghan, Gerry Byrne and Peter Thompson, would quickly show that accommodating the foibles of invading Scots – Ron, the extremely talented Billy Stevenson and me – was no obstacle to a superbly consistent display of team spirit. We were all carried along by the Shankly indoctrination – we were the finest team and Liverpool was the finest city, in any way you could imagine. When success came so quickly, with two league championships and the FA Cup – the first in the history of the club – the wild talk was suddenly wild reality. Liverpool, which had seemed so immense and sprawling when Betsy and I first arrived from Motherwell, had become our village – an excited, uproarious village. Other emerging stars could be seen around town – the Beatles, Gerry Marsden of Gerry and the Pacemakers, Cilla Black – but the big clamour was for the autograph of a footballer.

Injected into everything was that passion and driving obsession of Shankly. One Sunday morning he invited me to his house. It was a strange business. He spent much of the time talking on the phone to his great rival, Don Revie of Leeds United. He paced up and down the hall with the phone clenched in his hand. 'That was a good result you had yesterday, Don, but I have to tell you something — we were magnificent.' Then, hardly pausing for breath, he took Revie through almost every kick of the Liverpool performance. It was an epic of football brilliance, and as he talked I felt my chest swelling.

However, as I drove home in my new Vauxhall, I did speculate on the true status of the man who would now shape pretty much the rest of my football life. Was he a storm of improbable energy with more than a touch of genius? Or was he completely off his head? I had a shrewd idea of what Don Revie's verdict might have been when he put down the phone on that previously peaceful Sunday morning.

6

JUST A PASSING PHASE

S o MUCH of Bill Shankly's behaviour was bizarre, and so many football men over the years had the urge to shake their heads questioningly, that the temptation was to believe he was as much a clown as a messiah. The idea was utterly wrong-headed. Shankly always knew what he was doing, and what he was saying. His language could be extravagant and comic, but it never lacked a hard purpose.

He was obsessive and intolerant but at times he also had an astonishing warmth. More than anything, he focused on achievement, heroic effort and great character. A man of absolutes, he once said subtleties were for Malcolm Muggeridge, the great TV intellectual of the sixties.

'Aye, I'd have Muggeridge on board if he could tell me how to win football games, and I'd be parked outside Oxford University looking for talent,' he said, 'but Jock Stein never went to university, nor Tom Finney.' It was a family belief that football intelligence was the product of instinct rather than learning. Shankly's brother Bob, while manager of Dundee, was exasperated by the lack of development of one young player and declared, 'The trouble with you, son, is that your brains are in your head.' For Bill Shankly, football was a moral issue rather than mere sport. The effect was compelling, mesmerising at times. There was only one place to be when you were around Bill Shankly – on your toes. If you want to add up European Cup triumphs and the strong, lasting foundation of the empire he created, you are entitled to believe that his legacy remains the greatest in English football. His achievements flowed from an extraordinary will and energy. Most vitally, he could look into the mind and the heart of a player and almost instantly see what was there.

Shankly's command structure was strong and impenetrable. If Reuben Bennett heard a player spreading doubts about the boss, he would pin him against the wall. He had to be put right or sent on his way. One player couldn't be allowed to infect the barrel of apples with a hint of badness. Shankly once said that his power over the fans made him feel like Chairman Mao, and there was no doubt he had the ability to take hold of the emotions of a squad of players and a city.

Eventually, the loyal lieutenants Bob Paisley and Joe Fagan would step up to do the job, Paisley with astounding success in winning three European Cups and extending and deepening the strength of the team, but while they served Shankly their commitment was total. For so long, Paisley was content to operate in the shadows, the former player and army tankman, who drove into Rome with the first Allied forces, just happy to be around the game, doing his work as a trainer and confidant of a man whom he considered to be a unique force.

One moment Paisley was Mr Elastoplast, healing wounds, quietly trouble-shooting, sitting in the background as Shankly raged or exulted, depending on the way things were going. The next, after Shankly's departure in 1974, he was commander-in-chief, still as undemonstrative as ever but utterly sure of his judgement. When, a long way down the road, Kevin Keegan decided to make his future in Europe, much of Liverpool and the wider world of English football was stunned at the loss of a player who had become an Anfield icon. Not Bob Paisley. He had earmarked Keegan's successor some time before. The progression was seamless. Kenny Dalglish was in the bag.

Shankly inherited these veteran football men but when he grasped their knowledge and their characters, and saw how they responded to his ideas and his passion, they quickly became integral parts of his success. The old Boot Room legend paints a picture of ageing football men talking of dreams born of the past, but in fact they were defining and honing a brilliant future.

The new manager swept away the old ways. He blew in like a gale. Before he arrived, the custom was pre-season training runs out on the roads. Stories abound of players hopping on buses to take away some of the pain. Such liberties were banished from everyone's mind at the first gust of the new man. Shankly scrapped the road runs and, for the first few days of a new campaign, instigated gentle work. Quite a lot of time was spent with the ball – not kicking it, but caressing it, feeling it, creating the old urge to get playing again. Shankly wouldn't let us kick the ball in that early going for fear we might pull or strain muscles. When the preliminary stage was over, he would say, 'Right, boys, now we're ready to train.'

He always said that you could never be properly fit until you had played a few games. You didn't rush into a season like young, eager boys. You had to approach it, in the imagery of Shankly, like gunfighters, knowing men in their competitive prime. You had to prepare yourself perfectly. You had to be in the proper competitive groove.

You could see his mind turning over as you worked. Paisley was required to log every detail, including even hints of injury, right through the season. The value of this emerged on those rare occasions when we entered a bad patch in subsequent seasons. A key part of any inquest was Shankly's question to Paisley, 'What were we doing at this time last year, was it any different from now? Look it up, Bob.' In the scores of crazy incidents, times when you thought the guy might have flipped and finally gone flying over the top, the one consistent thread was Shankly's relentless need to move the team forward.

The process was not always perfectly achieved, however. Shankly insisted on upgrading the treatment room, and any new-fangled equipment he heard about had to be acquired, along with the wholesome food in the club kitchen and the daily lectures about how you had to respect your body. 'Jesus Christ, boys, you're nothing without healthy bodies . . .' he would say, as though reading from his private scriptures.

Albert Shelley, a former player who had come from Southampton and was the trainer before Paisley, bore the brunt of Shankly's first drive to improve the treatment of injuries. He was a great character who, like Reuben, would entertain the young lads with stories of the old days in football and during the war. Small lads were told they were wasting their time, they should be jockeys. Big lads were told to go off and join the police force. He wore a brown work coat and was always around the dressing room, keeping things tidy, and for a while he was the man you went to when you were injured.

The remedy for bad knees most favoured by Albert was hot and cold towels. He would have the towels in two buckets, one red hot and one filled with ice. First he would reach into the hot bucket with his tweezers and slap a steaming towel on to the offending knee, quickly followed by a cold one. Often you would cry out but Albert said it was the only way to do it. This wasn't good enough for Shankly. He brought in a fine piece of new machinery. He stood in front of it, hands on hips, as if it was one of the wonders of the world. Unfortunately, when Albert tried to operate the new gadget, he promptly received an electric shock. That was the end of his relationship with the wonderful machine. Shankly would come in and say, 'Albert, I want you to sort out this machine. It's a great invention, you know.' Shelley replied, 'Aye, okay, Boss,' and when Shankly left, he would say to the lads, 'Fuck that.'

Bob Paisley took the trouble to study the manual that came with the machine, and he knew enough to put us on it, but more often than not after doing so he would say, 'Right, I'm off to the betting shop.' If he was having a good day, he might not return. Those were the early days and Shankly was doing much to create a new climate in the game.

Joe Fagan was Bob's understudy and in charge of the reserve team. He, like Reuben, enjoyed a cigarette so, of course, the players christened him 'Smokin' Joe'. He was always held in the highest respect in the dressing room. He had the valuable habit of catching the mood of a player, detecting dips in morale and maybe suspecting that someone had a particular problem. In my last year at Anfield, when the romance with Shankly had been replaced by something colder, he had a word with me that I will never forget.

I was in the blackest of moods after being dropped from the team – the first time it had happened since I was selected by Motherwell for that game against Queen of the South. He said, 'Look, nothing is lost – this comes to the greatest of players. You have to deal with it in the right way. You have to remember that this is just a passing phase of your career, and your life. How you deal with it will decide what follows.'

It was the best advice and underpinned something Paisley said to me around that difficult time. The idea of being separated from the first team was terribly hard to accept, but Paisley said, 'We've had great times. Now in this situation, are you going to look at the big picture and maybe help us with the young players before getting something sorted out? Have a think about it. You've been in the game a while now, you know the score.'

Paisley and Fagan knew all the nuances of football. They charted the progress and the setbacks, the strengths and the weaknesses of everyone who went on to the field for Liverpool. They applied the psychology, the nuts and bolts, of the great tradition.

Shankly knew well enough Liverpool was the place where he had to make his name. He had scuffled along in football outposts. Now he had the chance to invest in all his instincts for how the game should be played. In the course of it, he would show both the richest of humour and the hardest streak.

The humour entranced the supporters. When, on our arrival in the First Division, we made a stumbling start, losing to Blackpool at home, he told the press, 'I can guarantee to the fans that we will win a game at Anfield this year.' Behind the bluster and the spiky comedy, always lurked that ruthless touch. In our promotion year Bert Slater, a goalkeeper Shankly much admired for his courage – 'That boy would jump under a bus if you asked him' – conceded a goal from a free kick at Rotherham. The ball flew into the top corner of the net and I thought it would have beaten most keepers. Later I heard Shankly say to Paisley, 'The boy's not big enough,' and I knew that was the end of Slater at Anfield. In Shankly's mind a flaw had been revealed, and he just couldn't live with that. The Anfield death sentence had been passed.

Ronnie Moran, who in time would take his place as a junior member of the Boot Room, was also pushed aside. He gave way to the ferocious challenge of Gerry Byrne. At training, even the young hard man Tommy Smith would look over his shoulder if Byrne was in the vicinity. Byrne was the only Liverpool player banned from making a tackle in the Friday five-a-side game. It was not that he was dirty or irresponsible, just that he tackled so hard. No one was better able to fulfil Shankly's demand that opposing wingers should have their 'bones shaken'. He never said 'kick 'em', nothing so crude; no, they just had to have their bones jarred from time to time. Once, in Europe, we were drawn against Vittoria Setubal of Portugal, a nice, ball-playing team with an extremely fast forward called Jacinto. 'Aye, he's quick,' said Shankly, 'but will he be so quick after Tommy Smith has introduced himself?'

Byrne delighted Shankly because he could send a winger flying into the crowd without provoking even the most vigilant referee into saying that he hadn't gone for the ball. On the other side of the field another emerging local boy, right-back Chris Lawler, was an entirely different type of player. Chris always stayed on his feet. He established a fine understanding with Smith. When Chris was confronting a particularly nippy winger, Tommy would say, 'Bring him inside, Chris.' Neither Lawler nor Smith had great pace, but they could control their side of the field with fine judgement and timing. Byrne's promotion to the first team was established when Moran was caught out too many times in a European tie.

One of Shankly's most important acquisitions was Billy Stevenson, who was known to the fans and everyone else except Shankly and me as Willie. I had known him, and admired him, in Scotland when he was with Rangers. He became increasingly frustrated operating under the shadow of the great Jim Baxter and eventually went into exile in Australia. When Shankly heard of this development, he quickly moved to get him to Anfield. He said that the boy was far too good to be wasting his time in kangaroo country. It was one of his best decisions.

'Stevo' was a valuable addition to the team, hard and skilled, and he was also a great favourite with Shankly. This though, as Stevenson, and so many other Liverpool players would find out eventually, was always conditioned by his membership of the first team. When that status was in question, or when you were out, you could quickly become a non-person. Partly, I think, this was because Shankly invested so much belief in the quality of a player, and when things weren't going so well, he found it very hard to deal with on a personal level. Bob, Reuben or Joe would come into play, trying to heal the wounds that in football are never too far away. In the good days, Billy could do little wrong in the eyes of the boss, and Shankly was always asking him, 'Hey, Billy, what's the latest gag?'

Billy was a character who, for one reason or another, persuaded himself that he was a little bit superior to the rest of the troops. He never quite said it but as he lit up a fine cigar and sipped a good brandy, the implication was that the rest of us were pretty much peasants. He dressed immaculately, favouring Reed and Taylor suits from Savile Row. They were beautifully cut with coloured thread woven into them. He always had an edge in the sartorial department, especially before some of us gave up on Lou Glanz's belief that he could measure us up without the help of a tape.

However, Billy's style left him vulnerable to an occasional slip-up. One evening some of us were invited with our wives, to his house after going out for dinner. He was very proud of a French brandy he had recently bought on a foreign trip, and asked his wife Carmel to bring it in. She said, 'Are you sure you wouldn't like something else?' She seemed quite perturbed. Billy said, 'Carmel, bring in the good brandy for my friends.' Soon enough we understood the reason for Carmel's concern. Billy took a swig of the brandy and said, 'Smooth, hey, boys,' but we were fighting the urge to double up with laughter. Carmel had obviously enjoyed it quite as much, if not more, than her husband. She had drunk most of it and replaced it with tea.

Ian Callaghan was quite different from Billy. He was a local boy, utterly unpretentious, willing to run all day in pursuit of Shankly's ambitions. He was laying claim to the right wing but first he had to fight off the challenge of Kevin Lewis, another home-grown boy, from the Wirral. There wasn't much of Lewis but he had a tremendous shot and for a while he doubled as a winger and my understudy at centre-forward. In the promotion year, he scored a couple of goals that were quite fantastic in their force. One, at Newcastle, threatened to tear away the net.

Lewis had great potential but some of the time you had the impression his thoughts were anywhere but on the game to which he brought some strong talent. He was a great man for hatching business schemes and dreaming about their success. Maybe Shankly's antennae picked up a certain ambivalence towards football as a way of life and, much to everyone's surprise, he sold him a year after we won promotion.

Before he left, Kevin provided Betsy, our daughter Elaine and me with quite a bizarre experience. He invited us to join him and his wife Pat for a caravan break in Wales. On the first day he and Pat had a row, which developed quite fiercely. She had told him she wanted to make a trip and he objected. It was quite embarrassing, and I said something to that effect. Quite soon, Kevin and I started fighting, which was not so easy in that little caravan. An extra difficulty for me was that Kevin had pulled the sweater I was wearing over my head, which meant that I couldn't see the target or swing a punch. All the time Pat was screaming at him, and finally she shouted, 'That's it, we're going. The holiday's over.' Fortunately for us, when they stormed off they left the key to the caravan. Many years later, when I was playing in South Africa, I met up with Kevin again. He had finally gone into business and was a different man, relaxed enough for me to say, 'Oh, by the way, we had a great time in Wales.'

Billy Stevenson, Jimmy Melia, Kevin Lewis and perhaps me if

I'd taken a careful look at myself, were the cross-section of football humanity – proud and insecure, affable and tense in the course of one game or training session. We had to fight our moods, our prejudices, and the changing flow of our form, but from time to time someone comes along who is devoid of all foibles, all doubts, who comes to play and simply gets on with it. The epitome of this was Roger Hunt. He went on to become a World Cup winner with England and a pillar of the team that Shankly was building.

When Roger was demobbed from the army he signed for Liverpool from Goldborne, a little club along the East Lancashire Road, along with his friend Tommy Lawrence. We said they were carrot crunchers or, as Scousers call all out-of-towners, 'woolly backs', but Hunt had everything that Shankly wanted in a forward and, above all, honesty. He was strong, he had pace, he could hit the ball with both feet and he was a great volleyer. If you picked up the ball, he was ready to run; if you suggested to him you were going to flip one forward, he was ready to run. In all circumstances, he was ready to run.

This was especially true on one of the most critical days of his career at Anfield. This story shows how profoundly times have changed in football. All the players would make their own way to the ground on Saturday and on this occasion Roger and his wife were driving along the East Lancashire Road, as was Tommy Lawrence, in good time for the 2 p.m. deadline that Shankly imposed. Suddenly they came to a traffic jam caused by a crash. The traffic was packed solid and both the boys were still several miles away from Anfield with no means of communicating their predicament. Separately, they decided they had to make a run for it. Roger said to his wife that she would just have to get to the ground as best she could. At around the same time Tommy was reaching the same conclusion and as Roger raced along the road he was joined by Tommy. Fans wound down their windows and cheered them on, and tooted horns. Long before they got to the ground they were soaked in sweat.

At Anfield, the clock was ticking down and Shankly was beginning to pace the dressing room, growling, 'Jesus Christ, where's Hunt, where's Lawrence? We have a disaster on our hands.' When it got to 2.45 p.m. Byrne was told to prepare himself to play in goal. As he pulled on the goalie's sweater, Bobby Graham was told to change. He was sitting next to me in the dressing room and when he got the order he just groaned. He told me that he had had a massive fry-up at his digs, which were just a few streets from the ground, and had washed it down with a couple of pints at a nearby pub. He didn't feel quite prepared to play First Division football.

With just eight minutes to go, Roger and Tommy burst into the dressing room, red in the face and with their shirts sticking to them. Paisley was going mad, but then he was just learning the business of management. Shankly listened to their story and said, 'Right, boys, you've done well, take your time – I'm going to see the referee.' He persuaded the official to delay the kick-off by eight minutes. It was hard to know who was more relieved, Shankly or Bobby Graham. The Football League fined Liverpool £300 for the late start. The opponents were Manchester City and the game finished a 1–1 draw. Our goal, you may have guessed, was scored by Roger.

That was Shankly's reassurance. It had been one of his nightmares. He always insisted that new signings lived on the right side of the Mersey tunnel and it was ironic that Roger and Tommy, who came closest to fulfilling the manager's worst fears, did not have to negotiate the tunnel. Eventually, Kevin Keegan beat the ban on trans-tunnel living when he bought a house in the hills of North Wales, but Shankly continued to worry that the passage under the Mersey would be blocked or would collapse shortly before the kick-off of a big game and send Liverpool's chances swirling out into the Irish Sea.

When Alf Ramsey chose Hunt for the World Cup final in 1966, it surprised some people but not at Anfield, not among those who knew him best, who saw the level of effort he put into everything he did. Shankly had just one problem with Roger – until the night he pulled him off the field and the great player's pride was so hurt he threw down his shirt in front of the Kop.

The problem was merely that Hunt had taken a liking to golf. Shankly didn't approve of footballers playing anything but the game through which they earned their living. He banned us from playing golf. The game involved too much unnatural stress on the body, he insisted. However, he suspected that Roger and Tommy Lawrence, away down the East Lancashire Road, were defying his orders. He rang their local club and roared down the phone to the secretary, 'Have you got my boys there?' They had tipped off the secretary that Shankly would probably call and asked him to say that he hadn't seen them, but the guy was terrified by the sound of Shankly's voice. He couldn't stop blurting out the admission that they were out on the course. 'Tell them to go home,' thundered Shankly.

Ironically, it was the boss who infected Tommy Smith, briefly, with the golf bug. We were staying in a hotel that had a par-three course and some of the lads were pottering around the course when the new boy Smith decided he would have a go. Shankly was sitting nearby, taking the sun. When Tommy's first-ever golf shot landed close to the pin, Shankly leapt up from his seat and cried, 'Jesus Christ, Tommy, you're a natural.' Tommy was so enthused that soon afterwards he persuaded some of the golf rebels, including me, to take him out for a game.

We took him to Grange Park, in St Helens, a nice course but

maybe a little bit tough for a beginner. This was certainly how it appeared when Tommy made a 12 on the first hole, then a 10 followed by a 14. It was, though, the build-up to an amazing pinnacle in the very short but eventful golf life of Tommy Smith. On the fourth – a tricky par three on the first full-length golf course he had ever played – Tommy holed in one. He was given the usual hole-in-one tie, had the ball mounted and walked away from the game, leaving me – still pursuing the dream after more than forty years playing the game – in some torment.

For Shankly any form of sport beyond football and boxing was alien and dubious and full of danger. Another example of this came when the club vice-chairman Sid Reakes had his company's cricket day and put Paisley in charge of team selection. When I heard about this I naturally made my off-spinning credentials known to Bob and he promptly put my name down. Unfortunately, Shankly got wind of the match and just before the start he drove to the ground with Reuben Bennett. Neither knew the first thing about cricket, a point underlined by the fact that they parked in front of the sightscreen. They were bewildered when the umpires and the cricketers turned *en masse* and waved to them to move. It had to be explained to them that the game couldn't start until the car was moved. Then Shankly was appalled to see me fielding close to the wicket and a batsman hammering the ball perilously close to my legs.

'Jesus Christ, Bob,' he cried, 'he could have had his fucking leg broken.' Shankly pointed out that he had just invested a vast amount of money in me. How would it look if I missed the start of the season with a broken leg, the victim of a cricket accident? 'Can you imagine the headlines, Bob, what do you think they would say we were running here? A fucking sports jamboree?' He let the full horror of the possibility sink in, and then said, 'Bob, there will be no more cricket . . .'

Football, of course, was everything, and that first season in the top flight Shankly fancied, along with the rest of us, that we might just see the moon and the stars. The team was coming along very nicely indeed. Another of our assets was Alan A'Court, who had been good enough to win caps for England.

He was quick, and had the knack of knocking the ball beyond the full-back and getting to the line to put in the perfect cross, which was a fine staple diet for the hard-running Hunt and me. Not only had we established ourselves solidly in the top division, we had made a serious run at the trophy that had always eluded the club, the FA Cup. It was said that the Liver Birds would have to fly off over the Mersey before Liverpool won the Cup, but in the spring of 1963 there was a growing belief that we might just defy the tradition.

Leicester City, our semi-final opposition, were struggling near the foot of the First Division, and we liked our chances very much, despite the setback of losing Melia through injury on the eve of the game. Shankly decided to move Lawler up from full-back into Melia's place, which would have been more of a gamble against tougher opposition. Leicester had some excellent players – Gordon Banks in goal, Davie Gibson in midfield and Frank McLintock organising the defence – but Shankly reckoned their strength was too thinly spread and that we shouldn't have too much trouble in reaching Wembley. He was entirely correct in all but one respect, for which you couldn't blame him – no one was entitled to believe that Banks could play so well. Even with Lawler out of position and our leading playmaker missing, we murdered Leicester, but Banks was in the form that served England so well in winning the World Cup and would deny Pele so spectacularly four years after that in Mexico. He dived everywhere and caught, flicked or punched everything. We felt we were caught by the curse of the Liver Birds, and this was confirmed when Leicester's big winger, Mike Stringfellow, got his head to a free kick and scraped home a goal.

In the following day's paper, a big picture appeared of me walking off the field with my head down and, behind me, Banks and McLintock laughing. Many Liverpool fans misinterpreted the photograph. They assumed the Leicester players were laughing at my expense, taunting a beaten hero.

The fans had got it wrong — the Leicester players were celebrating among themselves. Whatever they might have felt for their beaten opponents, however unlucky they might have considered us, the fact was they had survived to fight another, better day in the greatest venue in English football, Wembley Stadium. Banks told me that he was besieged with hate mail from Liverpool long after the game, a sad and stupid postscript to his superb display. Then a week later, the Manchester United of Denis Law, Paddy Crerand and Johnny Giles beat Leicester 3–1. To add to our pain that spring day, Banks felt we would have had the beating of the Old Trafford team. Aside from their stars, they had some quite pronounced weaknesses.

Of course, from time to time a goalkeeper will play so well that a result is shaped completely against the run of play and the balance of a match. Professionals are supposed to shrug their shoulders and say that's the way of the game and these things level out. I never doubted this theory more strongly than in the wake of defeat by Leicester. It was because I hadn't known such pain since Motherwell had stumbled at the same stage of the Scottish Cup — and for the similar reason of extraordinary goalkeeping. The additional twist was that we were supposed to be the boys of destiny, riding over a curse, delivering to Liverpool and their impassioned champion Shankly the great, elusive prize of the FA Cup. The final remained unchallenged as the shining day in English football. The championship might say more about you as a team as you took on your peers in autumn, winter and spring, but except for the moment of final triumph, it could never match the emotion generated by the season's climax at Wembley.

From down the corridor at Hillsborough, where the semi-final was played, you could hear the Leicester celebration gaining strength. Our dressing room was morgue-like. Shankly tried to bury his pain, not too successfully. He said we would pick ourselves up and win such an opportunity again soon enough because we were a team on the rise, but suddenly it seemed his conviction had dropped off by an octave or two.

The journey back over the Pennines could hardly have been more depressing. In Liverpool, Terry Littlewood, a devoted fan who knew some of the lads, was throwing a party. Terry was one of those people – Brian Welsh, Tex Williams and John Cantwell were others – who provided friendship that was constant down the years and had nothing to do with the celebrity 'pull' that seems to shape so many an entourage of the modern player. I decided to go along to blank out my disappointment, which wasn't the best idea I'd ever had. I went to the party and drank. I didn't have much to say, no philosophical reflections about the nature of football and how we had to heal the wounds and believe in ourselves again. I just drank. Drink after drink went down, and the more I drank the less likely it seemed that I would get drunk. I decided that losing at Hillsborough was the worst thing that had happened to me in my career. We could have been the Liverpool team that strode into history, but that possibility now seemed a million miles away. It was a cheerless binge. I just couldn't obliterate the sense of failure, so I said to my host, 'Set 'em up, Joe' – history would have to wait. In that mood, I could never have known quite how briefly.

7

GOD BLESS
THE MAID OF ERIN

L ESS THAN a year after that joyless bender in a house I didn't
know, I had another, better reason to reach for a glass. I was
in a pub situated among the warren of streets below Scotland
Road that were long ago razed by the bulldozers of urban
renewal. Well, that was the theory, but if the pub – a spit-
and-sawdust place called the Maid of Erin run by a great
character, Betty Hogan – has been gone for many years, the
spirit that pulsed through it that spring night in 1964 remains
vibrantly alive.

I was reassured of this still-powerful link with the past when
my old team swept into the final of the 2005 European Champions League – and so had the chance of a fifth European Cup
win – by beating Chelsea, the richest club in the world.

Of course, there are various ways of measuring wealth in
football, as in life, and at Anfield in May 2005 you could see the
extent of the riches accumulated by the tradition that Bill
Shankly and his team – my team – put in place. The human
richness was expressed in fantastically heightened emotion, a
force that plainly overwhelmed, at least for a few early, crucial
minutes, the belief of a Chelsea team that many had come to see
as invincible. They weren't. They were consumed by something
that went beyond man-for-man strength and market value.
Chelsea felt the force of something beyond their brief and, it
turned out, quite brittle experience of being winners. They felt

something that, I like to think, came roaring down the years. They perished in their most important game of the season after passing the old plaque put up by Shankly, the one that says simply, 'This is Anfield'.

On that distant Saturday night in 1964, Ronnie Yeats and I had gone to the Maid of Erin to join some of the fans celebrating the first major milestone of the Shankly years — the First Division title. We had finished four points ahead of Manchester United — Everton were five points adrift — and sealed the triumph with a 5–0 win over Arsenal. It was exactly as Shankly dreamed it would be, that final, irresistible rush after an Easter holiday burst that brought us maximum points from three games. 'There's the mountain top, boys,' said Shanks. 'You deserve the feeling that comes when you stand on top of it — go and get it,' and we did. We had quite a tasty Easter programme — Manchester United, still very much in the race, Tottenham, who had Dave Mackay and Jimmy Greaves and still much of the lustre of their brilliant double triumph, and finally Arsenal. We went out, really played and claimed what we believed to be our rights.

Anfield had throbbed in the afternoon, and in the Maid of Erin there was a tidal flow of Guinness. Eventually, our wives came to rescue us, taking us to dinner in some smart restaurant in the city centre, but for a few hours Ronnie and I were breathing the joy of the fans. I had known that intimacy before up in Motherwell, but not in such a moment of triumph, and some- times today I wonder at how much easier it was back in those days to feel part of a city, to go out on to the field knowing precisely the weight of the hopes and the dreams you carried on your shoulders when the referee blew the whistle to start a game. How easily do Rio Ferdinand or David Beckham associate with their fans as they make their carefully screened public appear- ances and peer at life from behind their dark glasses? Such lives of luxury were never imagined when Liverpool began ushering in new standards of achievement and professionalism in English football. Do they understand how hard it is for so many trying to make ends meet out there in the real world? I guess they never had to stuff cardboard into their shoes.

For me, one of the most amazing aspects of Liverpool's latest journey to the peak of European football was the contribution of Jamie Carragher, a Liverpool lad who seemed more than anything to be a throwback to my old team-mates Tommy Smith and Ian Callaghan. They both grew up in the city and running out at Anfield was the fulfilment of their greatest hopes. Carragher seemed to become a symbol of the best of the city in that run to the final in Istanbul, and each stunning performance from him reminded me of the regard in which I always held my fellow professionals. To be perfectly honest, that admiration had begun to wear very thin indeed.

Given my background, I suppose the dwindling of respect was inevitable. You read of Kieron Dyer talking about the new car he would like next, to put alongside the other seven he has littering his driveway, and Ferdinand shopping for furniture for his new mansion on the day he should have been taking a drugs test, and Lee Bowyer and Dyer, team-mates, fighting on the field before a great crowd at Newcastle. When you hear of, and sometimes see, these events, of course you despair of the direction being taken by a breed you were once proud to call your own.

Yes, I celebrate the fact that this new lot have played their way out of the tenements and the mean back streets, but the satisfaction drains away when I see what I suspect are the new priorities. When I read about three-million-pound new homes, and Wayne Rooney's teenaged girlfriend, who was raised in streets similar to the ones around the old, vanished Maid of Erin, spending on clothes, holidays and hairstyling in a few months what it would take an average family man half a lifetime to earn, it is not bitterness I feel so much as disbelief. Out of this new world of footballers, how can the old ambition and commitment possibly survive?

In the Maid of Erin, Ronnie and I felt the force that had shaped our contemporaries in the surrounding streets, professionals such as Tommy Smith, Gerry Byrne and Johnny Morrissey. Johnny, a fierce winger who played for both Liverpool and Everton, was combative enough to go into Jack Charlton's notorious black book, into which he claimed he had written the names of players he had earmarked for revenge.

Another product of those seething streets was Bobby Campbell. Bobby went on to have a good career after getting his pink slip at Anfield, and finished up manager of Chelsea, but he always retained his feeling for the club. He admired Shankly immensely, even though he had moved him on a year after his arrival at Anfield. The competition for places was ferocious then. Wages were poor, so clubs could maintain vast squads. Shankly had sixty or so players to sift through to find fourteen or fifteen who could serve as a first-team squad that he believed would deliver the major prizes. Bobby, who grew up close to Anfield, didn't make it but he always gloried in the success of the team. Throughout his career, he would look for the Liverpool result first on a Saturday afternoon.

That attitude, that love, was for me mirrored in the performances of Jamie Carragher in the run to the 2005 Champions League final as a Liverpool team drawn from all over Europe responded so brilliantly to the promptings of the home-grown hero. The kid took all of Anfield back to its most glorious roots. So much came back to me that night at Anfield when all the power and pretensions of Chelsea and their Russian owner, and all his fast-lane friends, were sent back to London beaten and, I suspect, a little bewildered. I thought of the mood in the Maid of Erin and of Bill Shankly, because I saw in his face that day we whipped Arsenal quite how much the breakthrough had meant to him. He was aghast when Arsenal won an early penalty but the normally immaculate George Eastham missed it. Then Shankly's voice bellowed above all the tumult, 'Now, come on, boys, this is it,' his fist clenched and punching the sky. He had no need to worry. We had moved forward strongly since the spring of our great FA Cup disappointment. Crucial to our development had been the width and the penetration provided by our now established wingers, Callaghan and the great dribbler Peter Thompson.

Callaghan was the perfect, functional winger, running hard, endlessly, and always getting in his cross. A shock ran through the club when, late in his career, which stretched to a staggering 800 games for Liverpool, referee Pat Partridge handed him a cheap caution, the first of his professional life, in a replayed League Cup semi-final with Nottingham Forest. Callaghan was yellow carded for a tackle on Peter Withe, who was well able to look after himself. Ian was stunned. I remember thinking of the match official, 'Where have you been in all the career of this great pro? Do you know what he has done – and what he means?'

Of Thompson, who came to us from Preston North End like someone who had jumped out of a magic box, all swerves and feints and mazy runs, Shanks would say, only half-ironically, 'If you're tired, give the ball to Peter – he'll look after it until you're ready to get it back. Mind you, there's every chance you'll have to tackle him.' At half-time in the trouncing of Arsenal, Billy Stevenson said, 'That was some run you had, Peter. You beat three of them, me twice and even the fucking referee.' It was true. Sometimes you just couldn't get the ball back off him. It became a bit of a joke in the dressing room and he was aware of it.

Once, though, the joke was on us when he weaved down the wing and, instead of crossing, shot for goal. Before we could scream at him, the ball was flashing into the net.

If Peter had ever learned the art of timing a pass, if he had moved the ball at the point when he had done most to devastate the opposing team, he could have achieved anything. Sir Alf Ramsey took a long look at him before the 1966 World Cup finals, and had there been more of that cutting-edge passing – if he had absorbed the message of Johnny Cash about knowing when to hold 'em and when to fold 'em – he would surely have added a World Cup medal to his other prizes. Ramsey held out for the basic value of a good old winger, but in the developing international game he saw a missing aspect to Thompson's play. It was so sad because, apart from being a great lad, he had huge talent. When he was chosen, with Callaghan and Roger Hunt, for the final England World Cup squad, we had the highest hopes that all three of them might go all the way. As it was, Roger was the Liverpool banker, holding off the challenge of even the legendary Greavsie.

For Peter the consolation was that he would always remain a great favourite at Anfield, particularly of the fans who gathered in the Kemlyn Road stand. It seemed that he always did his most spectacular work in front of them. He ran up and down the wing so cleverly, with great balance, agility and ball control, but too often the play broke down because of one extra touch, and when Roger and I had been making hard runs at a late stage of a game, that caused frustration. Once I heard Shankly say to him, 'Peter, for God's sake, why don't you cross it?' The truth was he had his style, and he couldn't do much about it. Eventually he went to Bolton, where no one questioned him and he was embraced all over again whenever he made one of his great churning runs through defence – but then that was Bolton.

At Liverpool, with the first title won, the need for a unit in which every individual understood his function perfectly was fully embraced. As the team developed to a new level of efficiency, so did the legend-builders on the Kop. The Liverpool fans used all available material, ancient and modern. They adapted the work of the Beatles and the Scaffold among others – 'We love you, yeah, yeah, yeah' and 'Thank you very much for the Anfield iron . . .' went straight into the portfolio. Much sentimental, meaningless talk is often heard about the impact of the fans but in Liverpool, the force of their inspiration was not in doubt. Once we were giving Tottenham a severe examination and it became even more intense when the sound of 'London Bridge is Falling Down' came rolling down from the Kop. It is not so hard to imagine the effect of such biting humour. You're playing well, on top of your game, which is exhilarating enough, and then you see the effect of your work, the response it is getting. Naturally, you re-double your efforts. In European action, the great Inter Milan team slipped behind at Anfield, and the moment they did so the Kop was booming, 'Go back to Italy.' You smile to yourself and you play, really play. When all the great teams came to Anfield, including the fine Leeds United side who were maybe a couple of years behind us, they knew that their backs would be to the wall. They knew that something close to instant mystique had been installed.

We won our first league championship with just seventeen players. I started the season scoring freely but as time went on I increasingly found myself supplying chances, especially for Roger. This didn't displease me because the effect of what I was doing was clear and I was enough of a professional to understand that the team was winning and I was playing a crucial part. Indeed, in later years, my need to score dwindled to almost nothing. My satisfaction came from helping to shape the play, seeing the moment to deliver the killer ball. I'll never forget one moment that came towards the end of our partnership. Roger was at the near post. The ball cleared him but as he turned around I saw that he was in a good position, so I nodded it back, precisely, to him. In my Motherwell days, and during the first years at Anfield, I probably wouldn't have hesitated to head for goal myself, but at that later stage of our playing careers, when I saw Hunt in a perfect position, I nodded the ball to him and he put it away. It was so nicely, easily done, and Roger turned, quite sedately, and waved his thanks. In its way, that was as memorable as the most thunderous goal I ever scored. One I scored at Wembley, though, had a rather deep meaning.

It was a great tribute to Shankly, his methods and his understanding of how to handle professionals that we were able to put in such a strong finish to carry off that first title. He realised that good rest was the key. When fixtures were piling up, to a degree modern players can scarcely imagine, and we found ourselves playing on pitches that resembled ploughed fields from as early as November, Shankly often scrapped conventional training. Once we reported to Anfield to be told that the usual work was off. Shankly took us to the local baths for steam treatment and massages, and fussed over us in his best mother-hen style.

During the build-up to a derby game with Everton, which came towards the end of a hard season, he was particularly careful about not extending us too much at Melwood, while all the time giving us a running commentary on the rigours the opposition were being put through by their manager Harry Catterick.

'You wouldn't believe it, boys,' he said. 'I've been getting a good look at their work and they're doing a commando course. He's running the legs off them. He thinks he can keep up with our training. He's delusional.'

Shankly lived next door to Everton's Bellefield training ground, but it was a little hard to know how he could have got such a clear view of their work. Bellefield was surrounded by high walls. One theory was that he had clambered on to the roof of his own house, which naturally had the front door and window frames painted bright red. It was a bizarre idea but it did provide the wonderful image of Shankly training his binoculars on his bitter rival Catterick – after one Everton defeat he called him the Town Crier – while his despairing wife Nessie pleaded with him to be careful.

Intermingled with all of this dedicated effort was the other life of the professional footballer, when fun, boredom, joy and, if you like, extended adolescence took over. One of the unshakeable realities of the professional life is that there will always be occasions when time weighs heavily, especially on the road. You know you have to look after yourself but there is a limit to how many books and newspapers you can read and how many hands of cards you can play. Practical joking was never far from top of the agenda on such occasions. It was activity in which I indulged quite relentlessly.

One prime victim was Davey Wilson, a good little winger who was bought mainly as cover for Peter Thompson. Davey could play on the right or left but Shankly decided he was a little short of what was required and so for some time Davey was twelfth man. On a trip to Sunderland, Ronnie Yeats and I were whiling away the Saturday morning in our hotel room. We decided that Davey would be the victim.

I got the job of imitating the voice of the Sunderland manager, Ian McColl, whom I knew from when he was manager of the Scotland team. I called Davey's room and said that I had noted his absence from Liverpool's team, which I thought was a terrible injustice, and that I had spoken with Shankly and received clearance to make him an offer I didn't think he could refuse. I would guarantee him a first-team place and give him £40 a week, nearly twice his current wages. I can see the cruelty of this prank now, given the boy's situation, but then it seemed like a natural part of footballing life. Davey's excitement crackled down the phone.

'That's a very generous offer, Mr McColl, and the most important thing is, of course, regular first-team football. I'd love to play for you.'

'Right,' I said. 'As soon as you arrive at the ground with the team, come to my office. There's no time like the present, we'll sort this out straight away.'

Over lunch I told the rest of the boys that the trap had been laid. Davey was a popular enough boy and there was no malice towards him at all, but that didn't deter the delight of the lads. They couldn't wait for the final stage of the drama. Once we had settled into the dressing room at Roker Park, Davey told Peter Thompson, 'I can't understand it. McColl just walked past in the corridor and he didn't say a word. In fact, I might not have existed.' Naturally, I stepped in again.

'Look, Davey, maybe he's being cute. Maybe he hasn't talked to Shankly and wouldn't want to be making a move so publicly. Why don't you just go to McColl's office and knock on the door. You can't let this situation slide away.'

Davey agreed and went striding off to McColl's office. A minute or two later he was back in the dressing room, his face contorted with anger. He was a mild enough person normally and it was suddenly a bit chilling to see him in this state. Apparently, he had knocked on the door and been told to come in. McColl, obviously preoccupied with the coming match, had said quite sharply, 'Well, what is it?'

'Well, you know,' said Davey. 'You want to see me, you told me so on the phone.'

McColl was quite icy. 'I've never spoken to you in my life before. No, I don't want to talk to you. I have no reason.'

Davey glared round our dressing room before saying, 'I know it was one of you Scots bastards. Well, somebody will pay for this.' I thought it wise not to own up.

Once, we were in Manchester on a Friday night – the eve of a game against United – and this time the victim was my compatriot and fellow Motherwell man Bobby Graham. Bobby was an extremely talented player, but like Davey Wilson, he couldn't break into the first team and was beginning to feel the frustration. By this stage, I had the voice of Shankly pretty much perfectly and I was nominated to make the phone call to Bobby, who was back in Liverpool contemplating another reserve game in front of a smattering of diehard fans.

'Hello, Bobby,' I said and I could almost hear the intake of breath. 'Hello, Boss, what's up?' he said. I told him that Peter had gone down with the flu and I was juggling the team. He was going to play.

'Go and see Joe Fagan. Get your boots and get over here as quick as you can. You need some good rest tonight, Bobby, this is a big chance for you.'

Bobby was elated when he knocked on Joe's door.

'Sorry to bother you on a Friday night, Joe, but I've got to get my boots from the ground and then go across to Manchester – I'm playing tomorrow.'

Joe adjusted his cigarette from one corner of his mouth to the other, without a helping hand, and said, 'Bobby, go home, you silly bugger.'

Why did we do this mischief, and why was I so often in the middle of it? Often we decided it was the best way to kill some time, and if you think it was a needlessly harsh way to do this, given the insecurities common to almost every professional footballer, you are probably right. Youth is often cruel and, in one way, football is nothing so much as a prolonging of boyhood. It is only later, when the cheers have stopped and the arthritis takes a grip, and you think of the paltry rewards that were available in those days, that you realise what we should all have known — one day there would be a price to pay. Back in the card schools — which I avoided whenever I could — and the bars, where the elaborate plots to fool and embarrass a team-mate were hatched, that day was always a million years away. We would play forever.

When the boys were playing cards, I generally read — spy novels, mysteries and the odd racy one that for plot relied heavily on the joys of sexual intercourse. The American pulp writer Hank Jansen had cornered that end of the market and although most of the lads didn't get far beyond the backpages and the form guide, Jansen's latest offering tended to get at least mildly dog-eared as it was passed around the team coach.

Shankly loved cards. He played back home in Ayrshire with the miners, and when he was a player, at Preston and Carlisle. He told us, 'Back in Ayrshire we played three-card brag and if you had a good day, you would come back to the house and tell your mother, "Here's some ten-bob notes. Would you mind ironing them because I want to go out tonight." ' He was at Preston with a group of other Scots and Shankly would talk fondly of how they used to gather on a Sunday morning, bringing crates of beer, and play all day.

I recall a long card game on a trip up to Newcastle. Shankly was involved in the school and so was Bobby Graham, who must have been relieved to know that his presence, on this occasion at least, was absolutely official. It was a tough school with Ronnie Yeats, Tommy Smith and Tommy Lawrence also participating, and it was fascinating to watch Shanks play. He squeezed the cards in the way that the miners did. He just took a quick glance and then clenched them up in his hand so that it was impossible to see what he had, even when you were standing behind him. Sometimes I wondered if he knew what he was holding, and that was certainly the case on the journey to Newcastle. Eventually, Shankly was betting £1 blind against Bobby. Then he took another look, squeezed the cards again and put £2 in. Bobby responded with his bet and it turned out that they both thought they had the winning hand. Shanks had three queens but Bobby held the perfect cards, three threes. When they showed their cards, Shankly growled, 'In Chicago, three queens wins.' Much to his embarrassment, Shankly had run out of money. 'See me back at Anfield,' he said to Bobby as he got up from the school. On the following Monday, Bobby wasn't sure about claiming his winnings.

'Christ, I'm not going to get it,' he said. 'Maybe I'll let it rest.'

Naturally, we all argued that he deserved his money and urged him to march into the manager's office and ask him for it. We went with him.

'Boss, I've come for the grabs . . .' Bobby began.

'Oh aye, son,' said Shanks, handing him the winnings. As Bobby was leaving his office, Shankly added, 'Bobby, son, stay away from the cards. No good can come from them.'

The following day he made it official. The blocks were on playing cards for money. That was fine, the card players said to Shanks, but would it be all right to play for matchsticks, surely an innocent way to pass the time on the road? 'Aye, lads, that will be fine,' said Shanks. For a while, a matchstick was worth 10p, or 2 shillings in old money, and soon enough the pretence was dropped.

Shankly was enough of a realist to know that you couldn't stop the way of the footballer's life. He had been through all of it himself, but occasionally he seemed to find it necessary to make a show of discipline. Of course, most of that discipline was implicit. If he had serious concerns about how you behaved, and how seriously you took your responsibilities to Liverpool Football Club, you would have been gone soon enough.

One of the oddities of travelling with Liverpool was that throughout my ten years there, certain rules never changed. When we were on long trips to places such as Newcastle, we would stop for a pre-arranged meal on the way home, but on hops back from Manchester or Stoke we returned non-stop to Liverpool. Bob Paisley would hand us all 10 shillings (50p) in lieu of the evening meal we had missed. Eventually, the amount became so derisory the card players just used it as a minor contribution to their betting resources.

Despite all the glory, our wages only inched up through the years. I started at Anfield on £30 a week basic, a £14 improvement on my rate at Motherwell, but for my last few years I was doing no better than £35 basic. At one point, when titles and Cup wins had been accumulated and the gap between our achievements and our rewards was beginning to seem quite grotesque, even in those innocent days, we formed a deputation to see Shankly and the directors to demand something more in line with the progress of the club. We asked for a £10 rise, a pittance when you considered the profits flowing from attendances of 50,000 plus. All we got was a fiver.

Win and crowd bonuses were the great saver. They put us on a standard of living that finally stretched beyond that of the average man in the street. For some reason, the figure of 28,000 was set as the starting point for the crowd bonus. We got £1 for every thousand above the mark. It was a simple equation. We made up to the princely sum of £100 a week if we filled the ground, and to do that we had to keep winning. That sort of incentive might concentrate the mind of Harry Kewell.

With his agent, Kewell cost Liverpool — the club who used to dole out ten bob a go for dinner — more than £4 million, and for what? Some of the most tepid, brainless performances I have seen from a professional footballer, a fact that is made all the more appalling by his great natural talent. Kewell has beautiful skill, good pace and when he is on the ball and alive, you wouldn't want anyone more talented along the left side of your attack — but where is the spark, the pride, the determination?

Shankly demanded all of that and although he was a man of the world, and gave us some leeway to relax when he felt it was necessary, there was always a hard and fast bottom line. It meant, inevitably, that Ronnie and I would be required to survive quite a number of scrapes. When he issued an order he expected it to be obeyed. On one occasion, we were dismayed when he announced in the lobby of our London hotel, 'Right, nobody's going out tonight. I want you tucked up in your beds, boys, you need some good rest.' We had played in a League Cup tie at Watford on that Wednesday night and were staying down in the capital for a game on Saturday. Ronnie and I were particularly aggrieved at the suddenly imposed curfew. We always assumed we were free to do a little socialising after a midweek game and had accepted an invitation to join the scriptwriter Johnny Speight, the creator of Alf Garnett, in one of his favourite London pubs.

Determined to make the date, we went through the motions of going to bed, gave it a few minutes, and then slipped down the backstairs and into the garden of the Hendon Hall Hotel. We were planning to go over the wall. Ronnie gave me a lift and I was just about to leap down on to the street outside when I saw, directly below me, Shankly and Paisley taking a late stroll, or perhaps it was a little security patrol. Ronnie hissed, 'Go on, what are you waiting for?'

'Shoosh, for Christ's sake,' I whispered back.

Miraculously, it seemed, Shankly and Paisley walked on, deep in conversation – well, Bob was deep in Shankly's conversation. When they disappeared around the corner, we jumped down and were away for drinks with Speight. It was dawn-chorus time when we returned, but we reckoned we were young and fit and could survive one late night without any serious loss of efficiency. In fact, it was always true that you worked that much harder when you were touched by a little guilt.

Looking back, it is remarkable that mostly we were so dedicated. I suppose our justification was that every so often you cried out for a break from the pressure, the expectation. You wanted at least a smattering of the wildness of youth, which most of the time you were obliged to put behind you. That it was quite perilous, both at the club and at home, possibly gave our adventures a little more spice.

Years earlier in Scotland, I had come rather badly unstuck when Motherwell played in Aberdeen and I told Betsy that the team would be staying over after the game. In fact, a boys' night out had been arranged. This would have been fine if Betsy hadn't been cleaning up the kitchen that Saturday night and looked up to see my team-mate Andy Weir walking up the tenement stairway. When I returned on the Sunday afternoon Betsy quizzed me quite gently, at first.

'So the team stayed over, did they?'

'Aye,' I said, 'all of us.'

'Oh really,' said Betsy, her eyes turning to flint. 'Then how did Andy Weir get home?' I was bang to rights and it was one of the longer Sundays of my life.

Maybe the best example of the line Shankly walked between hard discipline and a certain tolerance, at least towards players who had earned his respect by the consistency of their performances on the field, came on a trip to Ireland. Again, Ronnie and

I had gone over the wall and it was very late indeed when we straggled back into the team hotel. There, for our pain, was the sight of Bob Paisley standing on the steps of the hotel with an extremely severe look on his face.

'You lads are in real trouble,' he said. 'The boss knows you were out on the town and he's taking a very dim view of it. He will see you at Anfield.' Then Bob slipped in the knife. 'I think he's got it in mind to tell your wives . . .' It was not a good situation and while I was very concerned – I could see at least another long Sunday on the horizon – Ronnie was in a state of complete panic on the brief flight home.

'Look,' I said to him, 'this is what we tell the boss. It will be something he can relate to more easily than the fact that we were on the toot all night. We will tell him that someone took us to a gambling club, and we started off winning quite a bit, then we started losing and we were desperate to try to win some of it back. Then, of course, you lose track of time, and when we looked at our watches it was all hours.'

Ronnie nodded, rather bleakly. At Anfield the rest of the boys got into their cars to go home while we went down to Shankly's office. He came to the door with a scowl on his face and said, 'You first, Ronnie.'

So Ronnie told him the story, how we won, lost and then were battling back into the game – a classic story for a man who had spent so much of his youth squeezing the cards in the company of miners and old pros.

'Aye, aye, Ronnie,' he said. 'You never play with Irishmen – they're all cardsharps, but maybe you've learned your lesson. Okay, son.'

When Ronnie came to the door with a look of tremendous relief on his face, Shankly was standing behind him.

'Do you want to see me now, Boss?' I asked.

Shankly shook his head and said, 'No, you'll only tell me the same fucking cock-and-bull story.'

So there was Shankly walking the line again between discipline and accepting the world as it was and how it affected two of his best players, and making of it the best he could. He knew he had thrown a real scare into us and he was happy to leave it at that. He didn't want any escalation; he would keep the ship going forward smoothly through the odd little storm.

Shankly never fined a player in all the time I was at Anfield. His discipline wasn't about taking money off players. His discipline was his authority. He would give you a bollocking, and it would be a real one, the kind that makes you think a bit, but as he did it he would always know if you were the genuine article. If you were, he made up the rules as he went along.

In the matter of not fining players, the boss showed some contradiction. The old managers, including Shankly, Sir Matt Busby and Don Revie, never fought too hard for better terms for their players. In fact, many years later I joined Johnny Giles, who played such a key part in the rise of Leeds United, on a television documentary to suggest that the big managers operated something like a cartel. They kept wage levels down by never allowing one of their players the chance to claim, perhaps while on duty with their national teams, that they were on great wages. It was the kind of statement someone might make after a few drinks, and the big managers knew the possible repercussions. I don't believe it was meanness on the part of Shankly, Busby or Revie. More likely, they felt responsible for every aspect of the football club; they were the guardians of its future. Partly, too, they sensed that the more money the players received, the less committed they would become. They would be corrupted away from their first impetus to play the game for the sheer pleasure and excitement of it. When you look around today, who can say that they were wrong?

In reality, the attitude was both right and wrong. Someone on the board of clubs such as Liverpool and Leeds, who had come so far, so quickly and completely changed the prospects for the future, should have said, 'Look, these lads have worked so well, and really their rewards are not great. Maybe we could loosen the purse strings a little. Perhaps we could start a pension fund.' Such enlightenment never came and what we had was an irreversible march to today's situation, when the clubs are at the mercy of the players, often quite mediocre ones, and their agents.

In the sixties, instead of vision and a sophisticated understanding of what was happening, the game that was growing ever more popular throughout the world did so under a form of feudalism. While we were still being given ten bob for our dinner in a five-star hotel, we were also taken off to Majorca as an end-of-season perk. We were made to feel important and because we were so naive, so innocent of the world of money and business, most of us were happy to go along with it. That extended to the need, under FA regulations, to play a game, any game, to justify the trip. This resulted in one match that didn't amount to much more than a kick-around with a bunch of local waiters. We knew certain aspects of the system were deeply wrong, but then, as we were constantly told, we played football for a living and what could be better than that? Shankly cleverly exploited these realities, and he was far too smart not to understand that if you started fining players, you were admitting that you had lost them. Sometimes, though, even Shankly's best-laid plans went seriously wrong, as happened at a low point in that brilliant season of our first title win in the old Second Division, 1961–62. We went out of the Cup to Second Division Preston North End after two replays.

Before our league game at Anfield, Shankly came to me and said, 'Now today you're up against Tony Singleton — just think back to all the times he has kicked you from pillar to post. If you let it happen again today, you're not half the man I think you are.'

As Shanks was talking, I thought to myself, 'Jesus, what's he giving me here — a licence to kill?' He had never said anything like that to me before, or to any player. His sternest demand had been to 'shake their bones'.

As far as I was concerned, I had been given specific orders and it was true that in the past the big lad had given me plenty of punishment. My chance to gain a little revenge had been rubber-stamped and I didn't see any point in delaying the process. When the first cross came in, I didn't go for it as normal. I let Singleton make the header and came in late and very hard. Singleton went sprawling among the photographers while I strutted out of the penalty area, a man who had made a point with some quite dramatic force.

However, I was unaware that Singleton had clambered to his feet and was racing towards my back. I heard a roar of warning from the crowd but it was too late. As I turned, Singleton was landing a big punch in my ear. I was so angry at the sneak attack that I launched a tremendous kick intended for the place where you least enjoy such a blow, but he managed to turn in time and my boot finished up on his backside. Naturally, the referee sent us off. When I got to the touchline, Shankly was holding his head in his hands.

'Oh son, for Christ's sake, I didn't want you to do that,' he said.

Singleton came back into my life in 2004, the fortieth anniversary of Preston's march to the final with West Ham United. The club had gathered together their old players and Tony, who had moved to California and set himself up in business, was persuaded to make the trip, despite the fact that he was fighting cancer. Preston held a dinner on the eve of a Saturday match and Singleton's niece contacted me to say it would be a great surprise if I showed up. They brought me out from behind a curtain and we had another fight – this one faked. I said to him, 'You were an ugly bugger forty years ago and nothing has changed.' We sat down and had a good drink and went back over the old days. Shankly would have enjoyed that second collision, although I doubt that he would have accepted any responsibility for the first.

The kind of warm evening I had with my old foe is commonplace among Liverpool players of the sixties and seventies, which I feel is understandable enough. We may not have been the best-paid team that ever played but for a little while I think we were entitled to believe we were the best. The bond remains very close, and for that Shankly deserves great credit. He had one basic rule, which he laid down with great care to each of his players. He always said, 'Do your own job first, then help somebody else.' At times he was crazy, and soon enough I would have reason to feel less than warm about some aspects of his character, but I never doubted then, no more than I do now, that Bill Shankly had values that would hold true as long as the game was played.

8

SHANKLY AND THE GHOSTS OF WEMBLEY

THIS MAY be my story, one in which in theory I have control, but how do I shake off Bill Shankly? How do I scale him down and integrate him with all the rest of the passing cast that came in and out of my life, and why would I do that? Because of the madness, the contradictions and the cruelties that came with the brilliance and the often surreal fantasy? Because of a bad ending? Because when you were no longer of any use to him, the relationship that you thought was so vital and precious suddenly became history, an old affair, something he wanted to banish from his mind until sometime in the future, when it could be resurrected safely and without the need for daily care? No, that would demean both him and me.

I can't do it, anyway, not totally, not now, in the fullness of the years, any more than when I felt betrayed, when all the passion and the achievement seemed to have congealed into something that, for quite some time, would eat at my spirit. There is time to cover that, and meanwhile there is still so much of Shankly to pass down the chain of memory.

Maybe one day I will have a balanced view of the man who did so much to shape my life. I can still see so many vivid pictures of him in his prime, raging and exulting in the glory of his team when we won our first title and were heading off into a future that brimmed with the most exciting possibilities — and, as we seized our chances, appearing with ever-growing confidence and the strut of a fighting cock.

On a triumphant tour of the United States he often stunned and bewildered our American hosts. In the long run that tour proved to be more than anything a great folly, a draining of our strength. In modern football, almost certainly it wouldn't have been allowed to happen. At the Soldiers' Field stadium in Chicago, where we were due to play a game, he was intrigued and thrilled to learn that this was where Jack Dempsey and Gene Tunney had fought.

'Jesus Christ,' he said to the groundsman, 'you have to show me where the ring stood, and I don't want any guesses.' Eventually, when due allowance was made for changed configurations of the stadium with the mock Roman pillars, he was shown the spot.

'Right, boys,' he said, 'this is where we're going to train.'

We played five-a-side games where they had pitched the ring for Dempsey and Tunney and Shankly's eyes glowed as we did our work. He believed that somehow the spirit of those great fighters might be transferred to his team. He fed us the idea and, because so much of what he had said in the past had proved to be right, we half believed him. It is certainly a matter of record that we won the game – and I scored a hat-trick.

In New York, he had spent several nights in Dempsey's bar near Madison Square Garden, hoping to meet the great man, and he was downcast when he learned that the former heavyweight champion was out of town. At a press conference in New York he became impatient at some of the questions of American sports reporters, who plainly had only the dimmest view of the world game. He snapped when, after making one of his time-honoured references to Tom Finney, one of the reporters asked, 'Now, Mr Shankly, who is this guy Tom Finney?'

'Christ, that's it,' he said as he stormed out of the room. 'If you don't know who Tommy Finney is, you'll never have a fucking team in this country.' In the hotel lobby, Shankly's rage couldn't be contained. He stood with his hands on his hips, shaking his head and saying, 'Can you believe it, they've never heard of Tommy Finney? There's no hope for them.'

Meanwhile, the American journalists were asking, 'Gee, who is this Tommy Finney — he must have been some guy.' We said he was a great soccer player and in the eyes of our manager, a little more than that. Perhaps he was a god, like so many great players he conjured from the past.

In Chicago, he wanted to be shown the site of the St Valentine's Day Massacre, and when we travelled to the west he demanded to visit the local Boot Hill. Partly he lived in his own world of mobsters, great boxers and gunfighters, but however fascinated he was by new sights, and to see at first hand the places that so coloured his imagination — he once dismissed from Anfield a reporter who had been brave enough to criticise his team, with the words, 'Get out of here in your Elliot Ness overcoat' — he was always happiest when discussing the legends of his own game.

Finney, Wilf Copping and Peter Doherty were the true giants of his life. He lived to make heroes of men he played against or knew or signed to play for his team. His admiration for Celtic's great manager Jock Stein knew no bounds. 'John,' he once declared, face to face, after Celtic became the first British team to win the European Cup, 'you're immortal.' In the lobby of the Lisbon hotel where the two men spoke, Shankly noticed that his hero's presence was completely unnoticed. After Stein walked away from the brief, warm conversation, Shankly accosted a group of American tourists who were studying their travel guides and told them, 'You've just missed the greatest man you would ever have seen.' It was as well that Shankly passed away before Stein. Had it not happened that way, Shankly would have been shattered, inconsolable.

In all his sayings, he was most emphatic about the need for a player to operate to his strengths, to know himself. 'Never try to do what you can't pull off,' he would declare. 'Let the dribblers dribble and the passers pass and the tacklers tackle and the headers head . . . and most important of all, never think you can dribble if you can't. That's fatal.' According to Shankly, Copping and Doherty, in their radically different ways, were supreme examples of players who knew most precisely their own powers. He always used to tell Copping stories before we played Arsenal. It was as though it would strengthen the flow of our competitive blood against the great player's old team. 'That man,' said Shankly, 'was the hardest footballer I ever saw.' He recalled how the young Bobby Charlton had sat next to the formidable Copping at an FA dinner for former internationals. Bobby, trying to make pleasant conversation, said to him, 'Oh Mr Copping, my uncle Jackie Milburn always used to talk about you when I was a boy.' Copping glowered and said, 'Oh yes, what did he fucking say?'

Shankly's experience of Copping became one of the classics of man-to-man competition in football. Shanks told us, 'Copping did me with a terrible tackle and as they were taking me off the field on a stretcher, I shouted, "I'll get you for this, Copping." You said that all the time in those days. I just had to bide my time and, sure enough, the chance came the following season. It was a perfect situation for an over-the-top tackle, a fifty-fifty ball. I went in full steam but, would you believe it, he did me again.'

Shankly revered Doherty for his ability to throw the perfect dummy. 'Peter could do you every time. He went to kick, you turned your back and he was gone,' said Shanks. 'They were doing that fifty years ago and in fifty years' time the great players will be doing it. You can't teach that. You're born with it.'

That spring day in 1964 when we beat Arsenal to clinch the title, we were beginning to play in a way that convinced Shankly that we had the means to lay down a few legends of our own. It was the kind of powerful performance he loved, one that brought a good contribution from every player. There were no sleepers, no passengers, and that day I was delighted to get on the list of scorers with a headed goal.

We made a small imprint on football history. Arsenal, a decent team, just couldn't live with the force of our game that day. Gerry Byrne scared the life out of the opposition and Ronnie was a terror, mighty in his scale and his commitment. Thompson ran at the defence so potently that, whatever happened, they were undermined to some degree, and Callaghan was relentless on the right. We also had the craft and skill of Milne and Stevenson. For Roger and me, there would always be good space and good pickings. Vital to our self-belief, we knew that Shankly was always thinking ahead. The crunching power of young Tommy Smith was on the horizon, and so was the revolutionary switch to a flat back four.

This emerged in the season of our first European adventure, and our run to the FA Cup win that had become so central to the club's ambitions. Considerable confusion was caused because the fans were still thinking in terms of the old certainties. Full-backs wore numbers two and three, centre-halves were number five and wing-halves four and six. So when Tommy came in and played alongside Ronnie Yeats, they were obliged to ask what the hell was going on. Shankly knew, and so did we soon enough.

The boss didn't always spell out the last detail of our tactics, but he wanted more security along with width and striking force, with Smith playing beside Yeats, the plan was for Milne,

Stevenson and me to drop back when the situation required it. Roger Hunt would take a more forward position. Gordon Milne, particularly on European nights, would say to me, 'Just tuck in for a wee while and see how we're going.'

When Shankly was quizzed on the development of the team by one of the more tactically aware football writers, he would say, 'What's new in football?' Today we have fifteen-man squads playing some version of 4–4–2. Invariably, a couple of dummy players with defensive ability are included, who don't have a clue when going forward, and vice-versa. Wing-backs were invented, but to what effect? It is very questionable at times and I believe we always have to come back to the Shankly imperatives of players doing what they do best. As he said, defenders defend, attackers attack.

Our first European game was against Reykjavik, which was a formality but an historic one and I was sorry to miss the first leg in Iceland because of the need for an operation on my appendix. We were all filled with a sense of adventure and new horizons, and naturally I regretted I wasn't able to join the lads on this first step into a new world, especially in such an outpost of European football. I was able to play in the second game, however, when we ran up the score. Many years later, I was surprised when a Uefa official, a big man, introduced himself and said that he had played against me in that Anfield game, and what a great memory it was. The mystery was compounded by the fact that he had apparently played at centre-half.

The second round presented a much more formidable challenge. Anderlecht of Brussels were a rising team and supplied key players, including Paul van Himst, to an impressive Belgian team. Shankly went down to Wembley to see them play England and was deeply impressed.

'They have good skilful players,' he reported, 'and they play team football. We'll have to be on our toes, boys.'

Maybe as an antidote to this perceived threat, Shankly had come up with the idea of red shorts to go along with our red shirts. He thought the colour scheme would carry quite a bit of psychological impact – red for danger, red for power. He came into the dressing room one day and threw a pair of red shorts to Ronnie Yeats.

'Get into those shorts and let's see how you look,' he said. Ronnie stood there in his red shirt and red shorts and the manager was very pleased. 'Christ, Ronnie, you look awesome, terrifying. You look seven feet tall.'

'Why not go the whole hog, Boss,' I suggested. 'Why not wear red socks? Let's go out all in red.' Shankly approved.

On the afternoon of the first game with Anderlecht, Shankly took us to a hotel in Southport. We would rest there and make the perfect preparation. The manager was preoccupied with one point of team selection. His instinct was to play Tommy Smith, but the boy had scarcely any experience. Would he get lost among the polished Belgians? Shankly spoke to Ronnie and me and we were startled to hear that he was agonising over the decision.

'I know the boy can play, but is it the right time to blood him? I'm frightened of putting him on at the wrong time,' Shankly confessed. He was encouraged by our emphatic replies.

'Well, I don't think he'll let us down, Boss,' said Ronnie, and when Shankly looked over to me, I nodded my agreement. It was the first time we had been consulted in such a direct way and was a significant moment in the development of the team. That was the first time we played with a flat back four. It took a little bit of perfecting but came right soon enough; we were pacesetters.

Tommy was a strong new presence and Tommy Lawrence played a key role. Lawrence patrolled to the edge of the penalty area and this was the first time in English football that a goalkeeper had been seen beyond the six-yard box. The two Tommies both brought a vital ingredient to their tasks – they could read the game. Shankly called Smith his sweeper, which wasn't quite right because he was more proactive than that, but that was essentially his role, one that Nobby Stiles would also fulfil brilliantly for Manchester United on their way to the European Cup in 1968.

We didn't play an offside game as such – our defenders were obliged to cover the ground and make their tackles – but our system worked so efficiently that forwards had to time their runs perfectly to get into legitimate scoring positions. We knew we were well down the road to making our new game work when we played Southampton, who had the young Mick Channon in their team. Channon was making a strong early impact in the First Division but on this occasion he was made to look a novice. 'Let him run,' we said, and soon we lost count of the times he found himself offside.

Inevitably, for every young player, such as Tommy, who thrusts his way into the centre of the action, others, for one reason or another, lose their way. Two in that category were striker Alf Arrowsmith, who suffered a career-wrecking injury, and Phil Chisnall, a stylish player who couldn't quite fulfil the promise he had first shown at Manchester United. There was no doubt about Tommy Smith, however. He was clearly a stayer.

Tommy came in against Anderlecht as though he was simply claiming his destiny rather than facing the biggest challenge of his young life. He was strong in the tackle and confident on the ball. We swept aside the Belgians, who had caused Shankly so much apprehension, winning 3–0, but in the second leg in Brussels, the manager's instincts were proved, yet again, to be both acute and sound. Anderlecht played us off the park. They were quick and inventive and for most of the night we were tackling shadows. Yet in one moment that must have broken their hearts I got hold of the ball on the halfway line and pushed it through to Roger Hunt, who swept on and scored the only goal of the match. It was hardly fair, but it was football.

Anderlecht had been full of creativity but they just couldn't get the ball past Lawrence. The boys from the wrong end of the East Lancashire Road, who had come rushing into our dressing room that critical afternoon at Anfield, covered in sweat but ready to play, had pulled off an amazing victory. Tommy had never done more to enhance his reputation and we were sheepish about our win only for as long as it took to get hold of our first glass of strong, cold Belgian beer.

Yes, Tommy had produced one of the great performances between the sticks, but it was no better than the one Gordon Banks had come up with to deny us a place at Wembley eighteen months earlier.

Despite the display inflicted on us by Anderlecht, we had tremendous confidence now. We were champions of England, bearing down on the European Cup, and I will always believe that we could have successfully defended our title but for that long American tour in the previous summer. We were away for six weeks and I played in all ten games – not the best way to recover from a title-winning season. Another problem was that Ronnie Yeats finished the tour with his knee in plaster. Shankly had returned to England to make some plans for the coming season, and instead of being sent home for treatment, which would be automatic in today's game, Ronnie was allowed to continue on what for him had suddenly become an extended holiday.

We travelled all over America, visiting New York, Chicago, Boston, San Francisco and St Louis, and crossed the Canadian border to Vancouver. The start of the tour was bizarre enough when we got caught by a bad case of jetlag. Shankly refused to acknowledge American time, except when it was absolutely necessary, and went to his bed at 5 p.m. on our first day in New York. Quite sensibly, it seemed, we went out into Manhattan to see some of the sights, and returned to the hotel around midnight, dog-tired and ready to sleep. Unfortunately, Shankly greeted us at the door of the hotel, refreshed and excited to be in the great city. He was ready to talk the night away and, one by one, we had to slip away from him. In the end, he was left on his own, awake but with nowhere to go and no one to talk to in a heathen place that had never heard of Tom Finney.

Strangest of all, though, was the rivalry that developed between us and a now defunct German team, Meidericher. We played them three times and some edge developed in the first game because it followed a defeat by Hamburg, which Shankly took very sorely indeed. His determination that we do better and, as reigning champions, preserve the pride of English football was no doubt the impetus for an amazing record. The Hamburg defeat is still the only one suffered by Liverpool in forty-four matches in four tours to America.

Meidericher were an extremely useful team – they had just finished runners up in the Bundesliga – and the first two games were competitive without spilling into too much trouble. However, the game in the old Empire Stadium in Vancouver – where Jim Peters famously collapsed in the Empire Games of 1954 and Roger Bannister beat his great Australian rival John Landy – degenerated into something close to a full-scale battle. Several problems emerged, one of which was that the German centre-half decided to kick me for just about the entire first half. Eventually, I snapped and gave my marker a crack. I was sent off, something that at the time didn't seem to be one of the greatest disasters of my career. In fact, the *Vancouver Sun* said that I had been the victim of some terrible acts of aggression, a point over which I nodded approvingly at breakfast the following morning.

When I reached the touchline I sat next to Ronnie Yeats and told him he had been fortunate to miss the game. Apart from the flying tackles, the more the game went on, the more it felt like you were heading a cannonball. Ronnie explained that Shankly had got it into his head that the Germans were letting air out of the ball whenever they could. In response, Reuben Bennett and Bob Paisley were pumping a little bit back in whenever the ball came into our dug-out. The problem was that Shankly had got it wrong and long before the end of the game the ball was hurtling through the air with the impact of a small boulder.

In the last few minutes, the German coach, Rudi Gutendorf, came to the touchline wanting to make a substitution – each side could send on three substitutes, as mutually agreed before the game – and immediately Reuben dashed down the line and confronted him.

'You can't do that,' said Reuben. 'You've already used three subs.' Gutendorf waved Reuben away but our man wasn't to be dismissed and they finished up grappling with each other.

The following day the local newspapers, who said that shame had been brought to the game by this disgraceful exhibition, noted that the match had been played on the twentieth anniversary of the Normandy landings. The score, if anyone had been counting, was 1–1.

In common with all the other players, I arrived home exhausted. We had been playing in roasting conditions. In Chicago we were obliged to beat a Mexican team who ran non-stop as the temperature soared into the nineties.

Jet-lag was not recognised then and Betsy was extremely unimpressed with my condition when I took her off to another caravan holiday, this time in Morecambe. 'You must have had some great time in America,' she said as she shooed me to the beach with the kids and their buckets and spades.

Her mood might have been better if I'd managed to keep hold of the watch I had bought her on the last day of the tour. I had it in my pocket going through customs at Manchester Airport – where it seemed that United and City fans were less than overjoyed to welcome us back to the country – and my heart sank when I was called to one side and told to empty my pockets. The watch was confiscated and I was fined £20 on the spot. It wasn't exactly a homecoming for a champion of England – nor did it help when Bob Paisley explained that when he wanted to smuggle through a little bit of contraband, he tended to hide it among the used jockstraps. 'They don't dig around too much when they see those,' he said, without a trace of laughter.

Shankly was horrified to see that we were a tired team when we started the season and some disappointing results early on badly affected our chances of a successful defence of the title. Although we improved sharply after a few weeks, and strode confidently on to our new European stage, we always had just a little too much to do in the championship. This, however, still left plenty of scope for Shankly's dreaming.

He was still bruised from the FA Cup semi-final defeat at the hands of Gordon Banks eighteen months earlier, and the previous season's disaster against Preston, and no doubt he calculated that winning the great trophy – and maybe becoming the first British club to win the European Cup – would be achievement enough for one season. Shankly was once discovered alone in Wembley after watching a final that didn't involve Liverpool. The ground had emptied and rubbish caught in the wind was blowing along the terraces. He was asked if everything was all right. 'Aye, I'm fine,' he said. 'I'm just spending a little time with the ghosts of Wembley. I can see all the great ones now . . .'

When Manchester United decided not to defend the FA Cup in the 1999–2000 season and flew off to play in the World Club championship in Brazil, a bogus tournament including teams from such places as Iran and Australia, it was impossible not to imagine the reaction of Shankly. He would have been appalled. 'Jesus Christ,' he would have asked, 'what's money got to do with it?' No doubt it would have been one of the nastiest shocks he had received since he passed through Manchester Airport on his way home after spying on Cologne, our next European opponents in that first campaign.

He had felt confident enough about our chances of disposing of Third Division Stockport County at Anfield in a routine step along the road to Wembley to make the trip to Germany. As he was coming through the airport in Manchester some of the workers greeted him.

'Hello, boys,' he said, before asking if there had been any Cup surprises while he was away.

'Only your draw with Stockport, Bill,' he was told.

'Aye, you have a nice sense of humour today, boys,' he replied as he collected his bag and strode off in his best Jimmy Cagney style. Then he turned on the car radio and realised the baggage handlers hadn't been joking. He came rushing back to Anfield for a crisis meeting in the Boot Room. There, Bob Paisley and Reuben Bennett took quite a bit of time assuring him that in his brief absence the world he had been building with such force had not fallen completely off its axis.

9
FEVER IN THE BLOOD

Naturally, with Bill Shankly still so agitated, Bob Paisley and Reuben Bennett didn't dwell too long on how near we had been to catastrophe while he was away in Germany. They didn't describe how the gutsy Stockport team, riding the truth that, on his day, any football dog can come up snarling defiance, came so close to silencing the Kop and reinforcing the curse of the Liver Birds – or how Gerry Byrne kept us alive by kicking the ball off the line in the last minutes.

It was another reminder of the fineness of the line between the greatest success and the deepest failure, and it followed too quickly for our peace of mind an equally alarming incident at West Bromwich in the third round.

The score was 0–0 in a typically ferocious tie – the value of driving down Wembley Way on the last day of the domestic season was never in question – when Ronnie Yeats did the unthinkable. He bent down and picked up the ball in his own penalty area and asked the referee, quite nonchalantly, 'What's that, ref?' The official said, 'It's a penalty, Ron.'

Ronnie had heard a whistle blow, but it had come from the crowd and not the referee. It was a shattering moment and a ludicrous start to our drive to complete the unfinished business of adding the great trophy to the spoils of our first European campaign. There wasn't a lot we could say as Bobby Cram, uncle of athlete Steve, stepped up to take the kick that could so easily have carried us to an inquest that was just too terrible to contemplate. If Cram scored, it would surely not be a night when Bill Shankly would be inviting all-comers to take a tour around his colossus of a centre-half. We could only speculate how many nightmares, and recriminations, Ron was spared when Cram drove the ball just the wrong side of the post and we went on to win the tie.

Such were the margins in which we operated in a season that would be filled with extraordinary levels of both joy and pain. During a few days in spring, I would be carried from the most memorable moment of my career to an ugly street fight in Milan. Before that, though, the tension of extra-time deadlock with the fine Cologne team of 1966 World Cup star Wolfgang Overath had to be endured, followed by some excruciating moments when Yeats had to toss up to decide who would go through to the next round of the European Cup. The first time he threw up the disc – red for Liverpool on one side, white for Cologne on the other – it landed sideways in the mud and stuck there. No decison. Next time, Ronnie threw red.

It was an absurd way to settle such a big issue but in those days there was no alternative to such arbitrary acts of closure. Players of the leading clubs were routinely asked to play up to sixty-five games on pitches that began to look like First World War battlefields by early winter, and Don Revie's Leeds United were required to play their last and decisive title game forty-eight hours after appearing in a Cup final. It is sometimes amusing, in a sour kind of way, to hear complaints of fixture crowding from Jose Mourinho, Arsène Wenger and Sir Alex Ferguson – men with deep reserves and, certainly in the case of Mourinho, unlimited resources to strengthen and, if they choose, rotate their squads.

After the drama of Cologne, we had to fly back to England for our FA Cup semi-final with Tommy Docherty's gifted and extremely physical Chelsea team. Villa Park, where the game was played, was a sea of mud and after the physical and mental pressure of our European assignment, the prospect of meeting such hard men as Eddie McCreadie and Ron 'Chopper' Harris did not exactly flood us with pleasure.

The first hazard of the semi-final had presented itself before we left Germany, created by Docherty, one of the big-time game's more ruthless operators. After watching our match, the Doc came round to the team hotel, which in the circumstances, and upon reflection, was perhaps not the most diplomatic thing to do. Rightly or wrongly, Docherty had a reputation for being able to get hold of a few Cup tickets and, with such a big demand in Liverpool for the semi-final, we asked him if he might be able to supply us with a few 'spares'.

'Maybe I can help you,' he replied. 'Why don't you come round to my hotel for a few drinks?'

Getting Ronnie and me out for drink was perhaps not the greatest challenge of the day, and probably the Doc knew this. After the team dinner, Ronnie and I slipped away to Docherty's hotel. As soon as we arrived, he took us into the bar and ordered some beers. However, the glasses had hardly touched our lips when Shanks burst into the bar with Reuben.

'Oh shit, here comes Joe Friday and his partner,' said the Doc, in a reference to the popular American cop series 'Dragnet', a show that Shanks ranked almost in the same class as 'The Untouchables'. When I say the manager burst into the room, it is not just a figure of speech. At the most undramatic of moments, he never entered a room, or sidled into a room. He always burst. This time you could smell the cordite in the air. Plainly he suspected that Docherty was trying to get at two of his key players before the semi, maybe, as he might have put it, leading us into a night of degradation if not outright depravity.

'You two,' he snapped at Ronnie and me, 'out of here – now.'

We left our beers virtually untouched and hurried out of the bar. I cannot tell you what Shankly said to Docherty but I suspect it was rather more than the time of night.

In fact, despite our liking for some relaxation – especially after such a taut night as the one in Cologne – the Doc had no chance of compromising us seriously before the semi-final. We would have unwound a little, perhaps prised a ticket or two from the Doc's allegedly bountiful supply, had a couple of beers and returned to the team hotel. No one needed to tell us how important it was to win the game with Chelsea. We had seen the effect of semi-final defeat on Shankly two years earlier and, for all the ups and downs of our relationship with him, we badly wanted to win for him, for the club, for the people of Liverpool and, of course, for ourselves. Winning the title was a wonderful mark of professional application. It showed that as a team and as individuals we could go the distance, but winning the Cup was something different. Even for the most experienced and hardened professionals, the prospect created at least a little fever in the blood.

The game was played hard and unforgivingly. McCreadie and Harris would have caused pandemonium in today's game, as would Tommy Smith and the men who played such a vital part in the rise of Leeds United, Johnny Giles, Billy Bremner and Norman Hunter. They were involved in the other semi-final, against Manchester United. The players shaped the course of the game, making tackles of fierce and potentially crippling violence in the belief that attack was the best means of defence. If you gave quarter, if you didn't announce yourself physically, you might just lose all your ability to influence the game. Most of the referees had only the vaguest idea of what was going on.

However, I made it easy for the man in charge of our semi-final when the ferocious Harris lined me up for a desperate tackle as I swept towards the box from the right. Chopper was still in the penalty area as I bore down on him and I got the timing just right, nudging the ball to one side as he made his tackle. He hit me full force, which made his later claim that 'I didn't touch you' absurd. What he might have said more accurately was that I played for a penalty. I didn't make a dive of the kind that these days invites a furious debate centring on the need for the authorities to legislate against 'simulation' inside the penalty area. When the tackle came in, the ball had gone – but it was still available to me if I hadn't been clattered. The referee had the most formal of decisions to make when he pointed to the spot and gave us the chance to move into the lead.

The only problem surrounded the question of who was going to take the kick. So intense was our need to win the Cup that no one really fancied the responsibility. There was no discussion in this absence of a nominated penalty-taker. Later Tommy Smith, with his extraordinary confidence, would naturally assume the role for a few years but now there was a vacuum.

Suddenly, Billy Stevenson stepped forward. Casually he picked up the ball and placed it on the spot. No one said anything despite the fact that he had never taken a penalty before. With his belief that he was a little bit better than the rest of us, propped up by his liking for fine suits and the best cognac, he might have been saying, 'Step aside, you peasants, and let me do the job.' No one complained or challenged his decision. Later, he said that he had just fancied the task. It came to him that he couldn't really miss – and nor did he. He gave the Chelsea keep Peter Bonetti, one of the best in the country, no chance. You might have thought such a masterful moment would have given Billy an appetite for the job, but he would never take another penalty for us. He had his great moment and that, apparently, was enough.

We were all very grateful but, as always, a hint of ambivalence touched our reaction. Everyone knew what a fine player he was but he had something of a genius for irritating his team-mates. Once, indeed, he provoked in me a rage that led to a minor version of the Bowyer–Dyer incident, which caused so much outrage at Newcastle and throughout the English game in 2005.

It happened in a league match at Anfield. Stevenson had the capacity to play a beautiful forty-yard through ball in the style of the great Johnny Haynes but on this occasion he put slightly too much weight on the ball and, although I chased it with every bit of pace I could muster, it carried over the line. I plunged into the Kop and finished up on my back. The fans helped me up and lifted me back on to the field. I was in the process of gesturing my apologies to the team, suggesting to them that I had done my best, when I saw Stevenson standing with his hands on his hips shaking his head. As Haynes sometimes did, he seemed to be saying that I was just too slow to get to his brilliant ball. Nothing is more calculated to inflame a fellow professional and I'm afraid I reacted very angrily indeed. I chased after him, yelling in my rage what I was going to do to him. Fortunately, the incident was lost in the flow of play and not, as in the case of Bowyer and Dyer, endlessly replayed on national television. Ensuring this was so was the fact that Stevenson kept moving and stayed out of my way long enough for my blood to cool.

In the semi-final against Chelsea there was no such rancour and Stevenson's successful conversion gave us all the momentum we needed. Peter Thompson made our place at Wembley safe with a beautiful goal. He broke through the Chelsea defence and, with no unnecessary adornment, his shot flashed home sweetly.

We were going to Wembley for sure, but the identity of our opponents would not be known for a few days. Leeds, who had come so close to winning the First Division at their first attempt under Revie, had fought a knife-edge draw with Manchester United, and had to replay at the City Ground in Nottingham. My Scottish team-mate Billy Bremner decided the issue with one of his typically opportunistic goals for Leeds. It was a brilliant strike, but we remained confident that this time we would defy the big birds overlooking the Mersey.

I had just one regret preparing for the final, but it was a heavy one indeed. Gordon Milne would be missing from the line-up through injury and I felt responsible. We played Chelsea again in a league match before the final and, in the wake of the semi, they dug into us with some force, particularly their most menacing tacklers, McCreadie and Harris. It was the last kind of match in which you wanted to deliver a 'hospital ball' to one of your team-mates but, looking back, I couldn't shake off the guilt that I had done precisely that to Gordon. I knew the moment the ball left my boot that the pass was a bad one. It didn't have the proper weight or direction, and a less honest player than Gordon might not have gone for it. Of course, he did and to my horror I saw that he was running right into the path of McCreadie. My instinct was to close my eyes and say, 'Oh no,' because, in the run-in to a Cup final, the dread of serious injury to yourself or one of your team-mates was ever present.

The ball had run just a little too far in front of Gordon, which gave McCreadie the perfect chance to put the bite in. Milne was a great team-mate and a friend and even now I sometimes find myself thinking, 'God, it was my pass that kept him out of the Cup final.' Being the person he was, he never hinted at any reproach. I didn't have any long talk with him about it. I said I was sorry in the first bitter flush of the moment and then, briefly, after the game, but I'm sure he knew how badly I felt. Professionals understand these disappointments and they also know how quickly a game, a career, can be wiped out by one moment of misadventure. You do not dwell on the risks, or the mishaps, unless you want to give yourself an extremely hard time. Even so, everything that happened at Wembley, the build-up, the tension and the exhilaration of the game, was for me tinged by the absence of one of our best and most consistent players.

We went into the final favourites but, outside of the roaring belief of Shankly, not by much. The boss was, of course, doing his gangster walk on air. On the way to the ground he ordered the coach driver to turn up the volume on the radio so his boys could hear better his performance on the BBC's 'Desert Island Discs'. We were doubled up with laughter when Shankly's taste in music invaded the nation — Scottish songs mostly and one of his sentimental favourites, 'Danny Boy'. One of the non-Scots muttered, 'Oh Christ, any minute we're going to have Andy Stewart marching through the heather and down the glen.'

However, the atmosphere in the bus was tremendous, and skilfully manipulated by Shankly. As we got nearer the great stadium we began to pass supporters with their red banners and expectant faces. When he saw the fans, Shankly produced his usual exhortation, saying, 'See these fans, boys, they've travelled down to give you their support. They've spent money that some of them can't afford, and they've worked all week, so don't let them down.' On his lips, this wasn't a request or a plea. It was the announcement of a solemn duty.

Solemnity was not the mood of our dressing room. Whenever he could, Shankly liked to lighten the minutes before we walked out on to the field and this was reflected by his invitation to Jimmy Tarbuck and Frankie Vaughan to join us for the countdown. The comedian and the singer were well known to

149

the players, and they helped us to relax. Tarbuck, a fanatic Liverpool fan, knew what was needed on this occasion. He was witty and friendly but not overwhelming. Frankie Vaughan didn't overdo it, either. He was willing to give us a few bars, and steps, of 'Gimme the Moonlight, Gimme the Girl' but only on request.

Shankly certainly liked the feel of the dressing room as the minutes ticked away. 'This is great, boys,' he said. 'Revie has got those poor buggers locked up next door.' Almost all football men are superstitious to some extent, but Revie was quite notorious for wearing certain suits and ties and carrying a rabbit's foot. Of course, Shankly was working the theme quite relentlessly, and getting quite a few laughs at his rival's expense.

The point when the joking had to stop came shortly before the Wembley buzzer summoned us out of the shadows and into the glare and roar of the stadium. In the last ten minutes of the countdown Shankly got down to serious business. As he talked about what we had to do, including sitting on the creative forces in the Leeds team, the great midfielders Johnny Giles and Billy Bremner and the veteran Bobby Collins, Reuben Bennett moved around the dressing room giving each player a gentle rub-down. Bob Paisley largely stayed in the shadows, but from time to time he supported Shankly with a nod, and had a word with individual players. Between them, they were great wind-up men in those minutes before we got the call.

Shankly didn't batter you with detail in those flashing moments before you had to play. He covered the ground, though, and often reminded you of certain vital principles, and those little details that shape a truly professional, winning performance. Sometimes I applied a little mischief when some of his pre-match orders were particularly emphatic. Once, when we were playing against Burnley, a talented team who could produce quite a bit of fire, he said, 'Now, boys, go easy on them early on – don't get them riled up, don't get them really playing.' He had Burnley's big Scottish striker Andy Lochhead, a real force in the air, in mind. When Burnley won a corner I was on the edge of our box and as Ronnie Yeats was picking up Lochhead, I shouted out to him, 'Hey, Ronnie, is big Blockhead still playing for this lot?' Lochhead was furious and promptly gave Ronnie a bash in the face. It was not what Shankly, or Ronnie, had in mind.

Before a game, Shankly always conveyed one thought and feeling above all others – his yearning for the days when he had the thrill of going out to play. He envied us our ability to do this in the prime of our lives, and he was able to pass on the value of this in the most powerful way. On one cold afternoon at Old Trafford, Shankly's friend Sir Matt Busby invited him up to his office when we arrived at the stadium. The boss never drank, generally settling for tea or tomato juice, but this day we suspected that Busby had slipped a quite serious shot of Scotch into his cup of tea. No doubt the idea was simply to warm him up on such a biting day, but the effect was extraordinary. Shankly came bouncing into our dressing room and delivered an amazing speech on how lucky we were to be at this great ground preparing to play a legendary team. 'Boys,' he roared, 'I can't tell you what I would give to play today. This is our life . . . this is what we were born to do, it is the best we do.'

Without the fuel of Busby's whisky, Shankly was not quite so emotional at Wembley, but the usual message was as clearly expressed as ever – 'Enjoy yourselves out there, boys, do your work, be professional, do all your running and tackling, but don't forget to enjoy it all, every minute of it, and that way you will always remember what happens today. It will always be one of your best memories. This is a great day in our lives.'

Despite the picture of gloomy tension painted by Shankly, we could only speculate on how it had been in the Leeds dressing room before they joined us on the walk out to the field. They did seem to be a little tight. Their success had come in a great rush, and with the exception of Giles, who had played so well for Manchester United in their victory over Leicester two years earlier, and the richly experienced Collins, they did not have too much experience of such great football occasions. To a certain extent, the same could be said of us, but we did carry the reinforcement of being champions. We were proven winners at the highest level, and deep down that was as big an asset as all the brilliant psychological warfare waged by Shankly.

The Leeds player who seemed to be suffering most was Albert Johanneson, a quick, clever winger from South Africa. He seemed to be weighed down by the pressure of the day and looked drawn before the kick-off. As it turned out, he scarcely got a kick in the game, a sad foretaste of his future in England. As Leeds came through to the First Division, he was an eye-catching star, but the pressures of the top flight, the big crowds and the big expectations, proved too much for him. It was depressing to learn many years later that, as his career trailed away, so did his life. He died alone in a flat in Leeds, and it was said that he had spent quite a bit of time living rough. That was the other side of the glory of Liverpool's great day. It may have been that Johanneson was a victim of the regimentation of Revie's approach, particularly in his early days. Giles, Bremner and Collins, who was a vast influence on the development of the Leeds team, each had strong personalities, but Johanneson was much more vulnerable. Apparently, he vomited with nerves before the game. Maybe he needed someone to tell him that this was indeed an experience to see as a joy, not an ordeal. It's a nice theory anyway, but how it would have stood up to the great wall of sound that hit you when you came out at Wembley is no doubt quite a different story.

Many years later, over a drink in Spain, Revie said to me, 'I had a wonderful set of players at Leeds and my great regret is that I didn't let them off the leash until the later years. They were ready to play football much earlier, and would have won a lot more trophies to reflect their brilliance, but I was just too cautious about it.' When he went off to the England team, and then quit in controversial circumstances, Revie received massive criticism, and a lot of boots went flying in. For me, he was undoubtedly a great manager. What he did at Leeds was astounding, in many ways quite the equal of Shankly's work at Anfield. I always had a lot of time for him, and he was never less than courteous to me when we met. When he was slaughtered in the press, I thought, 'Well, maybe some of the criticism is valid — but one thing is certain, I would have played for him.'

At Wembley on that May day in 1965, though, there was only one team to play for and they were the ones all in red. I never had a serious doubt about the outcome all through the first, goalless ninety minutes. A goal in extra time seemed inevitable to me. Roger Hunt stooped to head in after Gerry Byrne got to the by-line and crossed, and we had the lead.

Gerry had a terrific match before Collins put him down with an over-the-ball tackle so violent that, to be honest, it could have broken a leg as well as a collar-bone. Byrne, his arm in a sling, was a magnificent inspiration, producing one of the great displays of courage and determination on a football field.

I had a lot of respect for Collins, partly through my experience of playing with him for Scotland, but he was one of the most cynical players the game had ever seen. He gave punishment and he took it, and he pressed on. Did he have regrets? Maybe, but as the Sinatra song says, perhaps too few to mention.

After our goal we fell victim to a phenomenon that often comes when one team forges ahead in such a closely fought game – we fell back a little. You never feel that one goal is ever enough, and that brings anxieties that are hard to repel. The pressure swings to the team defending the slender lead and so it was with us. Billy Bremner banged in a brilliant goal just before the break in extra time and, for the first time that day, I had doubts about the result. Suddenly, the spectre of the immovable Liver Birds hung over us. The curse was back. This was so, right up to the sweetest moment of my football life. Stevenson worked Ian Callaghan away on the right and Ian, as almost always, timed his cross perfectly. For some reason, Gary Sprake, the Leeds goalkeeper, came off his line to get the ball, against all the odds, and I went past him to meet it.

The Leeds line was guarded by their right-back Paul Reaney but the net seemed huge to me now, and I headed the ball with a heavy bump. It flew home. We were back in the lead with nine minutes to go. If you haven't found God in your life, you find him at times like that. You hear yourself praying, please God, give me this. I had never had such an attack of instant religion and it seemed that the game, and my conversion, would last forever. As the ball bounced dangerously in our box, Ronnie Yeats stretched out his left leg in the most amazing, telescopic fashion and lashed the ball to safety. Then it was over, gloriously, beautifully. The referee blew the whistle and finally the Liver Birds had flown out of our lives.

The next few minutes remain a blur of celebration, great relief and exhilaration. The Queen handed Ronnie the Cup and gave us our medals and we ran back on to the field to take the salute of the fans. Then we went back to the dressing room to get changed, and for most of us, to burrow down into our own thoughts. I found myself sitting next to Reuben Bennett as the bus rolled back to our hotel on Park Lane.

'Why are we not singing and dancing?' I asked him. 'We've won the Cup but I feel terrible.' The old warrior patted me on the shoulder.

'It's natural, laddie,' he said. 'You've been up for this for so long, and now it has come. You feel down right now, but it will soon be different. You'll get a few drinks down you and then you'll realise what you've done . . .'

As it turned out, Reuben was only half right. Yes, we all felt a surge of pleasure when we saw the girls at the hotel and received the heroes' welcome. We left the Cup at reception, saying, 'We'll be back for this,' while we got ready for the evening and had a few drinks. Then we carried the trophy the little way up Park Lane to the Dorchester for our victory banquet. Shankly made a rousing speech, and although the champagne flow was turned off quickly, with the challenge of Inter Milan now at the forefront of Shankly's mind, we all agreed it had been a great day. One year we were champions of England, the next winners of the FA Cup – a one-two combination that Shankly had dreamed about. Maybe we had picked up a little of the spirit and glory of Dempsey and Tunney when we slaved at our training out on the Soldiers' Field.

Yet flatness still pervaded my mood. I was told that the losers' dinner is generally the better do, but I remembered how I felt when we lost to Leicester City in the semi-final and I was sceptical about that. Eight years later, Leeds faced another night of Cup final defeat after they had been beaten shockingly by Second Division Sunderland. Don Revie couldn't hold back his tears as he vowed his great team would come back and show the world they were still winners, which they did with a record unbeaten run and the league title.

The point is that the emotions that come with winning and losing tend to blur and, in the end, you learn not to trust either event. The important thing, as Shankly always said, was to go out to do your best and make sure you enjoyed every moment. On that Saturday night, I wanted to feel that I owned the world. In fact, I had in my possession one great win, one great moment. Perhaps I should have realised that in the life of any footballer, any man, that was more than enough.

10

'WE DON'T DO SNEAKY THINGS'

Talk to any Liverpool player from the days when the club first claimed its place among the élite of the English game and began to campaign in Europe, and he will offer his choice of a night of nights at Anfield. He will speak of a football passion so intense that it produced an edge that could never be surpassed. It doesn't matter who it is — Ronnie, Graeme Souness, Tommy Smith, Alan Hansen or Ian Rush — he will tell you that night is the supreme example of his team's union with their fans, and who can argue with him? It affected him in a unique way and he will never forget it, no more than I will forget the night I'm about to nominate. All I had experienced in the game, all my feelings about how it could move the spirit of people and take them far beyond their normal lives, and carry me, out on the field, to a new level of experience, reached a new point of definition. It was an amazing sensation. It made me feel that I was virtually playing outside my own skin.

The debate is now neatly framed in the passage of the years, for the moment at least — forty years had elapsed between our European Cup semi-final with Inter Milan on 4 May 1965, three days after we had beaten Leeds in the FA Cup final, and the one our heirs, Jamie Carragher, Steven Gerrard and their team-mates, captured so tenaciously against the moneybags of Chelsea in 2005. I was present on both occasions, on the field against the Inter team of Luis Suarez and Joaquin Peiro, superb Spanish mercenaries, and the homegrown Italian stars Sandro Mazzola, Giacinto Facchetti and Mario Corso. I was in the stands when the boys fought their way through to the final against another powerful Milan team, the AC of Andrei Shevchenko, Alessandro Nesta and Paolo Maldini.

On an astonishing night in May 2005, I had to marvel at the force of the tradition I had helped set in place all those years ago. It was as though those ninety frantic minutes conjured up the best of forty years ago. When the ball flew to the Chelsea player Eidur Gudjohnsen inside the box in the last seconds of what seemed like a ridiculous amount of stoppage time, he had only to stab it home to wreck the night and send Liverpool toppling out of the Champions League at the end of a challenge that had stunned the football world. When the ball flashed past the post and we all knew that Liverpool were through, the eruption inside Anfield was immense. It sent you home with your senses shaken.

Which was the most dramatic of the nights, and which will linger most strongly in the memory? I cannot truly say because of the depth of my bias, but maybe I can return to my first assertion – if that night in 1965 could be equalled, it could never be bettered, certainly not in this football heart.

On the Sunday, we had the great parade with the Cup through the city streets and Bill Shankly rode the bus like an emperor. When it came down to playing Inter with a place in the final at stake – a final that would instantly plant the Liverpool flag on the high ground of the European game – the anticipation had been brought to an exquisite level. Again the FA Cup was presented to the fans, and when Gordon Milne, the man about whom I felt such unshakeable guilt, and Gerry Byrne, his arm in a sling, were sent out on the field, the reception was incredible. I felt a wave of emotion–I had never quite known before. I regretted again the pass that had denied Milne his great day in London, and then I thought of how Byrne had been so unyielding in those last minutes against a Leeds team who finally believed they could beat us.

Inside Anfield, the fans were going crazy and even the Italian players, used to the boiling atmosphere of the mighty San Siro, were clearly affected by the scale of the reaction on the terraces. It was so intense, so intimate. In San Siro you were in a great cathedral of the game. In Anfield, even more so than today, you were in a cockpit. Italian footballers have a wonderful aura, the kind of natural hauteur that our own Billy Stevenson aspired to, though not always with consistent success. In the tunnel at Anfield that night, the eyes of the Italians showed surprise, concern, the flickering of doubts – whatever it was, it was not such a distant cousin to sheer fright. Surely we could build on this surge of belief that filled every corner of our ground. Surely we could light the red touch paper.

We were astonished when we arrived at the ground because when we drove into the stadium car park the scene was eerily quiet. We had expected the usual milling crowd, a great splash of red scarves and banners, but the streets around the ground were those of a ghost town. The gates had been slammed shut an hour before kick-off. Everyone was inside. The pressure cooker was already hissing. It might have been a tribal pot into which we had a duty to place these brilliant, arrogant footballers from one of the strongholds of the European game.

The Inter coach, Helenio Herrera, an Argentinian, had a huge reputation in the game. In Milan he was called the Black Magician for the way he had taken hold of the men in the famous blue and black stripes and made a fortress out of their defence. He wore his elegant black overcoat over his shoulders in a fashion that would be adopted by the most brilliant of young English coaches, Malcom Allison, who would soon be working his magic at Manchester City. In his time, Allison was considered the hottest coach around, a fact reflected by an offer from Gianni Agnelli, owner of the Fiat car company and patron of the great Italian club Juventus.

As Herrera walked imperiously along the touchline, such a dramatic contrast to the intensely fired Shankly, he was still considered the most formidable football man in all of club football. He had been at Barcelona before moving to Milan, and carried with him an astonishing mystique. One of his tricks was to have his players hold hands before kick-off, so they could pass their ambitions and their energies through each other's bodies. Two years later, in 1967, Jock Stein would tear through Herrera's reputation in the European Cup final in Lisbon, but as the Kop hummed rehearsals for a mocking version of the song 'Santa Lucia', he was still the football tactician everyone in Europe had to beat. We believed implicitly that Shankly was the man to do it. Unflustered by the loss of Byrne and the continued absence of Milne, he brought Ronnie Moran in at full-back and rubber-stamped Geoff Strong as Gordon's replacement once more.

Shankly was radiant in the dressing room. He had never been so animated, every thought and vision coming out of him like machine-gun fire. He was a man who believed beyond any doubt that his time had come, and within three minutes of the kick-off he was punching the air as the Kop saluted thunderously a strike by Roger Hunt.

Strong fed Ian Callaghan, who did what he did best – he went down the line and crossed perfectly. Hunt came on to the ball and volleyed home ferociously. It was as if we had landed a big punch in the first round of a heavyweight title fight, and plainly the Italians wobbled. Champions are at their most dangerous when they sense they are in trouble, though, and Ronnie Yeats, of all people, for a moment forgot this old truth. Maybe he thought something fancier was required in European football but, whatever the reason was, he did something quite outside his superbly consistent defender's nature. He tried something showy out on the right, rather than knocking the ball away safely, and Peiro was on him, sending the ball to a perfectly placed Mazzola – 1–1 with just ten minutes on the clock.

'Christ, Ronnie, what are you up to?' I yelled into the tumult. There was no point in recriminations, however, and twenty-four minutes later, after building our rhythm again, we were back in front. Our confidence was boosted by the beautifully conceived goal, which came from a set-piece move that Shankly had had us working on at Melwood just a few days earlier. Peter Thompson was fouled a yard or two outside the eighteen-yard box and Stevenson and Callaghan lined up to take the free kick. Ian rushed to the ball, jumped over it and continued on a run towards goal. With the Italians confused, Stevenson played the ball to Hunt, who side-footed a pass into Ian's path. Ian shot home as sweetly as he had ever done on the training field. Just recently he told me it was the most rewarding goal he had ever scored. He said it was wonderful to work on something so hard, and then see it come off when it mattered so much.

With fifteen minutes to go on the great night, I made my mark with the third goal when a hard shot from Hunt bounced off the Italian goalkeeper and allowed me to knock home the ball. Three-one was a brilliant night's work even though we were aggrieved that the Austrian referee had earlier ruled out what we considered a perfectly legitimate goal from Chris Lawler. Shankly was enraged by the decision to wipe out the strike because a Liverpool player who wasn't interfering with the play had, it was alleged, strayed offside. However, when Shankly stepped back to consider the result, and how well we had played against such a highly rated team, he was as euphoric as the crowd. 'It was men against boys, tonight,' he rejoiced in the dressing room. 'You showed that magician and his boys how to play.'

He was confident but still wary when we travelled to a beautiful hotel on the shore of Lake Como for the second leg. Concerned by the noise of the local church bells calling the faithful to mass, he had a sharp word with the long-suffering Paisley.

'Bob, you'd better get those bells stopped, they're going to interfere with the boys' sleep.'

'Bill,' Paisley replied, shaking his head slowly, 'those bells have been ringing for centuries. Do you think they're going to stop them for a bunch of footballers from the other side of Europe?'

That was precisely what Shankly thought, and when he was finally persuaded that an official request was out of the question, he was not daunted.

'Well, you'd better do something about it,' he insisted. 'You'd better climb up that tower and muffle the bells. I'm depending on you.' Paisley continued to mutter and shake his head, but he did go around to the church and ask the priest if maybe some tape could be applied to the bells to muffle the sound.

Of course, the bells tolled on, as they had down the ages, but it wasn't the bell-ringers of Lago di Como who ruined our chances, or the combined brilliance of Suarez, Mazzola and Corso. It was the referee who, I will always believe, was a cheat — a Spaniard named Ortiz de Mendibil. He was so partial to the Italians that early in the game I turned to Roger Hunt and said, 'We'll be lucky if this bloody referee gives us a throw-in.'

Later, Shankly swore that he had seen an Inter Milan official hand an envelope to the referee, and if the claim seemed wild at the time — even after the grim evidence of the official's performance — it was rendered less so by the fact that de Mendibil, one of Europe's leading referees, always refused to discuss the game after his big-time career went into a sharp decline. Among various rumours going around, one was that the Spanish official had a sick child and had been offered medical assistance by Inter. Whatever the truth of such speculation, we would always believe we were cheated out of the game. Tommy Smith was so incensed he had to be restrained as he attempted to kick the referee all the way back to his dressing room.

Corso struck Inter's first goal direct from a free kick, but although we protested that de Mendibil had signalled an indirect kick, the official waved us away. The second goal was even more controversial. Peiro kicked the ball away from Tommy Lawrence as he bounced it in the goal area – which in Europe at that time was an automatic free kick for the defending team – and then ran it into the net. That was the truly sickening blow. It pulled Inter level on goals and meant that, with their away goal, they had only to play out time to go through to the final against Benfica. To us, the evidence seemed overwhelming. We were not to be allowed to get a result, and it was almost a case of simply shrugging near the end when Inter produced their one piece of authentic brilliance, a wonderful piece of interplay between Peiro and Suarez and a fine strike by Facchetti.

Driving away from San Siro I felt the same heart-sickness that had gripped me after the semi-final defeat at the hands of the inspired Gordon Banks – only this time it was compounded at least a hundred times by that terrible raw sense that we hadn't been given a chance. On the face of it, we had just played a great game in a great stadium for the greatest reward in all of football. In reality, all of it, the flowing play of the Italians, the fierce edge of ambition bolstered by the 3–1 lead we brought into the San Siro, had just been a façade for outright corruption. It was the worst feeling I had ever known in football, and once again a lot of regret was centred on the disappointment of Bill Shankly. The boss never got over what happened at San Siro, not really. It fuelled his distrust of foreigners on a football field. He believed that it was natural for them to cheat, something quite separate from his own culture, which was hard to the point of ruthlessness but purged of cheap trickery.

Certainly it was not hard to understand his distaste for some of the routine antics of European opposition, the diving, the spitting, the feigning of injury. It was beyond his comprehension that footballers could behave in that manner on a consistent basis. Only heaven knows how he would have reacted to some of the behaviour on show in today's Premiership. The blatant dives indulged in by some of the most honoured players of the day, stars such as Robert Pires of Arsenal and Ruud van Nistelrooy of United, would have filled him with scorn. He would also have been appalled that homegrown players had so quickly adopted the cheating tendency. 'Aye,' said Shankly, 'we may be hard, we may whack people from time to time, but we don't do sneaky things.'

When he finally quit, less than a decade after his breakthrough at Wembley and having won the second of two titles in three years, Bob Paisley was shocked that such a great football man, still in his fifties, should go so prematurely.

'Look, Bill, why don't you just go and rest for a while. Take six months off and you'll come back your old self,' he said, but maybe Shankly had asked too much of himself and of the game.

'No, I'm packing up,' he replied. 'I've had enough.'

Soon he would be telling Paisley, 'The man who invented the word retirement should be shot,' but he couldn't be turned back to the game. He worried about money, which he didn't understand, and feared that his pension would not sustain him and his beloved wife Nessie. My suspicion is that he also carried his wounds more painfully than some may have imagined, and there is no doubt that what happened in Milan was one of the heaviest blows he ever suffered. He would never shake off the memory of the refereeing of Ortiz de Mendibil. Had we got by Inter, we believed we had every chance of beating Benfica, the team of Eusebio, Torres and Simones. They were a talented team, of course, but had weaknesses the boss believed, with some certainty, that we could exploit. For Shankly, it would have been the coup of his football life. He would have beaten Stein, the man he hero-worshipped, to the great peak of the European game by two years, Busby by three. When you thought of his impact at Anfield and the speed with which he had turned us into a team who could compete properly with any force in football, who could say that it was a distinction he didn't deserve?

Bill Shankly would have been a worthy winner for the sheer vision and passion of his work. Bob, Joe and Reuben would have earned much reflected glory, because no football men have devoted themselves to a cause so thoroughly and self-effacingly. Later, both Bob and Joe had the exhilaration of managing European Cup-winning teams, but I know that deep in their hearts they felt, at their moments of triumph, that Shankly should have gone to the pedestal before them. I will always believe that this group should have gone down in history as British football's first European Cup winners, and this is after acknowledging the brilliant pioneering work done in Europe by Busby's Manchester United, and the terrible price they paid for their adventurous spirit at the Munich air tragedy. The United of Duncan Edwards, Eddie Colman and the other young stars was still developing, no doubt superbly, and it was several years before the genius of Di Stefano, Puskas and Gento began to fade in the white shirts of Real Madrid.

Maybe it was true that United would have been Real's natural successors, but that is in the realm of speculation. What we know for sure is that we had the beating of Inter Milan, and we would have done it but for a dishonest referee. That was the point on which we were impaled, and it would probably have driven Shankly mad (completely mad, that is) if he had dwelt on it for too long. Certainly, when I look back, it is the low point of all the disappointments that punctuated the great years at Anfield. It was another twelve years before Liverpool landed their first European Cup, in Rome against the German club Borussia Moenchengladbach. For Bob Paisley it was a triumphant return to the city he once entered in a British army tank, and there was a little moisture in my eyes when I saw the 3–1 victory on television. I was manager of Portsmouth then, and not having the easiest of times, but of course the win lifted me wonderfully. I was proud, too, when I heard Bob Paisley say that the foundations of this success had been laid many years earlier, when the first of Shankly's Liverpool teams had gone so close. That was typical of Bob, not to be lost in his own glory, and it was excellent that Shankly, despite his retirement and his strained relations with the board, was there in the Stadio Olimpico.

It would be less than honest, though, if I didn't admit to other thoughts as I sat in my house on the south coast of England, so far from the excitement of Rome and, no doubt, the joy welling up across the length of Merseyside. I said to Betsy, 'Wouldn't it have been nice if we had been invited to Rome; if one day, I'd picked up a letter from the club, at the same time as Billy and Roger and all the other lads wherever they are scattered, and read something like, "Come down to Rome, boys, we've got to the final at last, and you lads took us so close. Come down and enjoy the celebration." '

It wouldn't have taken too much style, or too much money, to make such a gesture. We had, after all, given Liverpool

Football Club the impetus to be great. In that one spring we had ended the curse of the FA Cup and been cheated out of what we deserved in the last but one stride to the European Cup. An old professional has always to be on guard against the destructive effects of bitterness, and so I tucked my complaints away with a sigh, as we all used to do when Bob Paisley handed us our ten-bob dinner money so long after we had made Liverpool one of the great names in English football.

Back in Milan after the Inter game, Ronnie and I were beyond comfort. We went out with some fans to a city restaurant but, locked in our thoughts, we were not good company. Towards the end of the meal it was clear that the restaurant were intent on stiffing us. The bill came in and it was outrageous. One of the fans, a businessman, was dealing with the situation, disputing some of the costs, and our table was surrounded by waiters. They were quite aggressive, which was not quite what Ronnie and I were in the perfect mood to handle. Fists started flying soon enough and a lot of anger and bitterness came to the surface very quickly indeed. At one point, I seemed to be fighting everyone, and this must have looked quite amusing to an objective observer.

Ronnie and I fought a rearguard action up the stairs and out on to the street. This gave me a certain height advantage, something that for Ronnie was not a dire need. We were, as they say in street-fighting circles, giving them plenty. Then I heard someone say they were calling the carabinieri and as the first howls of a police car could be heard, I said to Ronnie, 'It's probably time to call a halt.' We knew we had been recognised as Liverpool players – perhaps that was where the problems had started – and so we couldn't return to the team hotel, where the sight of two of his key players being marched to the Milan cells might easily have pushed Shankly over the top. We spent the night in the fans' hotel and, when we thought the going was clear, smuggled ourselves back to the team hotel and through the airport.

A little bruised and dishevelled, not to mention sick inside, we did not make the heroes' return for which we had developed an instant appetite after the FA Cup win, but if we were scarred both inside and out, we were far from a beaten force. Having healed our wounds during the summer, we were ready for the Shankly lash once again in the 1965–66 season, and full of running. Given our frustrations and self-belief – that at least had been untouched in Milan, both on the ground and in the street – it was not so surprising that we did quite well in the new campaign. We sailed to our second league title, six points clear of runners-up Leeds United and third-placed Burnley, equal on points. As a team, we had grown strong through adversity. Even now, at the distance of more than half a lifetime, I can see each member of that team as vividly as when we walked out at Wembley and then the San Siro to discover, in such quick succession, the best and the worst that is always waiting on the path of a professional footballer.

The greatest quality Tommy Lawrence brought to the team was calmness. Outfield players often scramble around, shouting and fighting and getting agitated, but it's the last thing you want in a goalkeeper. Brian Glanville, the leading sportswriter, wrote a novel entitled *Goalkeepers Are Crazy*, but Tommy could have sued him. The only time I saw Tommy truly incensed, apart from in the San Siro affair, was when we came in at half-time in a league game, having conceded a sloppy goal. Shankly heaped the blame on his goalkeeper, giving him a hard time in the dressing room. Suddenly, to everybody's amazement, not least Shankly's, Tommy stood up, tore off his sweater and said, 'If you can do better, do fucking better.' Then he sat down again and started taking off his boots. In those days, when no substitutes were allowed, this was truly alarming. Bob and Reuben rushed over to Tommy and started clucking over him, saying, 'Now Tommy, don't take it like that. Come on, lad, we've got the second half to play.'

The manager was stunned. He stood in the corner of the dressing room, no doubt reflecting that this had never happened to him before. You didn't need to be a mind reader to know what was going on in his head. 'Christ,' he was thinking, 'we've got to play the second half without the goalie,' but he couldn't say anything to Tommy because after berating him he could hardly say, at least with any credibility, 'Oh, Tommy, everything's all right, I didn't mean to upset you, son.'

So Bob and Reuben had to do the vital work, which they eventually accomplished with great patience and touch. Tommy went out to play the second half, for Bob and Reuben and his team-mates and the fans but not, most definitely on that occasion, for Bill Shankly. We won the title with the amazing record of conceding just twenty-three goals. That was quite phenomenal and a wonderful tribute to Tommy's resilience and ability to patrol the goal area. Later, in 1978–79, Ray Clemence would shatter the mark when letting in just sixteen goals, but no one would argue, not even Tommy I'm sure, that Clemence was not the better goalkeeper, indeed one of the best in the history of English football. Once, when I had stopped playing and Shankly had stopped managing and we were going over the old times, he suddenly said, 'I'll tell you something, if we had had Ray Clemence in our team, we wouldn't have lost for seven years.' On the way home, I chuckled over that classic Shankly pro-nouncement. 'Where in hell did he get seven years?' I asked myself.

Tommy's worst night was probably in a European Cup tie in Amsterdam, when Ajax beat us 5–1, provoking that bizarre Shankly claim that they were the most defensive team we had ever played. Fog had rolled across the pitch for most of the game and afterwards Tommy complained bitterly. He said, 'I just couldn't see the ball.' The game shouldn't have been played, but I couldn't resist responding, 'The trouble was, Tommy, their forwards could see it well enough . . . they scored five times.'

Shankly refused to accept defeat. According to him, we would pull back the tie at Anfield, and in this respect the goal scored by Chris Lawler was particularly valuable. 'Aye,' said Shankly, 'we've got the away goal and that means we only have to beat them 4–0.' Naturally, a few eyes rolled in our dressing room. Johan Cruyff, maybe the best player we ever faced, confirmed our scepticism. He played brilliantly at Anfield, scoring the Ajax goals in a 2–2 draw.

Shankly admired Lawler for a lot more than the slight hope he had encouraged in the middle of a North Sea fogbank. He loved Chris's consistency and stealthy work going forward, which was a great bonus on top of his sound defensive game, but the reality was that however much you did for Shankly, he wanted more. If you couldn't deliver at a certain time, he tended to forget what had been achieved in the past. One example of this swirls in the memory. During training at Melwood, Chris picked up a slight strain and, after the warm-up, Paisley said to him, 'You take it easy now, Chris. Just do a little bit of walking.' As Lawler was walking away, Shankly came out on to the pitch. He saw Chris's retreating back and yelled to Bob, 'Where does that malingerer Lawler think he's going?' Later, Paisley no doubt mentioned that Chris had been following his instructions and that, as a matter of detail, he did happen to be approaching his 250th consecutive appearance for the first team.

Chris was the ultimate quiet man. His temperament was, at times, astonishing. One night at Anfield, the kick-off for a European game against Cologue was in doubt because of snow.

The referee was required to make several inspections and at one point he said he couldn't make a decision for some time because the snow was obliterating the lines. We had all been getting revved up, eyeballing the opposition and saying things like, 'Come on, boys, let's get into these people . . .' – everyone except Chris Lawler. Having to go back to the dressing room after getting yourself so motivated is no easy task, but while the rest of us were thoroughly wound up and jumping around, Chris did something I thought quite amazing. He went to his corner, picked up his newspaper and stretched out to do the crossword. We were building ourselves up so that we could go out of this room and kill those people down the corridor, but he was picking away at the crossword, as though he was at home and in his slippers. I recall gazing at him and thinking, 'What a temperament this fella has.' What was so impressive was that you could look at Chris lying back there in the dressing room and know, with absolute certainty, that when we were told to go out there, Chris would be as ready as anyone to do battle. He would be up for it quite as much as, say, the warrior Tommy Smith, who, while Lawler was dealing with one across and three down, was practically chewing the furniture.

Lawler never said a word or made a gesture that was un-necessary, a fact that Shankly seized upon during a five-a-side game in which we had cricket stumps for goalposts, set just three yards apart. We were playing quite furiously when Shankly's team claimed a goal. 'No,' shouted the opposition, it was 'over' or it was 'wide'. Shankly turned to Lawler as the perfect arbiter, the quiet man who would speak the truth.

'You saw that son, was it in?' asked Shankly.

'No goal,' said Chris, and the boss was naturally incensed.

'You've never spoken for years, and when you do, you tell a fucking lie,' Shankly exploded.

While Gerry Byrne was distinguished by his extraordinary hardness, his nature was in many ways similar to his full-back partner's. After the 1965 Cup final win over Leeds, the flatness of the Saturday night celebration was lifted when you looked at Gerry and realised what he had done out on the field. You wouldn't have known he had an injury if his arm wasn't in a sling. No one should have been surprised by this, however. We should have known that his physical courage, his willingness to accept pain, were quite exceptional. This was evident when he was strapped to one of those new-fangled treatment machines for muscle problems. When you were receiving the treatment, a point was reached when you had to say, 'That's enough, the pain is too much.' In most cases, including my own, this was when the dial was about halfway up the gauge. For Gerry, the machine was usually applied at full blast. The rest of us would have been squealing like pigs.

When Tommy Smith came into the team he was something of a Wayne Rooney, physically mature way beyond his years. He was assertive, bossing around the other apprentices, some of whom were older than he was, and getting the cushy jobs for himself. He was the shop steward of the apprentices. Before he was seventeen, he was telling Shankly that he should be in the team. He went to the boss's office one day to demand a place, and was told, 'Aye son, you're right, but the problem is that they're not good enough for you yet. We'll try to get them up to shape to play with you.' Tommy came out of the office shaking his head. He said he didn't know what Shankly meant. Then he confessed, 'At first I was dumbstruck, then I realised he was fobbing me off.'

This was around the time Shankly asked Ronnie and me about Tommy before the Anderlecht game. Everyone knew that sooner or later the kid would be a foundation of the team. His official arrival came against Tottenham at White Hart Lane when he was still a teenager. Dave Mackay and Tommy found themselves in a fifty-fifty situation and for a fleeting moment you feared for the boy. The collision was awesome, but it was Tommy who got up first. When he looked down at Mackay, I thought to myself, 'There's a classic picture – the young gun shooting down the old gunslinger.' That was a defining moment. You knew then that the kid was going to be around for a very long time.

Of all his contemporaries, Norman Hunter of Leeds was most likened to Tommy. They were two hugely talented players and the fact that Hunter was such a fine player was often obscured by his ferocious reputation. In any comparison, though, you have to say that Tommy was the better rounded player, and this was to do with one basic fact – could use either foot equally as well as the other. That gave him his great strength and balance. His one weakness could be found out when he played in the orthodox right-half position, where he would sometimes drive Shankly to distraction with his ambitious crossfield passing to Peter Thompson. Too often Tommy was picked off when he went for the big ball and once, when he produced a terrific raking pass to Thompson's feet, the rest of us burst into applause. 'Well done, Tommy,' we shouted. 'You finally pulled it off.' Tommy was not pleased. Even the boss thought it necessary to tread carefully when he offered advice. Before games, he would sometimes say, quite gently, 'Let's try to ferry the ball across field to Peter, let's involve Billy Stevenson a little more.'

I'm not sure if Tommy ever removed that one blemish from his game, that yearning to play the perfect pass, and it could certainly be frustrating when we lost possession in that way. Nevertheless, Tommy emerged as one of the great Liverpool players. Apart from his footballing ability, he gave the side so much character and, being a local boy, such a connection to the life of the city, as did Callaghan, Byrne and Lawler, and as Jamie

Carragher does today. Carragher has emerged as Liverpool's best current player because, like those others before him, he has a passion and he has taken the trouble to learn his trade.

Whenever I think of Ronnie Yeats, Shankly's words flood into my mind – awesome, colossus, phenomenal. The manager may have had a tendency to overstate his case but in the case of the big man from Aberdeen, his instincts proved to be unerring. Ronnie was captain right from the start, Shankly's vast presence on the field. Shankly had him buttonholed for the role almost from the first moment he saw him run on to the field in a game in Scotland. Ronnie was rarely injured but it was only when he was out of the team that we got the true measure of his value. When he or Byrne were covering a dangerous situation, it was always so reassuring to the rest of the team. Ronnie was never flustered; someone might try to go around him in the box but the big left leg would stretch out and the danger was averted.

One of the things I admired most about Ronnie on the field was that, despite his vast physical presence, he was never a dirty player. Even when severely provoked, particularly in the pressure of European games, he always had a long fuse. His temper blazed on one occasion, though, when we were playing Standard Liège in Belgium. The Liège goalkeeper cracked Ronnie when they went up for a corner and there was no doubt it was a coldly deliberate foul. Ronnie accosted the goalkeeper in the tunnel at half-time. He was raging. Eventually, Reuben hustled him into our dressing-groom, shouting, 'Get in there, Ronnie, before it's too late.'

Ronnie and I roomed together for years. When we were away at hogmanay we would stay up in our room and toast the New Year with a glass of sherry. But for that isolated incident on the training field at a bad time in his life, we have always been the closest friends as well as team-mates. Ronnie would often ask me if I fancied a little flutter on the horses. He was keen on racing and spent quite a bit of time studying the form so I usually said, 'Aye, give it a go.' Each Saturday during the season, I would join him in a £5 double and on the way home I would inquire, 'How did we do today, big man?' Invariably, he would reply, 'Well, I came up on a couple but the double went down.' This went on for about six months without a break in the run of failure. Finally, I twigged. I realised that he was making his own shrewd bets based on form while he was going wild on the double, picking outsiders in the hope of pulling off some unlikely coup. When I put my theory to him, he just laughed, sheepishly.

I was delighted when Gordon Milne was capped by England, a fitting tribute to a tremendous career. In retrospect, I suppose it might have been some compensation for the angst he must have felt at missing the Cup final, made all the worse by the fact that Gordon's father, the Preston player and manager Jimmy Milne, suffered the same fate in his own playing days. Gordon appeared on the pitch as he did off it – neat and tidy, all of a small, efficient piece. His speciality was short, incisive one-twos that moved us down the field in a steady rhythm. He had terrific timing and it was just a shame that he wasn't a better finisher. So many times he worked himself into brilliant positions but he didn't have the killer touch of rivals such as England's World Cup winners Alan Ball and Martin Peters, the men who stood most discouragingly between him and a sustained run in Ramsey's team.

Gordon was deeply respected as a player, and much liked. One Saturday, after we played at Derby County, Gordon was chatting with some friends and missed the team bus. Shankly came bustling on to the bus at the last minute, took a quick glance around, said to the driver, 'Right, off we go,' and we had gone many miles through the Derbyshire hills before anyone realised Gordon was missing. He caught up with us when we stopped for a meal at a hotel, which had been pre-arranged. Gordon had got one of his friends to drive him there. We all felt a bit guilty when he came into the dining room. After that, there was always one big question whenever the coach driver cranked into gear. 'Is Gordon here?' someone would cry, usually Shankly. Gordon may have gone missing on that occasion but he was never invisible on the field.

The only time Ian Callaghan went missing when the team were travelling was at 9 a.m. on Sunday morning. Ian was a faithful Catholic but never hit you over the head with his religion. Apart from his visits to church, the only evidence was in his absolute refusal to use the industrial language of football. You never heard an oath or an obscenity on his lips. If he was ever outraged, and generally when he was he tended to keep it to himself, the worst he might say was something like, 'flipping heck'. That might have been considered lame or prudish if someone else said it, but not Ian Callaghan. He was always held in the highest respect. Off the field he was a decent, caring man. On it, he just didn't know how to give less than 100 per cent and it was a quality wonderfully enhanced by his understanding of the game. He was always a player who knew what was possible in any given situation.

I have already reported the tensions that existed between Jimmy Melia and me, and there is no point in suggesting now that they didn't run deep or that there was some moment when we put away the knives. He was a talented player, but maybe we were never destined to get along agreeably. However, it didn't matter in which camp you belonged, Melia was due everyone's sympathy when he became the first victim of Shankly's notorious German treatment machine.

When it was unveiled by Bob Paisley it was greeted with some awe. It had a black face and a battery of dials and wires were poking out from at least half a dozen places. When Bob, who was reading from the manufacturer's thick pamphlet of instructions, had made what he considered to be all the correct connections, he looked around and said, 'Right, boys, any of you got a bit of a knock?' When confronted by this piece of ferocious-looking machinery, I felt that it would be madness to confess to any problems, but Melia said, 'Well, Bob, I think I've pulled my knee a bit.' Bob told him to strip down and get on the table, which he did. Bob picked up two leads with large pads attached to the ends, wetted the pads and placed them on Melia's knee. He then picked up another attachment, which looked a bit like a microphone, and said in the most reassuring tones, 'Right, Jimmy, if you feel anything untoward, just give a shout and I'll turn it off right away.' For a little while Bob was twiddling with a knob to no effect and Shankly became quite impatient.

'Jesus Christ, Bob, haven't you read the instructions?' he said. Everyone but Melia, understandably enough, was now fighting off the giggles in quite a serious way.

'The instructions are in German, Boss,' said Paisley.

'Weren't you in the war, for God's sake – don't you understand German?' Shankly responded.

By now, Bob had turned all the knobs to maximum force and Melia was getting a bit tense.

'Is it full on now, Bob?' he asked.

It was then that Bob noticed the one thing he hadn't done was turn on the power. When he did, Melia's leg shot up in the air and jerked back uncontrollably. Those who weren't bent in two by now screamed for the machine to be turned off.

Melia survived, of course, as we all did in our different ways. Indeed, despite the hazards of the treatment room, we knew that what was being achieved at Anfield was something that would surely reach down the years. That was gloriously confirmed for me one night in May 2005.

11

SCOTLAND, OH SCOTLAND

S O MUCH of Scottish football has been about stealing disaster from the gates of heaven and so I suppose it was inevitable that sooner or later I would play my part. The timing, though, was as premature as it was spectacular. Liverpool were moving towards their zenith, and I was priding myself on becoming part of a sure-fire football legend, when I made myself a pariah in my own land.

I said something that I would never retract, but even as I said it I knew it would haunt me always. I said to anyone prepared to listen that I didn't care if I ever played for Scotland again. That, as I should have realised, was seen as a rejection of the Scottish shirt and my own blood. It was never that, and it could never be that, but there it was emblazoned in every Scottish newspaper – St John turns his back on Scotland, says he doesn't care if he ever plays again . . .

I wasn't rejecting Scotland, or the thrill of playing with John White, Dave Mackay, Jim Baxter, Paddy Crerand, Denis Law and all those other Scottish players who should have been given a proper foundation to beat the world. I was attacking – and with all the contempt I could muster – a system that allowed the men in blazers with badges, the committee men of the Scottish Football Association, to do the job of professional football men. They were picking the team as though they were handing out sweeties to their favourite pupils. They were divvying up the football honour of their country. They were pleasing themselves. What did the knowledge of Matt Busby, Jock Stein or Bill Shankly have to do with it? Nothing at all. When it came to picking the best eleven players in Scotland at any one time, such professional wisdom might not have existed. One committee man would say to another, 'Maybe it's time for your man to have a game . . .' It was a farce.

The English FA had discarded a similar system a few years earlier when they appointed Alf Ramsey, who had shocked football by guiding Ispwich Town to the league title in 1962. Ramsey had said that there was no way he would consider the national job if he wasn't given complete control over selection. The FA men apparently changed colour when they heard Ramsey's demand, but in the end they gave up their rights. The consequence was that England were on their way to their first World Cup win a few years later.

They had a settled team, the players knew the manager they were playing for and what it was he wanted from them. Ramsey was advised by his committee men that it would be good politics to drop the hard-tackling Nobby Stiles after a controversy over a tackle he made on French player Jacky Simon in a World Cup group game. Ramsey said, yes, he could drop Stiles, but they would then be without a manager in the middle of quite an important tournament. At that moment the battle for a professional approach was clearly won.

In the wake of the World Cup, when my connection with the team was gone forever, we beat England at Wembley in 1967 and Scottish fans dug up the Wembley turf. Some of them said the win made us world champions. Hadn't Baxter played like an emperor of the game? Yes indeed, but where did the victory leave us? Still locked in a competitive death wish.

Maybe I wouldn't have committed my act of harikiri if I'd had a little more time to reflect, to see that sometimes you have to accept life as it is and not how you would like it be.

The problem was that I'd just scored against England – always the highwater mark in the life of a Scottish striker – in a 2–2 draw. Along with what I thought was a decent performance against an England team who were already developing powerfully under Ramsey, I thought that was more than enough to guarantee my place in that year's summer tour. An adrenaline rush was still lingering when someone told me that I hadn't made the squad. I was raging. There was no question of an exclusive interview that day. Any reporter who approached me or called me was given a detailed account of how I felt about the Scottish selectors. Both barrels were fired. One line I remember, and perhaps it was the one that ended my Scotland career at twenty-one caps and nine goals – 'I don't know what those guys were doing at Wembley. They should have been on at the Palladium with Ken Dodd . . . they're Diddymen. I don't care to play for them. They are clowns.'

In the heat of that kind of emotion I couldn't be sure to what extent I'd contributed to a good Scottish performance, but certainly I felt it had been decent. At the very least I had played no better or worse that most of my team-mates, and I'd been playing well for Liverpool in 1965 as we moved towards the FA Cup triumph and that bitter European Cup semi-final with Inter Milan. Certainly, the team that drew at Wembley had helped the nation move another stride away from the shame of that notorious 9–3 hammering two years earlier, when Scotland's goalkeeper Frank Haffey had been put through a terrible ordeal of fire and humiliation. The previous year we had beaten England at Hampden.

Many years later, when Lou Macari was so embittered by the pantomime of Ally MacLeod's challenge for the World Cup in Argentina in 1978, he hovered on the point of a similar statement about his anger and weariness at Scotland's approach to international football. I was working for Granada Television in

Argentina, and the company had put a considerable amount of money on the table for Lou to go down to a studio in Buenos Aires and lift the lid on the chaos of the Scottish camp. The confusion had been highlighted by Willie Johnston's early flight home after testing positive for drugs and the fact that MacLeod's promise of triumph had turned into disaster with a defeat and a draw against the ill-considered Peru and Iran.

I could see that Lou was as angry as I had been thirteen years earlier and, although I was experiencing some conflict of interest as an employee of the television company, my instincts as a former player – and a Scot – came to the fore. I said, 'Don't do it, Lou. It will create tremendous pressure on you in Scotland. You will regret it soon enough . . . it's just not worth all the hassle that will come to you. You will be branded a traitor.'

Now, when I look at the state of Scotland's international game and see the massive job facing the latest manager, Walter Smith, I wonder if it might have been better if there had been more pointed protests down the years. Some of the reasons for the demise of Scottish football are, of course, quite complicated, but the history of wasted opportunities stretches back down the decades. When you think of the quality of native talent – indeed, in some instances, you can say genius without going over the top – you know that you are looking at one of the longest running scandals in all of sport.

One point to consider is the nature of the Scottish footballer, or any footballer, back in those days. He was paid poorly and given very little respect by the footballing authorities. Even when he was helping to fill Hampden Park and competing with the best talent in the world, he was taught to mind his place. So what did he do? He played football with great enthusiasm and passion, and he enjoyed himself, all the time not quite believing his good luck in being able to do something he loved rather than having to clock on at the factory or the pithead. The sophistication levels of the Scottish footballer when my international career crumbled, just when I thought I was touching the stars, are reflected in a couple of stories that were doing the rounds at the time. They were told with great relish in the dressing rooms of Scotland and among those Scots who inhabited influential corners of almost all the English First Division clubs.

The tales came from a tour of America by Third Lanark. The trip took the team to New York and the Celtic player John Colrain, a larger than life character who had been co-opted on to the tour, decided he was going to go to Jilly's nightclub at every opportunity in pursuit of his hero Frank Sinatra. This was after the disappointment of a team visit to the club when the great star failed to make an appearance, which the players had been told was more or less automatic. Colrain, though, was indefatigable.

While his team-mates drifted off to pursue other delights of Manhattan on subsequent nights, Colrain refused to be thwarted. Each night he showed up at the club asking if 'the chairman of the board' had made an appearance. Finally, some-one at the club weakened and said, 'Yeah, Frank's in tonight. He's in a backroom. I'll go and have a word with him.' John was summoned to meet Ol' Blue Eyes. The story goes that Sinatra, who as we know was not always the most accommodating of characters, poured Colrain a drink and quizzed him about his sporting life. 'So you play soccer, buddy boy,' said Sinatra, amiably enough. After a few more civilities, the audience was over, but Colrain walked into the streets of Manhattan on air.

He never quite established himself in the Scottish team, but he was a good player and had great passion for the game. It was also true that from that night on, his life was rounded enough. He was a crony of Frank Sinatra and within days of the team's return all of Glasgow knew about it.

His travelling companions were rather more sheepish about their experiences in New York. While Colrain was hobnobbing with Sinatra, the other boys were chasing their own late-night entertainment. When most of the bars had closed, some operator of the night approached them to say he could take them to a club. It was a members' establishment so he would need a little money to get them into the place. They stumped up $100. Their man took the money and went up some stairs and through a door. He said he would need just a minute or two to complete the negotiations. One minute turned into five, then ten. Eventually, the lads, thirsty now, grew impatient and marched up the stairs. They opened the door into an empty room. He had fled with their money down a stairway into the basement and back out into the street where, no doubt, he was hoping to find some more Scottish footballers.

Maybe the Scottish footballer was slow to organise himself, and more than a little naive, but then maybe there just hadn't been sufficient encouragement for him to recognise his status and responsibilities in the game that held his nation in such a firm grip.

There was a shifting cast of managers after I came on to the international scene, playing for the Under-23s and then the Scottish League in a 1–1 draw. That game was against an English Football League team that had the pick of all nationalities in the League, which meant that I found myself playing against Tottenham's flying winger Cliff Jones and Arsenal's goalkeeper Jack Kelsey, both of Wales. Matt Busby, recuperating from the Munich tragedy, did the job for a while as he felt his way back into the game after coming so near to losing his life. Andy Beattie and Ian McColl never had the natural authority of Busby and so their position, trapped between the all-powerful committee men and players who were picked up and put down on a whim, was basically hopeless. Beattie even burst into tears after an act of rebellion by Jim Baxter.

It was Beattie who told me I had won my first cap in that game with West Germany in which my ill-starred Motherwell team-mate Andy Weir stole a moment of glory with a goal and John White and I were written up as key elements in a new Scotland. I had gone along as a member of the Under-23 team and was watching, with mounting optimism, as the first-choice centre-forward, Andy Kerr of Partick Thistle, was put through a fitness test. In one area at least, Scotland had got something right, and that was the way the Under-23 team worked alongside the full team. It gave the younger players a feeling of being part of the big international scene. I have a picture from that time of myself and Jimmy Gabriel watching the senior players train, legendary men such as Bobby Evans and Bobby Collins, and you can see the awe in our eyes. When the full international match was played, the Under-23 team were given good seats in the stands, and before that we had played against the big men in training matches. It was invaluable preparation for the challenge of putting on the Scottish shirt for the first time, which made it even more sad when that sense of belonging dwindled so quickly.

The young boys usually won the hour-long training match. We tore around the field, thinking we were great, while the senior guys were much more careful. I understood their cir-cumspection when Beattie said that Kerr had failed his fitness test and I would play against the Germans. I would become a real-life player in one of those dramas that used to fill our little apartment from the first moment when the magic of radio came into our lives.

The bus that took us up to Hampden Park from our Turn-berry headquarters might have been a gilded carriage. It was a lovely night in early May. The grass was sparkling emerald. More than 80,000 fans filled the big, gaunt ground. John White stroked the ball around beautifully and Dave Mackay was Dave Mackay, arguably the best all-round player to come out of Scotland. Graham Leggat was on the right wing and he and Andy gave us plenty of width, but it was White and me who stole the attention in the 3–2 win. Our future was secure – at least, it was pretty to think so as we showered before taking our bows, but that pattern of inconsistency took instant shape. Despite the rave reports, the word from the Scottish FA offices was that I had to go back in the queue like some casual worker waiting for a shift at the dockside. I would not be going on the close-season tour and have the chance to build confidently on my promising start. Despite some press articles supporting my claims, it was pointed out that I had only made the team because of Kerr's injury. I had to wait my turn. Amazingly enough, considering his situation, the big man, a former full-back, was one of those making the case for my inclusion in the touring party. They didn't do that sort of thing in Scottish international football, though. They didn't respond to a moment. They went their own sweet, futile way.

On this occasion, I was far from devastated. I could see that I had put down an impressive marker for my international future, and I'd had plenty of experience of foreign football with the Under-23s. When I arrived at Liverpool two years later, I was a fully fledged international with seven caps, and that gave me quite a bit of weight in a team that was still fighting its way out of the Second Division.

World Cup and European Championship football were not as huge a factor in the minds of the players and the fans as they are today. When the qualifying draws were made for these competitions, there was no great rush to see who the opposition would be. I was nearly twenty years old before I became enthralled by the World Cup and that was only because I had the chance to see

Pele playing for Brazil. Grainy television pictures were beamed from the 1958 tournament in Sweden. That was wonderful, football as fantasy, but it didn't permit too much time for a build-up to one of my biggest performances in the blue shirt, a two-goal effort against Czechoslovakia in a qualifying play-off for the 1962 World Cup finals in Chile.

The venue was the ill-fated Heysel Stadium in Brussels and the Czechs were one of the best teams in Europe at the time. Despite some selection problems, including the absence of Alex Scott, we went into the game with great confidence. The Rangers right winger was a fine orthodox player but on this occasion he had to be replaced by the skilful but out-of-position Ralph Brand. We had some superb talent – players who had survived the selection process included White, Crerand, Baxter and Law – and the second of my two goals gave us the lead with just a few minutes to go.

As glory beckoned, so too did a Scottish football setback. The Czechs scored a late equaliser and we feared the worst as we waited for the start of extra time. Suddenly, Paddy Crerand and Jim Baxter were exchanging blows. I pulled them apart and said, 'For God's sake, let's fight them, not ourselves.' The issue was which one of them got first use of a wet sponge. It was not the most encouraging signal and, sure enough, the Czechs nicked the winner. It would be another twelve years before Scotland qualified for the World Cup finals, and there was much shared anger as we flew home.

Paddy took the defeat harder than anyone. He still swears that it was the night when Scotland missed their greatest chance of making a mighty splash on the world scene, and still bringing a hard edge to his dismay is that it happened just four years before England landed the great trophy.

Crerand's theory is not so far-fetched when you consider the weight of individual Scottish talent at that time. With proper discipline and preparation, that team could have held their own in Chile. The Czechs went on to reach the final and, in another haunting twist of fate, they lost to Brazil, who had never been so vulnerable in the absence of the injured Pele. Jimmy Greaves, who went to South America with England, said that he had one of the worst times of his football life. The tournament was poorly run and the conditions were bad. However, that didn't appease me too much. I agreed with Crerand. We should have been there. We should have been real contenders.

Such a missed opportunity should have galvanised the Scottish game, but still the committee men gathered over the malt whisky and then said to the manager, 'Here's the team, laddie, there you go.' So the great Scottish players, those with the talent that Ramsey would surely have given so much for the chance to inject into his brilliantly disciplined team, took their chances in the selection lottery.

It would have been a nightmare for any manager – as Ramsey had pointed out to the English – and maybe that is why the job became available to some frankly inadequate candidates. Neither Beattie nor his successor Ian McColl were up to the job. The latter came in at the end of his playing career and any doubts about the fact that he didn't have a clue about how to organise a team were dispelled when we played Austria in a tour game in Vienna.

We had been buffeted badly in an electrical storm on the flight from Turkey, where we had played our opening game without much distinction, but in Vienna the whole show fell apart. The Austrians were lively and very sharp tactically, and I spent most of the first half running offside. It was the first time I had encountered such a slick offside trap, but there was no guidance from McColl at half-time.

We just had to do it the Scottish way, which was hit and miss. If we sparked, if the individual talent blossomed, we were fine, we could give problems to any team in the world. If not, if we needed to adjust, come up with some kind of countering system, we were lost – utterly.

The Vienna experience was, in its way, quite as bad as that occasion when Beattie broke down in the face of the indiscipline of some of the top players. We were on tour and had been told to assemble for the bus at 7 p.m. Most of the team were on time, but there was the usual problem of the stragglers – Baxter, Mackay and Law. Beattie just cracked. He held his head in his hands to hide his tears. It was pitiful.

That set of players was a hard crew to master, requiring a strong manager, and football men of the calibre of Stein, Busby and Shankly would never have considered taking orders from a committee on a long-term basis. Unlike today, though, back then a pool of native talent was the lifesaver. If Scottish football's capacity to deliver pain always seemed to run a little bit beyond its power to achieve consistent results, there was always that potential to produce something special. Perhaps that was never seen more clearly than at the end of the Ally MacLeod mis-adventure in Argentina in 1978, when, with Scottish football rendered a laughing stock across the world, the boys rose up to beat a superb Dutch team – a gesture of unfulfilled defiance that was as agonising, when you thought about what might have been, as it was brilliant.

No one more exemplified Scotland's potential to beat the world than the tragic John White, the brilliant, ghostly product of Bonnyrig Rose. He was from the little pit town near Falkirk and at times he seemed to represent not just the talent but the spirit of the Scottish game. On top of a classic ability to pass the ball, which was so much heavier in those days, he could hit it in the spectacular side-to-side fashion of David Beckham manip-ulating today's lightweight model. John could hit it any distance, and he always did so with tremendous vision, subtlety and weight.

He was a natural athlete, a cross-country star in his youth and, in many ways, he ran ahead of his time. When he died, the blow to both his club, Tottenham, and his country was terrible. I played in the testimonial game for his family at White Hart Lane after his death, and I doubt that there was ever a more poignant sense of loss at the disappearance of a single football player.

You couldn't shake off the dismay at how freakishly he had gone. The ring on his finger was the catalyst of the tragedy. He was sheltering under a tree with a club in his hand when the lightning came. He was a fanatic golfer and he had gone out on his own to play a few holes. The lightning struck his ring and, they said, that was what killed him. They found him sitting under the tree.

I was in hospital at the time, seriously ill after an emergency appendix operation, and when I heard the news that my team-mate and companion in that most optimistic of headlines after the German game, had been taken away so randomly, it was a sickening shock. 'John,' I thought, 'if I'd snuffed it too, it would have been some double act.'

In some ways, John was a curiously elusive boy, almost with a streak of madness. Sometimes he would dress up and play the clown and he would have his team-mates roaring with laughter. On another occasion, if you were on the bus, say, and you'd left something lying around, you would quite often see it flying through a window. Dave Mackay, a giant authority on the field, was also capable of such adolescent behaviour, but Baxter was the manager's nightmare, the always ungovernable factor.

Slim Jim was at his worst on an end of season tour to Norway,

Ireland and Spain, a trip that, when you looked back, seemed to encapsulate all of our problems. We lost to Norway, 4–3, despite the fact that Denis Law was in blazing form, as sharp as he had ever been – which is to say as sharp as any player could possibly be – and he scored a hat-trick. We lost to the Republic of Ireland. My place went to Jimmy Millar of Rangers and I came on late as a substitute for him. Then we went to Spain, played without Mackay who was injured but won 6–2. We travelled across a slice of Europe, all the way lurching between anarchy and world-beating brilliance.

Baxter, naturally, was at both ends of the spectrum. He arrived at the airport in Glasgow dishevelled and without his boots. He had been on a bender – but, by his standards, a hugely successful one, having won around £1,000 in a casino. He gave Billy McNeill the money to keep so he didn't blow it all on the horses. McNeill confessed to being seriously uneasy. He wondered if there could possibly be a tougher role in all football than minder and treasurer to Jim Baxter.

After the game against Norway, Baxter came into the hotel in Bergen and sat at a table occupied by the manager, McColl, Willie Allan, secretary of the Scottish Football Association, and a few of the players. The first thing Baxter did was pick up a glass of beer and throw it over one of the lads. Allan leapt up.

'Baxter, sit down, behave yourself,' he ordered. Baxter glowered at Allan.

'It's Mr Baxter to you,' he said. Then, after a moment's reflection, he added, 'You can stick your team up your arse. I'm going home.'

In fact, he simply disappeared to his hotel room but the rest of the trip was spent on a knife-edge, wondering what Baxter was going to do next. That was the story of his football life – he was given the most beautiful talent, but also a genius for self-destruction. When he was in drink, his personality changed. His career displayed all the glory and tragedy of Scottish football.

Mackay's devilment was centred mostly on that classic footballing habit of pulling a prank. I heard just recently that when Mackay was told of John White's death he burst into tears – and then reported that he had a pair of his fallen friend's trousers in the boot of his car. They had been taken after training, requiring White to drive home in his shorts.

Dave had one supreme party piece, and he patiently coached the rest of us in the fine technique involved in tossing a coin in the air, catching it on his foot, flipping it on to his forehead and then sliding it into his top pocket. Great applause would follow a perfect rendition of the trick. I cannot easily imagine such a scene in today's game. In the era of mobile phones, the outside world is constantly coming at the players, but nobody was coming at us. We were just ourselves with each other, and most of the time it was fun – we were just a bunch of lads going away for a trip and to play a game of football.

On one of my first trips to London with the Scottish League team, one of my team-mates said to me, 'A press guy has been looking for you – he said a London paper wants to do a piece and there's twenty quid in it for you. He said he'll meet you here in the lobby at 6.30.' I was waiting there when the boys were leaving to see a movie. One of them said, 'What's up, aren't you coming to see the film?' I explained that I had a very profitable engagement, but then I saw him beginning to smirk, and the rest of the team were laughing, too.

I've told a number of such stories already in these pages, but I make no apology because if football is now a huge business, larded with attention in every corner of the media, it is also a game for boys. Players will retain a little of that status as long as they play, or watch, something that has touched every corner of the world with its beauty and its simplicity – and, of course, nowhere more so than in my native land.

Inevitably, I have regrets, both for Scotland's ultimate frustration in the international game and my own early departure from that stage. Certainly, I felt it acutely when I missed the chance to play in the Wembley victory that came two years after my last appearance for the team. Beating England at Wembley was more than an ambition, it was a compulsion. As the novelist and poet Willie McIlvanney, once said, 'The moment a Scotsman gets on the train for London, he gets a bad attack of paranoia along with his ticket.'

An additional pain was that I left the Scottish team at a point of genuine maturity, aged twenty-seven and playing, in a more withdrawn position, some of the best football of my career. Shankly always said that a player should deliver his best in the years between twenty-seven and thirty. That was the time when everything should come together – skill, judgement, knowledge of his own powers. If that was true of me – and I believe it was – I can only regret all over again that the results were not at the disposal of my country. However, I do think I can reasonably distribute some of the blame.

Today, the challenge facing Scotland goes far beyond a mere improvement in the abject levels that have been touched by the national team in recent years. Walter Smith, a man who knows the game at all levels, should have a far wider remit than merely picking and preparing the team. He should be asked to review all levels of Scottish football, right down to the schools, and then be given the power to take some action. The most pressing question – one that is relentless when your mind plays back over the quality of Scottish talent when the lightning struck down John White – is simply, 'Where did all the good players go?'

Look at the history of the great English clubs and consider for a moment the impact of Scottish players. Then look at the force of Jock Stein's Celtic team that beat the best of Europe and was drawn from the environs of Glasgow. It is a staggering legacy. Walk down an English street and ask someone to name a current Scottish player and the certainty is that you will get a blank face. Scotland's best player is probably Barry Ferguson, who made such little impact with Blackburn Rovers before returning to Rangers. The brutal truth is that he would be lucky to get a run in the Republic of Ireland team.

Even though England hold an advantage over Scotland in their much bigger black population, it is not the main issue. The make-up of the current England team includes such key figures as Ashley Cole, Rio Ferdinand and Sol Campbell, and the outstanding prospect of Shaun Wright-Phillips, but England have also produced Wayne Rooney, Michael Owen, David Beckham, Paul Scholes and Steven Gerrard. Scotland can only fantasise about players of such quality.

In the end, if you really want to get an answer, you find yourself probing into changes in the life of Scotland that go beyond the boundaries of football. You think of the hold that television and video games exert on today's young people and see that something has to be done not only for the organisation of Scottish football but also its appeal. Football has to cause a spark, it has to lift boys and find some of that old spirit. It has to recapture whatever it was that made the great players, and persuaded kids to play deep into the night on the cold street.

Those conditions of life can never be recreated, thank heavens, but at least the follies that have dogged Scottish football can be banished. We cannot have our time over again — no one knows that better than I do — but we can remember what we once had and maybe that can be a spur as well as a regret.

12

BAD DAY AT NEWCASTLE

I F YOU are very lucky, you know days when you don't believe you can be beaten, when you feel that all you have worked for, and dreamed about, has become reality. The Scottish misadventure was sad but it never touched the fact that I had such days and they reached their peak in the middle sixties. The greatest of victories was no longer a gift. It was a right.

I walked down the street in Liverpool the master of everything I saw, as did all my team-mates. Maybe we lived in modest houses that we didn't own, and would never earn similar fortunes to the pop stars – who seemed to be springing up in every corner of the city – but, as footballers, we were in the right place at the right time, following the lead of the right manager. He made our football lives.

When we beat Everton 5–0 on the way to our second league title in 1966, we played so well that it seemed we could do anything. We were not so much a football club as an empire, and I lived at the heart of it. As well as slaughtering Everton, we put five past West Ham, Blackburn Rovers and Northampton Town, who were taking a brief tour of the First Division. In the Cup Winners' Cup we were equally imperious, disposing of Standard Liège, the great Juventus, Honved and, in the Battle of Britain, the Celtic team Jock Stein was building towards European Cup triumph. Shankly likened me to one of the best middleweights, quick and hard, and for an old fighting man that was another reason to believe in a future without bounds.

Our second title was virtually in our pockets by Christmas, and if there was some disappointment in the final against Borussia Dortmund on that filthy night at Hampden Park, when Roger Hunt was injured and the whole team unaccountably misfired, it seemed like the merest slip along the way to unlimited glory. We were fighting cocks who had to resist the urge to strut on to the field, a resolution that was not always kept. We believed it would never end.

In all of that, I never imagined the situation that unfolded in the pre-match lobby of Newcastle United in the autumn of 1969. Well, maybe that's not quite true. I always knew I had to play out the scene one day, because it is one no player can avoid forever, but I assumed the circumstances would be rather different. I didn't expect such a gut-wrenching surprise, an ambush that came without a hint of warning.

I had just performed one of the rituals of match day, as I had done countless times before. I had gone out front to pass on some tickets promised to friends, and exchanged a few pleasantries, all the time my mind ticking down to the forthcoming action. In the lobby, the great legend of the north east, Jackie Milburn, who had become a football writer, was handed copies of the team-sheets by a club official, and we amiably shared the latest gossip. As Milburn ran his eyes down the teams, I said I had to get back to the dressing room to change. Then he looked up sharply and said a few words that might have been, for the impact they had, imprinted on my brain with a branding iron — 'Bonnie lad, you're not playing.'

Bill Shankly had dropped me without saying a word, without even meeting my eyes. This was the day I stepped down from one of the certainties of my life — the one that said I always made the team and the anguish of omission was somebody else's fate. Of course, like death and taxes, it was inevitable, but I thought it was

reasonable to believe that the day would not come unannounced, like a thief in the night to rob me of a confident
expectation that, suddenly, I realised how much I had always
cherished. Somehow the blow might have been softened. I always
thought that I would get the chance to absorb the blow before I
had to deal publicly with my new, diminished status. I didn't
expect to get the word so suddenly, in a room full of strangers,
and from a man who knew right down to his bones the
implications of what he was telling me. He couldn't keep the
shock off his face.

I rushed back to the dressing room spitting with anger. It was
only later I realised that maybe I should have picked up on a few
of the Indian signs and the blurted words of Jack Milburn should
not have landed with the force of a sledgehammer. I should have
grasped that, when a newspaper headline had read 'A wind of
change is blowing through Anfield', I too was standing in its path.

Malcolm Allison, whose Manchester City were producing
some brilliant football, had sneered publicly that the great
Liverpool team had become a bunch of 'trial horses'. He said
Liverpool were living on yesterday's reputation rather than
today's performance. Naturally, Shankly was enraged, pronouncing Allison a maniac, but the master of Anfield had always
known, as all managers are obliged to know, that the time would
come when he had to make changes to his team. He had to re-
seed, shape the future before it overwhelmed him. He signed
Tony Hateley from Aston Villa and Alun Evans from Wolves.
Emlyn Hughes was going to be the engine of a new team, and
soon enough there would be a new, famous alliance – Kevin
Keegan and John Toshack.

The old guard was breaking up. Billy Stevenson went to Stoke
City, Geoff Strong to Coventry, Roger Hunt, who fell out of
Shankly's favour before I did, joined Peter Thompson at Bolton,

and Gordon Milne went to Blackpool. Me? I was immune. I had adapted my game to the drift of time. I was playing farther back, and enjoying it. Hadn't a Wayside Pulpit notice secured my position well enough with a scrawled answer to the question 'What will you do when the Lord comes?' – 'Move St John to inside-left.' Now I could make goals with the same satisfaction that I once had scoring them. I was part of the furniture of Anfield. At least, that was something comforting to tell myself.

As I hurried down the corridors of St James's Park, I thought of the great relationship I had had with Shankly, all the warmth and the intimacies, the endless laughter and the deep sense that beneath all the passing pressures of the game, and sometimes the terrible tension and the cruelties that from time to time it produced, we had a deep understanding. If it wasn't father-and-son understanding, it was something very close indeed – or so I had thought.

To this day, I cannot shake the belief that, at the end, Shankly let me down. I was terribly disappointed he didn't handle it better. He should have taken me to one side, even in the hotel in Newcastle on the eve of the match. He could have said any of a hundred things. Anything would have been better than the blow administered by Jackie Milburn. Neither Shankly nor I could change the realities of football, or the ageing process, but he could have shown a little courtesy. He could have taken away some of the rawness of the pain. Shankly could have said – and how could I have denied it? – that the greatest teams have to change and every player has his time. He could have said that I had been part of a great team, but the time had come when I had to think of my future, just as he had to move on with a new challenge and new players.

Ironically, I had already begun to deal with the fact that there was only so long I would be able to resist the 'wind of change'. I went to the FA's coaching centre in Lilleshall to get my coaching certificate and, in another irony, Shankly hated that. He distrusted the coaching culture — and who can say that in the broad sweep of his thinking he was wrong? — and he was dismissive of my efforts at the converted country house deep in the fields of Shropshire. One day I was talking to some of the lads about the game and, apparently, slipping in a few coaching phrases. When Shankly overheard this he barked, 'Naw, lads, never mind all that Lilleshall shit.'

He had also been unimpressed by the fact that I had been working with an amateur team, Skelmersdale United, and helped them get to the FA Amateur Cup final at Wembley in 1967. As he saw it, I had enough of a job to do as a Liverpool player — until that afternoon in Newcastle.

When I got to the dressing room, my boots had been placed beneath the number 12's peg. Shankly was nowhere to be seen and I presumed he was lying low. I ranted and raved. Bob Paisley and Reuben Bennett were trying to calm me down but it was futile work. I got changed and went down to the dug-out in the sourest mood that had ever possessed me around a football ground. I sat on the bench, head down, and shrugged away Bob when he said, 'Go on, have a little warm-up.'

'I'm not warming up unless he comes down to tell me to,' I snapped. Shankly stayed in the stands. We were both being stubborn. We lost the game.

I rode the team bus home wordlessly. On the Monday morning I went straight to Shankly's office.

'Why didn't you tell me I wasn't playing?' I asked. 'After all these years, didn't you think I deserved something better than hearing it on the steps of another football ground?'

He said that I should have been in the dressing room when he made his team announcement. I said that wasn't the point. He had all Friday night to tell me, all the time up to the game. I told him it was the first time I had ever been left out of a team, and it was very hard that it happened that way. He wasn't sympathetic. The conversation slipped into a full-blown row, with yelling and cursing.

Later, before training, Bob Paisley pricked my conscience. He reminded me of some of the truths of the game — the hard ones that everyone had to learn to accept if they didn't want to be torn up by bitterness — and he made me think of how great Shankly's staff had been to the players down the years. Yes, I would have to get hold of myself but, as I had said to Shankly and repeated to Bob, it was the hardest thing I had faced in football.

Nothing was worse than what happened after the warm-up before that first training session I had at Melwood as a former member of the first team. I was told to join the reserves. More than anything it was embarrassing. I had the terrible feeling that I had come to the end of the road. All that I had achieved had suddenly come full circle and I was on the outside of the charmed circle. The greatest moments of the past roared through my head, but now I knew that all of them had irrevocably gone, even if I returned, briefly, to the glory of the first team. Something had snapped. I just wanted to hide. I didn't want to look at the kids, those hopeful kids, because I might just imagine I saw pity on their faces.

Later, during my time as a manager, I came to realise how hard had been the task facing Shankly when, having led us all to so many great moments, he had to discard us, one by one. I remembered the pain of my own experience, that awful sense of suddenly becoming a non-person in a place where once you had been a king, and unlike Shankly, I tried to soften and explain the blow.

Joe Fagan did all he could to make me feel important as a

reserve player, asking me my opinion on some of the young lads, but he couldn't take away the harsh impact of turning out at an empty Gigg Lane, Bury, when I knew that somebody else was wearing my shirt in a big, pounding game at Anfield. I had done it before, while returning from injury, but that was different. Everyone knew you were making a brief appearance among the 'stiffs' before returning to the important action.

I didn't slack in the reserve games. I knew that if I wanted to extend my playing career as I headed into my thirties, I had to do my work and keep my professional values. This attitude apparently registered with Shankly. I made a couple of appearances on the first-team bench and Shankly brought me on. I did well enough. In a Uefa tie against Bucharest, the team were struggling and I was able to liven up the performance, laying on a goal for Emlyn Hughes. Such cameo appearances from the bench were, maybe inevitably, sparse because my presence was invariably seized upon by the crowd, particularly in the Kop. They chanted my name and Shankly didn't like that. He saw it as a threat to his authority, and so it was clear enough that my Anfield days had just about run their course.

My last contribution to the club came in the campaign that returned Liverpool to Wembley for the 1971 Cup final against Arsenal, the double winners, who beat us on the strength of Charlie George's brilliant goal. I was on the bench against Swansea in one of the comfortable home ties that helped the team, now strengthened by the £110,000 signing of Toshack, to move easily through to the semi-finals. I was brought on to change the pattern when the boys began to stutter a little. I managed to raise a few of the old cheers from the Kop and scored a goal. Then on the Monday morning, Bill Shankly called me into his office to say that I was wanted by George Eastham in South Africa.

It was a rather cold conversation and Shankly was quite matter of fact. He simply told me that Eastham, who was manager of Cape Town Hellenic, had called to find out if he could speak to me. Shankly told Eastham he could do so if I agreed. So there it was, officially confirmed. I had become part of the history of Anfield.

I had maintained warm relations with Paisley and Fagan, but had scarcely exchanged a word with Shankly since the bad day in Newcastle. The bruising I had suffered that day had gone too deep. I couldn't be other than offhand with him, even though the feelings between us had been so strong and warm for so long. I knew what I had meant to him in the best Liverpool days, and certainly what he had meant to me. I suppose the last few months had been like a marriage breaking down, when you have to wonder where has all the love gone?

What do you do when a marriage fails? It was a new experience for me but I realised that you cannot nurse your wounds for too long, not in the brief years allowed a professional footballer. By the time George Eastham arrived at Anfield for our discussions, I had shaken myself into a more positive mood. As always, Betsy was a strong and steadying voice. Usually, we discussed the events of the day, and the current situation of our lives, on our nightly walk with the dogs around the neighbouring park, and it was there that the possibilities of South Africa were examined. Betsy was enthusiastic about the prospects of a new adventure, as she had been when Bill Shankly first came calling at our little flat in Motherwell. Assuming the terms were right, it would be a good experience for our family.

After the pain of Betsy's miscarriages, we had felt blessed by the arrival of our son Ian, a brother for Elaine. I suppose it is true of most men that when they have a son they feel complete in some inexplicable way. Having a little girl was on precisely the same plane of joy but I suppose when Ian was born, my feelings were intensified by the fact that I had lost my father when I was such a young boy. Now, at an age when I had mourned the father I had known so briefly, Ian would have both his father and a great adventure. Betsy applied the seal of approval. We would go to Africa, a land of brilliant light and new experience. As we walked through the park, I found myself picking up my feet a little, and felt a stirring of the blood that hadn't been there since Wor Jackie had delivered those killer words. Betsy said, quite dryly, that whatever Cape Town offered, it would almost certainly be better for her than seeing me moping about the house in Maghull.

Eastham underpinned our growing excitement. I would be paid £100 a week – the same as I was getting from Liverpool – and I would be player-coach, which was a tremendous bonus because I had worked to become a coach and manager when the playing had to stop. The club would give us a beautiful house over-looking Sea Point, one of the most desirable areas in the city and where, later, Margaret Thatcher's son Mark would take up such controversial residence.

When Betsy and I look back on this episode, it is with great warmth except for one source of regret. We were still quite young, and had been living through a time of considerable tension. Maybe that was why we neglected someone who had become a cornerstone of our lives – Betsy's mother. In the rush to get on the plane and catapult ourselves into this new thrilling phase of our lives, we left her in the terraced house in Liverpool into which she had moved so happily after we had been whisked away from Motherwell. She was settled well with her second husband, enjoyed the city and spent a lot of time with Elaine and Ian, but suddenly we were gone and, with us, a large part of her life. Much later, we realised we should have been a little more thoughtful and at least arranged for her to pay us an extended visit so that she could see South Africa and be with her family. Betsy felt this keenly but by then it was too late. We had to reflect that, in the chase to get on with business, Bill Shankly wasn't alone in forgetting the feelings of those who had served him so well.

Liverpool Football Club's lack of appreciation for past services was in a different category. It was simply the way it was in the game. That was certainly my feeling when, soon after listening to Liverpool's Cup final game against Arsenal on South African radio — a campaign to which I had made that small contribution in the Swansea tie — a letter from Anfield landed in the mailbox at Sea Point. It was a two-line note signed by the secretary, Peter Robinson, announcing that the club would not be taking up their year's option on my contract. Of course, this was no surprise. I hadn't carried any illusions with me on the flight to Cape Town. There would be no reappraisals of the value of an ageing St John, but maybe there might have been a note of appreciation, some registering of the fact that the prime of my career had been spent with the club. No, I had been paid my wages, received my bonuses — £1,000 for winning the title, the same amount for the Cup — and I had always been given my ten-shilling dinner money. The account, no doubt, was closed.

I showed the letter to Betsy and said, 'There's ten years of my life covered in a two-liner . . .' Even just a few months earlier, it might have been the spark for some indignant speech from me about the inequitable treatment of the professional footballer, how the best of him was taken and the rest thrown away. I could have rehashed the story of Andy Weir and a thousand others, but all that ground had been covered and perhaps nowhere more comprehensively, or comically in a bleak way, than in a little room at Anfield a few months earlier.

At Christmas time the club gave the players turkeys. The birds were laid out on a table and the lads were told to collect them after training. There was just one, roughly applied, rule – players who had families were given a choice of the bigger birds. I was still raw from my Newcastle experience when I went to collect the Christmas bird. The man in charge of the turkeys was an assistant secretary, Bill Barlow. It was plain that he disliked me and the feeling was mutual. Quite a background existed between us. From time to time, I had taken the mickey out of him. He was in the snooker room guarding the turkeys when I walked in. He handed me a scraggy little bird and I asked him if he was joking. I put down the turkey he had given me and reached out for a bigger one. He got in my way and said, 'No, those are for first-team players.'

After ten unbroken years, I was out of the first team for hardly a week and I could see the pleasure in Bill Barlow's face.

'You bastard,' I replied, and had to fight hard to resist an urge to lash out.

'If you've got a problem with this, you'd better go and see the boss,' he smirked.

I walked down the corridors of Anfield in some rage before knocking on Shankly's door.

'What do you want?' he said. I said I just wanted to let him know that I knew, finally, the writing was on the wall.

'How's that, son?' he asked.

'Because I just went to get my turkey and some bastard gave me a budgie.'

It was not the exit I had ever had in mind.

13

AND SO TO CAPE TOWN

Now the four of us were flying to a new life in Africa but, just as my mind had travelled back to the old battlegrounds of Scotland when Betsy and I headed to Liverpool in the Rolls-Royce for the first time, once more it was not so easy to break the chains of the past. Anfield may have been a dot receding quickly behind the wings of the airliner, but I knew then, as much as I know now, that I would never be totally free of its influence. I couldn't just cut away the tentacles that had taken ten years to grow. The place was a football planet out on its own, and it came back to me in so many different ways as I thought of where I had been for the last decade, and dozed and dreamed on the long flight to Cape Town.

I thought of all that past and then tried to imagine the future of Liverpool without Ronnie, Roger and me. Shankly, who always needed a hero or two, had a new one in Emlyn Hughes. Word was that another would soon be on his way, a Yorkshire kid of little pedigree, playing in the old Third Division, but one with bite and ambition and who had apparently deeply impressed the boss. His name was Kevin Keegan. Shankly had seen another spark with which to make a fire, but then, who really knew about the future so clearly? Some aspects of the past were still a riot in my mind. Quite often it had been so in the most literal sense. Even in those days, when referees were so much more tolerant of the harshest physical action, I was sent off six times, and invariably for retaliation. Growing up in Scotland, I had been told so often by the old pros, 'Get your retaliation in first,' but, with the single exception of the Tony Singleton incident, on those occasions when I was dismissed, I was not guilty of that crime. In every case but one I had simply given a little back.

The most bizarre incident, and sequel, came when I was sent off in a Boxing Day game at newly promoted Coventry City in 1967. At a free kick, one of their players, Brian Lewis, did to me what many years later Vinnie Jones would do to Paul Gascoigne. He reached behind and squeezed my testicles very hard. Not unreasonably, I thought at the time and, when I think back, still do, I whacked him on the chin and was sent off instantly. There followed a brief conversation between Shankly and me.

'What the hell happened there, son?' he asked.

'He grabbed my goolies, Boss,' I said.

'Come in tomorrow and see me,' he snapped.

After going over the details again the next day, Shankly took me to the treatment room where Bob Paisley was waiting. I was told to strip off and get on the table. As I lay there, Bob was dabbing a piece of cloth into iodine and boot polish. He then proceeded to daub the mixture on to my groin and genitals. As he was doing it, I asked him – ironically, of course – if he was getting as much pleasure as I was. Very quickly I looked as if I'd been in a road crash.

'That's enough, Bob, that'll do,' Shankly ordered, and Bob grunted agreement as he put away his painting materials.

Shankly then opened the door of the dressing room and summoned the press – the usual Sunday morning detachment sniffing out a story, or at least something dreamed up in the musings of the manager.

'Come in here, boys,' said Shankly, 'and take a look at this outrage . . .'

Naturally, the press were aghast and, much to Shankly's satisfaction, marched off to file dramatic stories of the sickening attack on my manhood. Unfortunately, the disciplinary commission were less impressed. I got the statutory three-match suspension.

When I was sent off for responding to some hair-pulling by Fulham's Mark 'Pancho' Pearson, Shankly made another attempt to score an upset victory in the football court, this time with an historic move. He was the first football manager to present film evidence in support of a player's appeal. The result, however, was another suspension.

I had come to Anfield blemish-free, but that was largely because of the extraordinary influence exerted by Rangers over the affairs of the Scottish FA. I was playing for Motherwell when I got involved in a scuffle with Willie Telfer, the Rangers centre-half who had been signed from St Mirren after Willie Woodburn was finally banished from the game for battering one too many opponents. The referee booked both Telfer and me and a few days later I got a letter from the SFA, demanding that I appear before the disciplinary committee, who were said to be in the mood for a crackdown. I got the day off work and went up to Glasgow where I found Telfer and a Rangers official looking very respectable indeed in their club blazers and ties. Telfer came up to me and said, 'Look, son, we'll just tell them we were having a wee discussion and everything should be all right.' After about two minutes' discussion, the committee chairman announced that the case was dismissed.

Right at the end of my career, some years after the flight to Cape Town, I would have one last eruption on the field. It came during a short stint at Tranmere, where I went to help Ronnie Yeats, who was the manager. I played just twelve games for Tranmere, who were doing well and heading for promotion to the Second Division, and had two serious mishaps. One was when I was sent off for the sixth time. The second was when someone fell on top of me at training and broke my leg.

I was enraged by the sending off in a night game against Blackburn Rovers at Prenton Park. I was tussling with their inside-forward Stuart Metcalfe. He was a clever player but he was plainly intent on winding me up, and eventually he succeeded. We came to blows. Ronnie pleaded my case but the referee would have none of it and sent off both Metcalfe and me.

As I headed off the field I saw Metcalfe disappearing down the tunnel and the red mist descended again. Here I was, an elder statesman of the game, being sent off the field in a Third Division match, and I was determined to take some revenge for this humiliation. I raced down the tunnel and burst into the Blackburn dressing room, where Metcalfe was untying his boots.

'Right, you little bastard,' I shouted. 'Now we can really sort this out . . '

At that moment, a guardian angel appeared. He was dressed in blue. A big policeman, perhaps atoning, so many years later, for the callousness of the one who hauled me into court in Motherwell for kicking a football in the street, wrapped his arms around me.

'Come on, Saint,' he said. 'Get in your own dressing room. Leave this be.'

Had the policeman not intervened after reading my body language so clearly as I charged off the field, there was every chance that my career would have ended in that little dressing room across the water from where I had known such glory. It was another occasion on which I had to be grateful that my instinct to right wrongs instantly, with my fists – a tendency that, if I'm honest, still had many years to run – had not led me into much deeper trouble.

Ronnie and I had been lucky enough to emerge unscathed after fighting our rearguard action in the restaurant on that bitter night in Milan, and if some of the flavour of my life in what passed for football's fast lane in those days is to be properly reproduced, a few other incidents probably need to be mentioned. One of the more hazardous came in a club in Puerto Banus on the Costa del Sol. Dave Sexton, who was manager of Chelsea, was in the company with his wife, who was talking with Betsy when some local character started getting fresh, asking for a dance. He was discouraged politely enough, but he persisted, at which point I gave him a belt. Dave and I agreed it was best to get out of the place. I was a little concerned about the possibility of guns – the Costa del Sol was, after all, not exactly a crime-free zone – after seeing the guy I had hit talking intently with someone in the shadows.

As I drove Betsy back to the house where we were staying – it had once been owned by Eric Sykes – I became aware that we were being followed.

'I'm going to deal with this,' I said to Betsy, and got out of the car. Two guys got out of the other car. I kept up an aggressive front, asking if they wanted some more. Clearly, they were intent on giving me, at the very least, a serious working over but I went in again and landed the first shot on my original opponent. Fortunately, it was a good one and plainly his friend was not so keen on joining in. They retreated to the car. Betsy had not been terribly impressed with any of this and, to be quite honest, I was quite relieved when we bolted the doors on the holiday house.

Betsy had been still less overjoyed by events on another holiday, this one in Majorca. We had bumped into George Graham, a friend of his from Glasgow, and George's then colleague at Chelsea, John Hollins. I was given dispensation by Betsy for a night out with the boys, which proceeded in the most sedate way until we strolled home around midnight alongside the empty beach of Arenal. Suddenly, two Spanish guys, one of whom looked extremely powerful, came rushing up to us shouting angrily. They accused us of wrecking their bar and were not interested in our claims of innocence. The big guy threw the first punch, and then, briefly, there was mayhem. We won the argument but as we left we heard them shouting, 'Police, police . . .'

Apart from rather sore hands, I was fine when I got back to the hotel, and gave Betsy no reason for alarm. Unfortunately, we were woken up by the police banging on the door. Both the police and Betsy were demanding to know what I had been up to. The police took away my passport and the following morning all of us had to report to the police station. I was particularly concerned because of the presence of my family; to be abroad, under investigation, and separated from your passport is not exactly an ideal situation when you are supposed to be taking a break from the pressures of big-time football.

The interrogator noticed our job descriptions as professional footballers and that seemed to impress him a little. Finally, he said, 'No more, no more,' and handed us back our passports. I didn't feel the need to confer with my co-defendants. In the face of that threat of Spanish justice, and the continued displeasure of Betsy, I had no doubt about where I now had to go – back to the buckets and spades.

One of George Eastham's selling points, I now reflected a little wryly, was the number of breathtakingly beautiful, golden beaches to be found around Cape Town. There was also the enticing prospect of a good life coupled with an opportunity to draw out some of the last of my talent for playing football, and as I did that, before big, enthusiastic crowds – Hellenic drew 30,000 plus for their big games – I would get the chance to develop my coaching experience. These new realities brightened my mood, and took away much of the angst I had felt in the last days under Shankly, but of course it could never be a matter of drawing a veil over the Anfield days. I knew that well enough as we flew towards the brilliant African dawn.

The new young giant of Anfield, 'Crazy Horse' Hughes, upon whom Shankly was now placing so many of his hopes, was obviously a key to the future, but back then at the start of the seventies there were no guarantees that he would play such a significant role in the development of the club's history. He didn't earn his nickname lightly as he charged about the field, and it was only thirty-five years later, when he succumbed to a long and painful illness after a brave fight, that I, along with some of my old team-mates, was able to take a totally dispassionate look at the player. Unlike most people I've ever known, in and out of football, Emlyn had two personas, one for public con-sumption, and one that in the dressing room, particularly, was often received rather less rapturously. But in the last analysis, late in 2004, Emlyn Hughes deserved all the accolades that came when he died. The one minute's silence so scrupulously observed at Anfield spoke of a respect due to the man who led the team for so long and with such passion and conviction. As Keegan would do later, Hughes made himself a great player by the sheer force of his will and desire.

My own team had longed to see Ronnie Yeats lift up the European Cup, and we would always believe we had been cheated of the chance to win the greatest prize that infamous night in San Siro. We knew it would be the fulfilment of all our work and our hopes, but when the veterans saw the honour fall to Emlyn there was no option but to be thrilled — for both him and the club. Emlyn came in to play alongside Ronnie Yeats and, like so many new Liverpool players, not least

Ronnie, he carried the weight of expectations built to the sky by Shankly.

When I came to assess Emlyn as both a footballer and a man on that day when the phone rang constantly and I was repeatedly asked to re-create those distant days, I tried to apply to the judgement all the knowledge I had acquired over the years while looking at my own successes and failures, and of all those around me. The most basic quality you look for − and it was one that Emlyn had throughout his career − is a tremendous basic enthusiasm. You can't instil that into a young player. You can tell him to work on his technique, improve his fitness, have a better sense of positional play, but you can't order him to be enthusiastic. He either is or isn't. In this respect, there was never a question about Emlyn Hughes.

Keegan arrived at Anfield four years after Emlyn, but it was uncanny how similar was the appraisal of the old guard. 'You should see this new kid,' they said. 'He's just like Emlyn. He never stops running.' But of course the years − and the knowledge and guidance of Shankly and Paisley − had to come into play before anyone could begin to see that either of them would be a great player. The most basic point is that when you are running around at 100mph, it is not that easy to get a look at the big picture. You only enjoy that when you take a step back, and that generally doesn't happen until a player is in his mid-twenties. You come into the game galloping and you never stop to look around and sometimes, if you have enough energy and talent, you find yourself at the top of the game, but it is utterly obligatory to take that pause. Then you see that, in the past, everything you have been doing has been spontaneous and you haven't really understood much of it at all. So you have to work towards a better understanding of the game. You have to see how you can retain an edge of effectiveness, exert yourself over all the other good-hearted lads attempting to make their names.

The problem, as Oscar Wilde said, is that youth is often wasted on the young. When I was growing as a player at Anfield, learning new tricks, developing my instinct for getting into the hurtful places on the field, I would think, 'My God, I wish I'd known this back in Motherwell − I would have been so much more of a player.' There are so many things to learn − where the ball is going to go, what the opposition is trying to do, what you should always do in certain situations, and always, vitally, how much of a risk you are ever going to take. Such decisions become automatic as you get older. At first, you do the right thing from time to time, with a flash of insight or instinct, but as time goes on, and you truly know the game, you are doing it all the time.

Emlyn faced all of this challenge of understanding how to play for others and not just himself with his inherent enthusiasm, listening to Shankly always telling him that the great profes-sionals did their own job first and then looked to see how they could help their team-mates. There was a reluctance in the Boot Room ever to play more than one youngster at a time because it meant that too many of the older players would be trying to help them at the expense of their own jobs on the field. It was for the same reason that, when Bob Paisley took over, he was wary of the new freedom to send on substitutes, especially late in the game and particularly if your team happened to be winning. One day Paisley explained his thinking quite eloquently by his standards, saying, 'I'd really rather have someone limping around, as long as he isn't doing damage to himself, because if you bring on some young sub, he just raises the whole tempo of the game, running around like a blue-arsed fly, and then all of a sudden the whole flow of your game can disappear, and you can finish up losing it.'

The first thing that struck you about the young Emlyn was

that he was completely self-absorbed. A small but telling indicator of this often came on the Friday before away matches, when the pre-booked lunch always had steak for the Protestants and fish for the Catholics, with the usual breakdown being seven steaks and five fish. Emlyn used to sit closest to where the waiters came out of the kitchen and would claim whatever the first one was carrying, be it fish or steak. As a result, one player would quite often be handed the opposite of what he wanted. This began to happen so frequently that Paisley, who was in charge of such matters, decided to investigate. Soon enough he identified the problem and delivered his report to Shankly, who immediately challenged his young hero. 'Christ, Emlyn,' he said, 'don't you know whether you're a fish or a steak?'

In the bar, Emlyn was the same, eager to get his hands on the first drink and picking up the first one that was put down, whatever the order had been. The older players quickly became restless, mumbling remarks along the lines of, 'Who's this kid coming along taking drinks that he hasn't even ordered?'

At that time, the players' wives had to sit in Shankly's pokey office beneath the old main stand while we showered and changed and returned to the real world, and it was only after several requests that the club eventually agreed to supply them with a cup of tea. When Fred Hughes, Emlyn's dad, a former rugby league international, found himself in the little office amid the tinkling teacups, he was very unimpressed and promptly invited himself into the directors' room for the after-match drinks.

Emlyn was often accompanied by his brother Gareth, who acquired some of the privileges of a member of the first-team squad. Whenever some new gear, perhaps sweaters or tracksuits, were being handed out, Emlyn would always say, 'Give me an extra one for our kid.' The advancement of the new boy ruffled quite a few in the dressing room and no one more so than Tommy Smith, who felt that he had been rather usurped after being for so long the rising star at Anfield. Tommy's resentment came to the surface during one match at Anfield when a dog ran onto the field and was gathered up by the referee, who ran with it towards the touchline. Emlyn got out of the dug-out to collect the dog and as he did so, Tommy muttered in my ear, 'What's the betting Emlyn asks the referee for another one for "our kid"?'

Such resentments were maybe inevitable as Shankly brought in his new order without any clean break with the past, with old players including Ronnie Yeats and me fighting for places with a gathering sense that our time was just about through. After my departure, Ronnie was moved to left-back but it was plain he was fighting a losing battle, and when I listened to the 1971 Cup final from my house in Cape Town, it was sad to note that he hadn't made the team. Ronnie had given way in the middle of defence to Larry Lloyd. Shankly had announced that Lloyd was the new Yeats, a new 'colossus', but that part of the manager's dream didn't quite happen – through no lack of encouragement from Shankly. Once, after Lloyd and I had quite a fierce collision in a training session, Shankly was enthusiastic about the aggressive approach of the big man as we drove back to Anfield. 'Christ, Lloyd didn't pull out against St John,' the manager said in a loud voice. He said it in a very approving way, and of course it was another signal of change. I pointed out, quite sharply, that it was to be hoped Larry never avoided the odd confrontation with someone just a little more than half his size.

Shankly was talking himself into the belief that he had a new breed of super-player at Anfield, but some of the results were a little irrational as he had to cope with the reality that from being an all-conquering force, we had lapsed into the status of nearly men. Of course, there were some stirrings of the old greatness.

Emlyn Hughes might be an irritant at times but no one seriously doubted that he had the makings of a great player. Ray Clemence had arrived at Anfield and Keegan was on the horizon. The signing of Alec Lindsay from Bury proved to be significant but before he emerged as a fine left-back, he brought a lot of confusion to Shankly's heart.

The fact was that Shankly hadn't closely supervised the signing but had entrusted it to his fine scout, Geoff Twentyman. This was the basis of an hilarious scene at the training ground. Lindsay had been an extremely solid left-back at Bury but he was being played in midfield in the reserves. Shankly was never slow to vent his feelings during a training session and suddenly he shouted at Lindsay, 'Look, son, we brought you here to do certain things and you're just not doing them.'

One of Lindsay's big problems in Shankly's eyes was that he wasn't Emlyn Hughes. In fact, he was the complete opposite. He was frank about his distaste for training and also candid about his chief passion in life – following the greyhounds. On the field he was always quick enough, but at training he was the slowest man any of us had ever seen. If he was lapped during a run, he would show no concern. Once Shankly bellowed at him, 'Christ, son, if I was you I'd trip up the man in front of me if it meant I wouldn't be last. You can't be last!' Lindsay shrugged his shoulders. Slowly, over the weeks, Shankly's anger was moving to boiling point as he considered the quite substantial transfer fee he had paid out for Lindsay. His distress flooded over during a training game and he called a halt.

'Alex, son,' said Shankly, 'when you were at Bury, you could go into the box and score.'

'No, Boss, that wasn't me. That was Jimmy Kerr,' Lindsay replied. Kerr was a very useful midfielder with plenty of poise and, as Shanky had pointed out, a flair for biting moves into scoring positions.

'No, no, Alex,' Shankly sailed on, 'at Bury you could take people on and stick it past the keeper.'

'No, Boss, that wasn't me,' Lindsay said again, 'that was Jimmy Kerr. I'm a full-back, that's all I do.'

Shankly, distraught now, turned to Paisley and said, 'Can you believe it, we've signed the wrong player.'

However, the mistake was rectified soon enough. Lindsay was moved to left-back for the next reserve game and he played quite beautifully. He had a perfect left foot, sculpting passes down the left-hand side of the field. He didn't get any quicker, but then it wasn't necessary. While Emlyn Hughes was pounding his way to the old football truth that sometimes mere running isn't going to get you very far at all, Lindsay was one of those who had an innate sense of where to be at any particular time. When Ronnie first saw him play at left-back for Liverpool, he too knew that his playing days at Anfield had come to an end.

In Cape Town, we were engulfed by the excitement of our new lives. Then, one spring day, I couldn't resist tuning in to my old and all-consuming existence at Liverpool Football Club one more time. I sat beside the radio, as I had in Motherwell as a boy, and listened to a football match. Liverpool lost the Cup final to the double-winning Arsenal, but they played well and for me there was a strong sense that another empire was in the making. Clemence was in goal, Lindsay played in the back four with Lawler, Lloyd and Smith, Heighway and Callaghan were out wide, Hughes and Brian Hall were in the centre of midfield and Alun Evans and John Toshack were up front. Peter Thompson was on the bench, Ronnie Yeats was in the stands and I was thousands of miles away. Then I went out to tend the barbecue, grateful to have something pleasant to do.

14
A MATTER OF DEGREE

SETTING foot in South Africa gave me rather more than a breath of new life. The invasion of sparkling colours, and possibilities, was captured perfectly by Betsy's remark that suddenly we were operating in Technicolor. From our rent-free house at Sea Point we could see the sweep of the coastline where the Atlantic met the Indian Ocean. Table Mountain loomed above us as we sat round the swimming pool and I made my first tortuous moves towards becoming a master of the barbecue.

The first of these ended in disaster. We bought the finest meat and the special wood for the cooking fire and parked on a stunning beach, but in my enthusiasm, I ruined the meat in the flames. A local, mourning the disaster, explained that the wood needed to burn down to a fine, white ash.

An irresistible urge to see more of this extraordinary country took hold. A few days before an away match in Durban, we piled the kids into the car and, without so much as a spare wheel in the boot, drove up the long and breathtaking coast. We went through native lands, and if we were taking risks, as it was suggested to us later, they could not have been more handsomely rewarded than on this great family adventure. More than once, Betsy and I marvelled that we had come so far from the twelve shillings and sixpence flat in Motherwell.

On a professional level, I could hardly believe my good luck. In my first big game I played well and we beat Johnny Haynes's

Durban City team before a packed house. It was so satisfying to play alongside the old Arsenal and England man Eastham. He still had a beautiful touch and a fine eye for the game, and he gave me free rein to develop my coaching ideas.

It was also a pleasure to be reunited with my old Motherwell team-mate Billy Hunter. After playing for Scotland he broke his leg, which more or less finished his career as a front-line performer. However, he had been touring the byways of football, done a stint in North America, and now he was enjoying something of an Indian summer in Cape Town, bringing a lot of craft to his new stage, if not all his old pace. We strode confidently to the championship.

It would be good to report that this tide of well-being was hazard-free, that after the strain of my last days at Anfield all points of conflict had disappeared from my life. This might have been true if one of the team, Calvin Palmer, the former Stoke City player, had not made an amorous remark to Betsy one night in a rather sedate sports club bar. Calvin was not a bad lad at heart, but he could from time to time say and do the wrong thing and it just happened that he was going through a tricky patch in his marriage. His wife and family were back in England and whether or not this was a cause for resentment, I didn't know. The fact was he made his remark and I hit him, quite hard. We went sprawling over the tables. The consequences were humiliating. We were marched off the premises and told never to return.

For obvious reasons, as the coach of the team and with quite a high profile in Cape Town, I would have been happy to express my regrets and let the matter slide away. Unfortunately, the affair nagged at Palmer and not so long afterwards, when we were sitting on somebody's veranda having a few cold beers, he raised the issue again.

'You know,' he said suddenly, 'you caught me off-guard that night in the sports club.'

I was a little taken aback and wondered why he would want to go over it all again, but instead of saying something innocuous like, 'Well, maybe so, Calvin, these things happen,' I found myself speculating out loud, 'Are you on-guard now?'

'Yes, I'm here,' he said.

The urge to hit him again was very strong, but this time I resisted it. Calvin could, however, see that I was ready and he just got up and walked away.

The lingering tension didn't help my coaching task of getting the most out of a player who was undoubtedly strong and useful but seemed to me to be suffering from a terminal case of the disease that had afflicted the young Emlyn. Palmer was a run-around player, one of those who too often made his moves without thinking too deeply about where they would leave him and his team-mates on the field. I spent quite a bit of time trying to explain to him that when an opponent played a one-two, you had no option but to go with the runner. 'You can be the best player in the world,' I said, 'but if you go for the ball and miss, you're dead. The best thing you can do, always, is fill the space behind you.'

However much I hammered it home, Calvin went his own way. In the end, I just had to shake my head and get along with him the best way I could, taking his strengths and living with the rest.

That was one of my wiser decisions. If sometimes I believed I could paint a message in big letters on the dressing-room wall and Palmer would miss it, he certainly had some good days, when he played powerfully, and at the finish of the season, when we were handed the league trophy, I could shake hands with him on the fact that he had, overall, made a genuine contribution.

Meanwhile, after the mishap at the sports club, life had flowed seamlessly, brilliantly. The schools closed at 2 p.m. and, with training done, the St John family could devote themselves to having a fine and unforgettable time. Every day was a gift of sky and sparkling water and beautiful flowers. Scott Street, Mother-well, and even the upwardly mobile Maghull were located on another planet – one painted in grey.

So, too, was Stoke City, Palmer's old club, deep in the Potteries, but that made it no less warming to receive a call from the famous old club's manager Tony Waddington towards the end of the 1971 South African season. 'Waddo', as he was known affectionately in the game, had made himself something of a legend in the way he secured Stoke's place in the First Division with the clever use of older players who had made their names at big clubs and come to the Victoria Ground to eke out the last of their talent.

The list of such players stretched out from Sir Stanley Matthews, who was brought back to Stoke in a brilliant publicity coup at the age of forty-six. Down the years, the Stoke payroll read like a lexicon of some of the game's most skilful players – Jimmy McIlroy, Jackie Mudie, Peter Dobing, Jimmy Greenhoff, my old team-mate Billy Stevenson and my current boss George Eastham. All of them had headed to Stoke for a late flowering of their talent. 'Stevo' swore to me that he had never been happier in his career than when he settled in at Stoke. He said that the players were treated well, and always with respect, whatever the state of their current fitness. Now, Waddington was coming for me.

Apparently, he had been talking to Eastham, who had given a good report on my performance. When Tony came on the phone I told him I was most anxious to continue my coaching work but he said, 'Ian, I want you as a player, that is my need right now . . . but I'll pay you a £10,000 signing-on fee.'

Ten grand! In all those years at Anfield, when the great prizes of the game were always within touching distance, I had never sniffed such a reward. It made me rail all over again about the way Shankly and his friend Sir Matt Busby had worked to keep down the wages at two of the most successful clubs English football had never known. When Waddington made his offer, I tried to bury my surprise at the scale of it, pausing for a decent moment or two before saying, 'That sounds fine, Tony. We have a deal.'

Within a day or two, and while I was still congratulating myself on my good fortune, the phone rang again. This time it was Noel Cantwell, manager of Coventry. I told Noel, whom I liked a lot, about the Waddington offer and said that, unfortunately, I had given my word to Stoke. Noel was persuasive, however. He said that he would match Stoke's offer in every respect – and add the bonus of a coaching job. Regretfully, I told myself it was only a dilemma if I entertained the idea of breaking my agreement with the good and generous football man Waddington.

Given the appeal of the offer from Coventry – who had shown a lot of ambition since their promotion to the First Division – I thought that I could at least put the situation to Waddington, while stressing that I realised I had already said yes to him. I told Tony that Noel had offered me good terms with the promise of a staff coaching job. Even though I stressed my willingness to go to Stoke if he felt we had a firm arrangement, Waddington was emphatic that I consider myself a free agent.

'Look,' he said, 'you've had a great playing career but, whatever you've done in the game, it can be hard getting your foot on that first rung of the ladder. Go to Coventry with my blessing.'

Eddie Plumley, the Coventry City secretary, flew out to Johannesburg to seal the deal. Hellenic were playing there and the formalities were swiftly concluded. Eddie Plumley was one of the game's outstanding administrators and he should really have gone on to play an important role at the Football Association. Instead, he moved to Watford and was there during their years of prominence in the late seventies and early eighties. Everything was as agreed between Cantwell and myself and the confidence created in that meeting in Johannesburg was confirmed the moment we arrived back in England.

We needed a house – we were still paying rent for our old club house in Maghull. Liverpool, who had paid £2,500 for it ten years earlier, always refused to sell it to me for the price they paid and now they were demanding the market value, £5,000, which I couldn't afford. My wages at Liverpool had never permitted the luxury of saving, and I had to find a new house with virtually nothing in the bank, my signing-on fee having been paid in stages. The problem was solved the moment one of the Coventry directors, a Mr Mead, heard about it. He took me on one side and said, 'Don't worry, here's three grand – give it back to me when you can.'

It was an amazing feeling to be treated like that. Suddenly, I didn't feel like Oliver Twist holding out his bowl. I felt like somebody who had something of real value to offer. It meant that, after more than fourteen years of marriage, Betsy and I could finally get our names down on the deeds of a house. It was, for me, as quite a famous footballer, an extremely late rite of passage. We moved into our new and splendid house in Armorial Road in the village of Stivichall, with great pride. We were just across the road from Noel and Maggie Cantwell. We had joined the ruling classes, or at least it was nice to think so.

There was a tremendous atmosphere at Highfield Road, the sky blue stadium. Jimmy Hill had left the club in excellent shape. Before that, as chairman of the Professional Footballers' Association, he had led the fight for players' rights and, with the help of the courtroom battle of George Eastham, he had broken the maximum wage limit. I worked on the PFA committee that waged the campaign, with brilliant guidance from the canny secretary Cliff Lloyd. Jimmy was the front man and more than a match for the old-school Football League types led by the long-time secretary and old navy man Alan Hardaker, who so often made his contempt for the professional footballer quite clear.

If there were any doubts on the Coventry horizon, they were to do with my ability to justify myself in First Division action. I had done well in South Africa, in spite of the knee injury and a back problem, but I was thirty-four now and I worried that the greater pace and physical hardness at the top level of the English game might at some point find me out. Noel was emphatic. He thought I could be a good influence on some fine young players out on the field, whatever else I contributed as a coach.

Without question, there were some fine young players to nourish at Highfield Road. Dennis Mortimer was an outstanding young midfielder, quick and skilful, and in Willie Carr we had a midfielder of classic Scottish guile and trickery. Ernie Hunt was a character from the West Country, who showed off his ability when he wasn't leaving us creased with laughter or ducking training. Once he was sent off for refusing to give the referee his correct name. He insisted his name was Roger Hunt despite the referee's warning that if he didn't stop taking the mickey he would be dismissed. The trouble was that Ernie – who was also known as the 'Fastest Milkman in the West' after a Benny Hill record and TV sketch – had indeed been christened Roger.

Strength was nicely distributed through the team. The line was led by young Billy Rafferty and, at centre-half, Jeff Blockley was a potential England player. He was soon partnered by an extremely tough Scot, Roy Barry, and Bill Glazier was a solid goalkeeper.

The problem for the team – and for me as a player – was that too many players were too inexperienced, and the benefits of my background had to be spread too thinly on the field. We needed a bit more iron – and nous. I also had some injury problems. One consequence was the basic one that we were simply not winning enough games. Inevitably, Cantwell was getting some heat from the chairman, Derek Robbins, a man who was very sure of his opinions before running off to South Africa with his secretary.

However, I did have one supremely satisfying moment in the blue of Coventry. The club had never beaten Everton, which meant that I had rarely gone on to the pitch with more determination than on the afternoon I was greeted with waves of the old taunts that had been so fiercely applied in all those derby games. I have to admit I don't remember the details of my winning goal that day at Goodison Park, no more than those of my hat-trick in that first appearance for Liverpool, at Goodison, but I will always remember the satisfaction that swept through me when the stadium fell silent.

That uplift was one of the sweetest moments of my career. However, I would have given anything to have traded it for my experience that season against Liverpool. I raged to do well and maybe that was a big part of the problem. My better judgement should have told me that I just wasn't fit enough to play against my old club with any chance of doing myself, or the team, justice.

A few days before the game at Highfield Road, I'd injured myself in training. At Liverpool I'd never sprinted for more than thirty yards, but Noel was straining to get a bit more out of the Coventry lads and he had us doing hundred yard stretches. During one of these I felt a pinging sensation in my calf, as though someone had fired a gun at it. I went straight to the treatment room with the heavy suspicion that I had done something quite serious.

During the build-up to the game, I tried to mask the damage while I jogged around the training field. Noel would come into the treatment room and ask, with anxiety in his voice, 'How are you doing? What do you think about your chances?'

'I think I'm going to be all right,' I reassured him.

Unfortunately, it wasn't so easy to reassure myself. I knew I was in trouble but I was desperate to prove a point. I kept telling myself, 'You're going to play and you're going to show Shankly how wrong he was. You may never get a chance like this again.'

In my desperation to play I convinced Noel I was fit and broke the cardinal rule of professionals that says you should always be honest about your fitness. I was playing in midfield against Ian Callaghan, who, as always, was motoring along quite relentlessly. I didn't have a chance. To compete with a man such as Ian you have to be 100 per cent and on top of your form. Long before the end of the game I had to signal defeat and limped off the field. I felt angry with myself, and embarrassed. I had handed vindication to Bill Shankly on a silver platter, and I knew as I hobbled back into the dressing room that I would always regret this day when, like some optimistic kid, I had refused to face reality.

Liverpool won the game, which was a great personal defeat for me and another heavy blow for Noel. Nothing compounds a crisis more than a home defeat. The directors are embarrassed, they feel pressure from the fans, and it was of little surprise when soon afterwards I received a Sunday morning call from Cantwell.

'The chairman wants me to drive over to his house in Leamington,' he said. 'I think it could be serious. Do you want to come along?'

The case for Noel's defence was clear enough. He had to argue that the club had to be patient and invest a little time in an outstanding bunch of young players. In this, Cantwell would certainly be proved right. Most of them would go on to excellent careers with other clubs. I could hear most of the discussion from the hallway of Robbins' big house, where I was parked while the other two went into the lounge to battle over the future of the club. Noel argued that this was the time for a good chairman to be strong and look to the future. He gave examples of the benefit of this policy, but he wasn't making much progress. Indeed, voices were raised before he marched out of the door to tell me, 'I'm finished.'

Robbins said that he wanted me to stay on, but I told him I couldn't do that. Noel had brought me to the club, I was his man, and I couldn't profit from his downfall. Tony Waiters, the former England goalkeeper, who had worked at Anfield as a coach and had earned his FA badges with me at Lilleshall, made the same decision. Robbins appointed a caretaker from the scouting staff before bringing in my old team-mate Gordon Milne under the watchful eye of Joe Mercer. Coventry didn't go down. They survived another thirty years in the First Division and then the Premier League.

I had put myself out of work with the decision not to walk in Noel Cantwell's shoes, but I didn't regret it for a moment. Back then, a certain rough code of conduct existed and one of the more basic rules said that you had to be loyal to the guy who took you to the ball. However, I never lost my feeling for Coventry or forgot the exhilaration I felt when they gave me such a warm welcome. Much later, when I was working in television in London, whenever I could I would make Coventry's Saturday afternoon game a staging post on my return home to Liverpool, where Betsy and I eventually set up home again.

My reward for loyalty to Noel Cantwell was an immediate invitation from George Eastham to go back to South Africa. I asked George if I would get my old coaching job back. It was a pointed question because I had heard from my old team-mate Billy Hunter that George's father – also George – had taken over the Hellenic training, a fact that had sparked Billy's defection to the rival Cape Town City. George reassured me that everything would be as before, so I promptly agreed to return to what had been one of my happiest hunting grounds. Only a month or so of the season remained, so we decided that, apart from a brief holiday trip, Betsy would stay at home with the children. It was just as well because it turned out to be a tumultuous time.

My reunion with George didn't go well.

'Well, Ian,' he said, 'the old man is doing a bit of coaching and I don't want to upset him.' I was angry.

'George,' I said, 'you've brought me out here under false pretences. We talked about this. You agreed I was coming back as player-coach.'

George said that we just had to hang on for a little while but I wouldn't accept that. The club made some efforts to keep me but I said no. This was a point of principle and I was heading home.

It was a depressing situation but I decided to make the best of it and spend a few days in a city I had come to enjoy very much before going back to re-make my future career once again. Then Billy Hunter intervened. He said that he was very happy at his new club and that the coach, Frank Lord, was very interested in my joining them for the rest of the season. Cape Town City offered me the same money I would have been receiving at Hellenic, and I was pleased to take the opportunity.

As is so often the way in these affairs, my first game for City was at Hellenic's Green Point stadium. It meant that I would return not as an old favourite but a new enemy and I quickly confirmed that status when I 'did' George in just about the first tackle. The crowd were in uproar and, after the game, the fiery Hellenic chairman Babbalatakis came storming into our dressing room. He pointed his finger at me and roared, 'You kicked my players, you kicked George . . .' This was unfortunate because Mr Babbalatakis had been one of my great champions. It was clear that the old relationship was over.

I had immediately regretted my action because I'd had a great relationship with George, the club and those passionate Greek characters on the board. I had submitted to a fit of pique and had already decided it was not my finest hour. I was wrong to react so fiercely. I had shared a lot of affection with these people, and they had looked after me well, right up to the moment George found himself entangled with an obligation to his father. I should have been more understanding, and I like to think that I learned a lesson.

The wounds inflicted when I decided my friend and former colleague was due a bit of a kicking ran deeper than I ever imagined they would. This was confirmed to me many years later when I was walking down a platform at Euston Station and a porter, who had a broad South African accent, came up to me and said, 'You're the man who kicked Mr Eastham.' Babbalatakis also received something of a kicking from the South African government. He was sent to jail for a swindle involving government coal.

Despite the arguments with my old club, the new stint in Cape Town mostly went well, even though Lord was a little too keen on physical preparation, even for my liking. He listed all the great players he had brought out from England, including Bobby Moore. Malcolm Allison had also been along to advise him on training and game preparation. However, I told Frank, 'Come on, at our age we don't need running or weight lifting. Just give us the ball. We won the League at Hellenic last season without any great physical regime. We just played football and won the League, surely that's a good way to go.' I also made the point that running down Table Mountain was a little hard on my constitution. 'Bloody hell, Frank,' I said, 'when you're running down that mountain, you can't stop.'

Frank was a good coach — he now works for Manchester

United in pursuit of talent in Cape Province – but he did over-emphasise the need for super-fitness, especially in ageing players, and for me there was a price to pay. I still live with it today. Frank had me playing in my old position up front, even though I pointed out to him that it had been years since I operated there. In one game, I stretched up for the ball, lost my balance and fell on my head. Frank took me to a chiropractor the following day, named, appropriately enough, De Beast. After explaining that something had popped out in my neck, he put me into a kind of dentist's chair and proceeded to attack me. This went on for quite some time. I was swearing and shouting as he twisted me about and cracked away at my neck. Finally, De Beast stepped back.

'Is that it, then?' Frank asked.

'Oh yes, he will be able to play in your next match,' said De Beast.

I walked out of the surgery feeling like Frankenstein's monster. In the next game, I got up for the first ball that came to me in the air, flicked it on and felt my neck go again.

I was walking around with a neck collar for quite some time. Then, when I returned to England, my daughter Elaine was one day talking enthusiastically about her progress as a gymnast. She demonstrated a backward roll and asked me if I could match it. Of course I could – for a trained athlete it was a basic move. So I did my backward roll and went straight back into a neck collar. Plainly, I had been marked by De Beast.

When Ronnie Yeats, now manager of Tranmere Rovers, called to say he needed my help – 'I'm a desperate man,' he said – I felt my neck, quite gingerly.

'Aye, Ronnie, I'll be along.'

Desperation in football, after all, is almost always a matter of degree.

15

AN APPETITE
FOR THE JOB

Tranmere Rovers, as it turned out quite quickly, and brutally, were at the end of the road, but when you are a player with not too much left, you don't think in that way. You always believe you still have another season in you – you can hang on, find from somewhere a last vestige of all that made you a force, a natural-born winner. You want that last season because who knows what might happen? Something magical, maybe. At heart, footballers will always be dreamers, always have a bit of the boy in them, and this is true even in the most unpromising circumstances.

Ronnie, Tommy Lawrence and I, reunited in the Third Division, agreed that this still held true in 1972 when we changed in the little dressing room of South Liverpool, a junior club who played on a wind-blasted field near Speke Airport. We were playing there in an early round of the FA Cup, and we knew it would be a tough afternoon in front of a capacity crowd of 2,000. South Liverpool had a long, battling tradition, a fact always underlined when one of their most rugged and accomplished products, Jimmy Case, ever went on the field for Liverpool and then later Southampton. South Liverpool's Holly Park stadium would never be mistaken for the headquarters of the Red Cross.

I looked up from tying my boots and said to Ronnie and Tommy, 'It's a long way from Wembley, boys.' We laughed in the half-sad, half-mocking way of veterans heading for the last round-up, but the important point was that we had a game to play, and to win, and we duly did this, despite the fierce opposition and the jeering catcalls of the locals. We lost the next Cup-tie at Bradford, but we were going well, fighting Bolton Wanderers for the Third Division title and, apart from the bitter skirmish with the Blackburn Rovers player Metcalfe and the sending off, I was doing better than I could have expected at this combative level after my injuries in South Africa.

Dave Russell, a Scot, one of those classic football men so immersed in the game they never stop to consider the odds they are facing, had managed Tranmere through the sixties, and now he was acting as club secretary and adviser to Ronnie. When I arrived at Prenton Park, Dave outlined my deal. I would get a £5,000 signing-on fee, paid in instalments, which wasn't bad for a Third Division team, and a wage that would eke out the days until I could find something better as a coach back in a higher division.

The end of my playing days came during training at the Birkenhead Oval, a big, flat sweep of a dozen council-owned football pitches. I suspected right away that it was all over when a young player, Malcolm Moore, tackled me and then fell on me awkwardly. My leg was trapped beneath me and I knew immediately that it was broken. I shouted, 'Don't touch me,' as I lay in the muck. The trainer Johnny King, another Tranmere veteran who would later serve a total of fourteen years as club manager in two stints, supervised the rescue operation. He had me lifted, very carefully, on to the back of one of the younger, stronger players who carried me to a car.

When we arrived at Prenton Park, Ronnie was just about to leave for the training ground. He had some papers in his hand and looked harassed. His face fell when he saw me hobbling on one leg. He drove me to the hospital after I'd showered, very tentatively. It was a horrible, rain-lashing day. I had always imagined a more glorious exit, but then I did go in a tackle, I fell in the traces, on the most basic of duty.

When Russell saw me a week or so later he seemed a little embarrassed. He said, 'Ian, we know we owe you half your signing-on fee, but with you not being able to play again, and with money being so scarce here, we wondered if we could make an arrangement.' I cut him short. I said that he could forget about the other two-and-a-half grand. It was almost certain that I would have finished at the end of that season, Tranmere had been as generous to me as they could be, and I appreciated that very much, given their circumstances. I said that it was my contribution to a good little club. They didn't make promotion that season, but they would have many successful seasons, and when these came along I was always delighted. It is as though a part of your life has risen up again, igniting old hopes for a set of colours you once wore.

However, the bleak day at Birkenhead Oval meant, more pressingly than ever before, that I had to fight to make something of the rest of my life. I had the familiar problem of the ageing footballer — a still young family to support and uncertain prospects. Still, it transpired that the terrible moment on the muddy training ground had brought a very substantial financial benefit.

Bill Shankly had imposed an unwritten but hard and fast rule at Liverpool. Ex-players could have their testimonial only when they could no longer play. It was something that had come into his head about not having current players distracted by the effort to come out of the game with something in their back-pockets. As far as he was concerned, there could only be one priority and that was the next match. If the club decided you deserved a testimonial, well you could get on with it in the rest of your life when you were no longer part of the club. Suffering a broken leg as I headed towards my mid-thirties made me eligible immediately.

My friend Dave Sexton said that he would bring his Chelsea team up to Anfield at the end of the season, and Liverpool confirmed that the ground would be available. That was all a club did for their old players on such occasions – they lent them the ground for a night. With the help of a committee – mine was headed by a friend, Liverpool businessman Wilf Preston – all the other costs have to be met by the player. I was grateful for the swift granting of the testimonial because I was among the last wave of players in English football who didn't enjoy a pension. This was my great chance to gain a little financial security, something to put against all those years at the top of the game.

I was excited by the possibilities when I thought of Roger Hunt's testimonial. He had quit before me, and more than 40,000 attended his farewell. It was depressing, then, on the day of the match, to look out of the window of my mother-in-law's flat, which was just around the corner from the ground, to see the rain pouring out of a grey Liverpool sky. I knew what I was looking at; I knew the psychology of the football fan. He would be coming home from his work soaked and, however fondly he remembered the great days of which I was part, he would think doubtfully about going out again into the wet and dreary night.

I was thankful that 28,000 did make the effort and when the proceeds were counted, and the stewards and the police paid, and the electricity bill met, I was handed £15,000. For the first time, I had a little financial security and in those circumstances, I always told myself, it would be wrong to envy the beautiful night that Roger enjoyed or the fact that later, after Bill Shankly left, Tommy Smith had his testimonial a few nights after he had helped to win the European Cup.

I trained hard for my last appearance at Anfield because I wanted to go out with a touch of style, but it was an ordeal, the worst I'd experienced in all my career of fighting injury and often playing only with the help of a pre-match jab. The worst thing was trying to get full weight on to the broken leg. The Tranmere trainer said, 'Just hop over the line,' but the message from the brain was difficult to transmit to the leg, and there was a desperate fear that, once again, it would snap like a twig. I got through well enough and, with the help of the Chelsea boys, I managed to score. The new stars, Kevin Keegan and John Toshack, were among the first to congratulate me on the field and a great roar surged through the rain, creating a little more moisture, this time in my eyes.

Finally, it was over. I would never cover this ground again as a player. I would never again pass under the sign that proclaimed simply, 'This is Anfield'. I was told Bill Shankly was at the ground but I don't recall any contact between us. That would have been the perfect time to restore some of the best of our old relationship, but perhaps too many hard words were too fresh in the memories of two stubborn men.

Such musings were cut short by a phone call from Motherwell. I was wanted back at Fir Park as manager, that first significant rung of the ladder Tony Waddington had said could be so elusive. Bobby Howitt, an old professional, had had eight years in the job and, after a bout of relegation and immediate promotion, hadn't been able to move them above mid-table. The word was that the team had grown old and needed a shot of new blood and new ideas.

It was strange going back to the old ground; because of the tricks of memory, I had forgotten how pleasant it was around the stadium. When I thought of the old town, I had remembered the tenements and the factories rather than the pretty parkland that separated Fir Park from an industrial landscape. The meeting with the chairman Ian Livingstone, a young lawyer who plainly cared a lot for the club, went very well. I had my coaching badges and my experiences at Coventry and in South Africa but it seemed that I didn't have to sell myself very hard. I had a name in the town and the game, he said, and he thought with my background I could have a good impact. My basic salary would be £5,000 a year with a £2,000 bonus if we did well. Flushed with the testimonial money, we bought a fine big, stone-built, semi-detached house near the ground and just down the street from the chairman.

When I thought about the pressures of the job, and the expectations that I carried, the money wasn't so great, but I was delighted to get the job and a car – and, most importantly, the chance to make my reputation as a bright young manager. I would take the best of Bill Shankly and all the other great men I had got to know in the game, and I would inject my own feelings about what was right in the handling of footballers, and I would make a great career. It seemed a relatively simple matter back then.

One of my first tests lay in how quickly I could identify the weaknesses of my new team and then rejuvenate it. One key was how accurately I applied the old Shankly verdict – which invariably signalled that a player was about to be shipped out of Anfield – that somebody had lost 'half a yard'. Half a yard is not a physical measurement so much as the spotting of dwindling ability to deal with the vital tasks. Half a yard is no more than a single outstretched stride, but in football it is everything. It is the difference between getting to the ball first, and then getting clear, and losing it. From the first training sessions it was clear that too many of my new players had lost that mythic half a yard. I had to do a rebuilding job.

Acquiring good basic fitness seemed to be a challenge for most of the players and I immediately recruited Ian McCafferty, a local boy who had been an Olympic distance runner. He had a tremendous impact on our pre-season training. He was so fit he could stay with the leaders when we ran through the woods, then go back to check the stragglers, before returning to the head of the group. He was doing twice the running of everyone else and it seemed as though he was scarcely drawing a breath. I couldn't expect such a standard through the club, but he was an impressive model.

Apart from pushing up the fitness level, the other priority was the classic chore facing all new managers. I needed to get a few new players in, but I could do that only after moving a few out. Here, I could not have been more fortunate. Manchester City's manager Johnny Hart needed a goalkeeper and had taken a fancy to our Keith MacRae. He was quite a spectacular shot-stopper but I wasn't so sure about his basic soundness, his judgement in controlling his area. This weakness was well concealed, however, when MacRae played brilliantly against Celtic, with Hart sitting in the stand. The following day, the City chairman Peter Swales came on the phone to me with an offer of £50,000. The chairman was excited by the prospect of such a windfall, but I said, 'No, we have to turn them down. In this situation, the kid is worth a lot more than that. They want a goalkeeper badly and they think that Keith is a great one.'

I worked the price up to £80,000 but by then Livingstone was beginning to sweat. His instinct, enforced by my telling him that I could more than adequately replace MacRae for a fraction of the City money, was to grab at Swales' latest offer. The chairman was in his office down the corridor and we would confer after each call.

'I really think we should say yes,' he said after I reported that Swales had just insisted he was making his final bid at £90,000. I told him we could still do better. I had told Swales that, as far as I was concerned, my main concern was that I had a goalkeeper for the next match, and I was happy that I had a good one. I didn't want to change that until he met our evaluation.

Finally, Swales said, 'We'll go to £100,000.'

'Well, that's what I was thinking of – we're talking business now,' I replied.

The club had never got their hands on so much money. The chairman was delighted by my negotiating technique and, just to round off the operation, I was able to tell him that with the help of our chief scout, Peter Keachie, we were able to sign an excellent replacement in the experienced and extremely sound Stuart Rennie, who at the time was a Falkirk reserve.

Rennie made 176 appearances for Motherwell and is generally rated as one of their best post-war goalkeepers. A few years later, he confirmed that status by refusing to leave the field after suffering a gash in his face when the team were losing 2–0 to Kilmarnock. Stitches were inserted in his cheek at half-time and the rest of the team were so inspired they finished up 5–4 winners.

The success of the Rennie signing, on top of the chairman's pleasure that such a profit had been made on MacRae, gave me the perfect chance to do something for Keachie, who had been such a brilliant servant of the club since the days when he took John McPhee and me to Fir Park. One of the first things I did when I arrived back at Mothetwell was to look up Peter's wages. They were a nonsense, scarcely more than basic expenses, and I told the chairman that this was a man who just had to be looked after if we really expected to compete with the likes of Celtic and Rangers.

When I told Keachie that I had managed to get him a substantial rise, he said he was grateful but that I shouldn't have done it. I said, 'What are you talking about? Nobody at this club deserves it more than you.' He loved the club and he brought to it the vital instinct to spot the boys who had the makings of good professionals. This is something that has to be separated from the mere recognition of natural talent. Most people can see that a kid has a good touch and a bit of flair but Keachie, like all the great men of his business, could go far beyond that. He could see a boy play for ninety minutes and take a perfect bead on his character. Such a talent will always be the lifeblood of a successful football club.

My first move was for my old Liverpool team-mate Bobby Graham. He had joined me at Coventry and was disappointed when I walked away with Noel Cantwell. When I called him, Bobby said he would be delighted to join me again – Motherwell was his home town – and he remained at Fir Park long after I left the club, forming a tremendous partnership with another local boy, Willie Pettigrew, whom I had promptly lifted from part-time professional status.

That proved to be one of my better decisions as a manager. Willie won five caps for Scotland. He had genuine pace and a terrific eye for half a chance. In 159 games for Motherwell he scored at fractionally more than one goal every two games – a phenomenal strike rate. Bobby's fine touch perfectly complemented Willie's talent, and after he had done very well in a victory over Celtic, Jock Stein called Bill Shankly to deliver a mock heavy reproach.

'Bill,' he said, 'you didn't tell me about Bobby Graham.'

Shankly, chastened by this rebuke from the man he adored, sheepishly admitted, 'Aye, John, the boy can certainly play.'

Bobby's move to Motherwell provided him with a fine and satisfying run in the game after his career appeared to have been wrecked by a broken leg. I was still at Anfield when the disaster occurred, and Ronnie and I went to see him in hospital. We took some beer along and were sipping from the bottles when we heard Shankly clattering down a corridor. We put the bottles under the bed for the duration of his visit. Bobby represented some of the best of Scottish football. He had craft and skill, and plenty of wit and imagination. He came straight from the bargain counter at £15,000.

This was more than I could say for a player known around the club as Billy Bungie, real name Campbell. He was one of the first to greet me when I arrived. He came into my office unannounced and when I asked him what he wanted, he said, 'I just wanted to let you know that I'm the best player you have here.'

'Well, Billy, I think you need to let me be the judge of that,' I said. Maybe it is needless to say, but he was one of the first out of the building.

Another good acquisition to place alongside Bobby and the emerging, fully professional Pettigrew was Willie Watson, a big defender who had threatened to become a star as a schoolboy, winning fifteen Scottish caps at that level. He got lost in the competition at Manchester United and played just twenty-five times for them in eight years. He looked a very sound prospect indeed and came straight into the team, helping us to the League Cup victory over Celtic on that night when MacRae drew the attention of Manchester City. We also beat Celtic at home – the club's first league win at Parkhead since the Second World War.

While this rebuilding process was going on, we played some eye-catching football and never looked like slipping below the comfort zone in mid-table. That was as much as I could reasonably have hoped for in a season of major reconstruction. I felt very much at home in the manager's office and confident that I have given myself the right preparation for the challenge. The years at Anfield were, I thought, swiftly proving their value.

The coaching courses had no doubt been beneficial but dominating everything I thought and did were the lessons learned under Bill Shankly and his brilliant sidekicks. The most valuable of these, I was sure, was the one about the need for honesty in all your players. That conviction led me into a brief but fierce dispute with one of the team's more popular figures, Jim 'Jumbo' Muir. After playing up front he had been converted into a centre-half, where he had considerable physical presence. He was an extrovert character in the mould of Jack Charlton but, to my mind, that was where the comparison ended.

I was furious with Muir when he failed to get back quickly enough after making a mistake – a lapse that cost us a league match at Morton. I blasted him in the dressing room and a few days later told him that I didn't see any future for him at Motherwell. We did a deal with Dumbarton but before it went through Muir came to my office demanding a loyalty bonus. I told him that time-serving – he had been at the club for seven years – was not necessarily the same as loyalty deserving of a pay-off. I said that if he had been straight and honest with me I would have done all I could to get him something, but I didn't think that had been the case. So it was time to say goodbye. It is only by such small but significant rites of passage that a manager can prove to his players that he demands serious professionalism of them.

My appetite for the job had also been stimulated by an invitation to join a party of managers analysing the World Cup in Germany that summer. Bertie Mee, Arsenal's double-winning manager, had put together an interesting mix of football men, including Bobby Robson, Terry Venables, Bobby Campbell – who had played a vital role in developing Mee's all-conquering team – and Keith Burkinshaw. Later, as Tottenham manager, Burkinshaw startled English football with the major coup of signing Argentina's World Cup-winners Ossie Ardiles and Ricky Villa.

One vital aspect of the job, I believed, was creating a winning psychology at the club, and a key aspect of this in the Scottish game was standing up to the might and the aura of Jock Stein's Celtic. In this, I got a flying start with the League Cup victory at Fir Park. Before the game, Jock Stein told me his team wanted a 'bit of a stretch' out on the field and asked for some balls. I agreed, as any young manager would have done in that situation, but I did think the request a little odd, especially as it took just a few minutes to drive from Glasgow to Motherwell. Were Celtic really saying, 'We run the show here. We do what we want, when we want?'

Whatever the truth of that suspicion, I decided that I would make a similar gesture when we went to Celtic Park for the return leg. When my players ran out on to the field well before the start of the match, I said to one of the groundstaff, 'Get us some balls, son.' He said, 'Oh no, I can't do that. We don't do that.' I said he had better see the manager and tell him that Motherwell wanted to loosen up after their journey up to Glasgow. Jock came along to say that we couldn't use the balls out on the pitch, we had to go behind the goal. I didn't make an issue of it, but I did think Jock's response was interesting. It confirmed my instinct that you had to stand up to him and his club.

We beat Celtic that night and it would have been by a more convincing margin if one of our free-kick routines had met with its just reward. We sent a short ball forward and the guy who received it got to the goalline and cut it back. We had a man on the six-yard line who should have scored easily, but he missed and Celtic were extremely lucky to survive. It wasn't the most inventive free kick that had ever been conceived, but it was sharp and we had worked hard on it in training. Jock looked over to me from his seat in the directors' box and his expression said, 'Okay, that was a bit special.'

Above Forget the Liver Birds, the Cup is ours. Big Ron is hoisted on to Willie Stevenson's shoulders while the rest of us celebrate on the ground. *Left to right:* Geoff Strong, Peter Thompson, me, Gerry Byrne and Ian Callaghan.

Below Liverpool parade the Cup. *Left to right:* me, Geoff Strong, Ron Yeats, Willie Stevenson, Gordon Milne, Chris Lawler, Ian Callaghan, Peter Thompson, Roger Hunt and Tommy Smith.

Above Jack Charlton of Leeds United gives me the big, bony shoulder as Gary Sprake gathers the ball.

Below The header of my life – the great Johnny Giles looks on as I send the ball past full-back Paul Reaney, guarding the line.

Sometimes I found the game so easy I could play it standing on my head – well, it's a
pretty thought.

Above Celtic goalkeeper Ronnie Simpson dives at my feet and smothers the ball in the European Cup Winners' Cup semi-final at Anfield in 1966.

Below A moment of celebration – the ball is in the back of the net for Liverpool's first goal in the European Cup Winners' Cup semi-final with Celtic.

Right Jock Stein meets Bill Shankly at Renfrew Airport before Celtic's semi-final first-leg game with Liverpool. Stein was still a year away from winning the European Cup but Shankly was already convinced that he was one of the great managers.

Below The Anfield High Command – (*from left*) Shankly with some of his 'general staff' Bob Paisley, Ronnie Moran and Joe Fagan.

Above Leave this to me, Emlyn – I still have something to show the rising star Emlyn Hughes in the 1969–70 season.

Below My last Liverpool hurrah – I turn away after scoring against Swansea Town in the FA Cup in January 1971. I came on as sub, wearing number 12, in my last game for the club.

When I think of that moment, all the excitement of that time comes rushing back. I felt as I had done in my early days at Anfield. I believed I was on the brink of something major. I loved this business of being in charge of a team, getting players to gel, opening their minds to new possibilities. We trained like demons and there was the wonderful sense that the boys were enjoying every minute of it.

Every day I went to work with a new idea buzzing in my brain. Sometimes it worked, sometimes not, but always there was a new thought, a new attempt to improve. I had been dazzled by the strength and movement of the Dutch in the World Cup – they would surely have won if they hadn't got a little carried away after jumping into an early lead against their bitter rivals West Germany in the final – and I wanted some of that from my team.

I have to admit that occasionally my short temper flared in the heat of all that ambition and, maybe inevitably, it led to an explosion on the training field. The recipient was Jim McCabe, a skilful, crowd-pleasing player who had grown up in the Coatbridge area, a place so tough that it was said a local custom was to eat the first born. The day before a match I told him I was leaving him out of the team and I was curious to see his reaction. 'Caby', as he was known affectionately by the Fir Park faithful, responded poorly. At the Friday session, I told McCabe to keep tight on a certain player but he seemed to be making a point of ignoring my instructions. Repeatedly, the player he was supposed to be marking was allowed to run free. I stopped the play on several occasions to remind McCabe of what he was supposed to be doing and on the last one he began to talk back. The red mist swirled and I whacked him. He went down, and when he got to his feet I ordered him to the dressing room.

I carried on with the training session as if nothing had happened and, naturally I suppose, I had everybody's attention.

I told someone else to pick up McCabe's marking duties and we got through our work quite effectively. However, by the end of training I was filled with remorse. I gathered the players together and told them, 'I'm sorry, boys, I lost control of myself and I shouldn't have done that. You have my apology.' There was a short silence and then, from the back of the group, one of the players said, 'He fucking deserved it.'

There was no excuse for my action, I knew, but however roughly and ill-advisedly it had been done, another point had been made. I felt that the reaction to the incident confirmed my best hopes that I had most of the players with me. Thus encouraged, I marched to the dressing room and delivered McCabe a severe dressing down. The result was that he was a good player for the rest of my time at Motherwell. He had plenty of natural gifts and for a little while he produced them consistently.

The trouble with McCabe was that he had a crucial lack of deep ambition and application, and less than two years later, when I had left the club, I was not surprised to see that he had been given a free transfer. Jim McCabe was one of the lads who would produce his best only so long as someone was prepared to drag it out of him, and in the team that I was hoping to build his presence was never likely to be long-term.

I didn't know that my own stay would be so brief. Looking back, I see that perhaps I was learning more than ever before that nothing in life is as simple as you would like. I was enjoying my job more than I ever imagined I would. I could see the pieces that go into a winning football team falling into place in front of my eyes, but there was a complication, and it was a serious one.

Betsy, my wife and the greatest support I would ever know, was not enjoying her return to Scotland. Yes, we had a fine house and my job was going very well. She had joined a golf club and was developing a passion for the game, but the return to her home town had not been as she had imagined and hoped. Her old friends could never be as close as they had once been. They had their lives and she had hers. They had gone along different routes. Betsy's mother was still in Liverpool, where she had made a life. We were paying a price for the dislocations of football life. This was a growing tension in our lives when suddenly everything changed. I was rushed to the crossroads of my football career, taken there by a phone call from Jock Stein.

16

THE WORST SIDE OF FOOTBALL

APART from being the all-conquering manager of Celtic, Jock Stein was the highest point of contact in Scottish football for all the major English clubs and so his question in the summer of 1974 sent my head whirling in the wrong direction.

'How would you like to return to England?' he asked.

My first thought was that Liverpool, with Bill Shankly having just resigned, were calling me back to Anfield. In that flash of time, it made a certain amount of sense to me. I knew the place inside out. I was popular on the terraces, a fact that would win some breathing space for a club no doubt reeling from the sudden exit of the man who had made them what they were. It was also true, I didn't think anyone could deny, that I had made quite a dashing debut at Motherwell.

It wasn't Liverpool, of course. It was Leeds United, the reigning champions of England, a team filled with players I liked and respected – players who, I believed, shared my view that if you played the game, there was a heavy obligation to win. Ten years earlier I happened to have scored the goal that ruined one of their first big days as a great team, but they had earned my admiration and never, not even in the most bitter battles between us, had they lost it.

'Don Revie is going to run the England team,' Stein told me, 'and a contact of mine on the Leeds board has been on. I've put your name forward.'

Stein asked me if I was interested. I said I was but first I had to speak to the Motherwell chairman. I had it in my contract that if an English club came in for me I could speak with them, but sometimes these matters are not as straightforward as that. However, the chairman was fine, saying, 'Ian, I've told you all along, if a club in England is interested, we won't stand in your way. You've been honest with me and now I'm being honest with you.'

I called Stein back and asked if he would meet me in the car park of Glasgow Zoo. Jock was waiting in his big car when I arrived. He told me that he had arranged a meeting for me with Leeds at the halfway point of Scotch Corner on the A1.

'Go and see them there,' he said, 'and do your interview, but I think you'll get the job.'

Three Leeds directors, led by the chairman Leslie Silver, were waiting for me at the hotel, which immediately told me that this was serious business. Leeds were offering me £15,000 — three times my Motherwell salary — and I couldn't get one thought out of my head — 'God, I've just won the football pools.' Most exciting, though, was the idea that I would inherit a brilliantly professional team. I knew them all — Johnny Giles, the brains of the team, Billy Bremner, my old Scottish team-mate, Norman Hunter whom I admired despite his assassination attempts, and of course my fellow Lanarkshire man, Joe Jordan, one of the most formidable young strikers in football. As the Leeds directors asked how I would approach the job, I gave what I considered sound professional responses. I talked about the need to evaluate the team, but any point I made was prefaced by my respect for all that had been achieved at Elland Road down the years. What I was reserving for the team, when I walked into the club as manager, was something the Leeds directors might, or might not, have wanted to hear. I knew that Revie had difficulties with some of the directors, so I thought it better to hold back on the speech I intended to give to the players.

It was going to be simple enough. I was going to say to them, 'Let's keep it going in Don Revie's memory. You guys have had the best boss and the best team. Keep it going, even though he's gone. Show all of football what he left behind.'

I knew they all loved Revie and I wasn't going to try to get in between them and their feelings for the man who had shaped their careers. This wasn't mere strategy. I believed it was right as I considered the good luck of any man who took over this team, one that would be competing in the European Cup after running away with the English championship. The meeting went well with the directors. I drove home to Scotland with the warmest feelings. Betsy would get to go back to England. I would get a fast track to the top of football and the chance to show what I could do with some of the best players the game had ever seen. I wasn't going to make a revolution at Leeds. I was going to go with what was right, qualities that had served the club so well.

When I arrived home, Stein called. He said, 'My man says that everything went great and the job will be yours.' I told Jock that I, too, was optimistic but that I wouldn't get carried away. As I left the meeting, Silver had told me that he had one other interview.

That other person, as the football world would learn with some surprise, given the background of relations between the man and the club, was Brian Clough. He was appointed within twenty-four hours. To say that I was gutted scarcely covers the scale of my disappointment. It came over me again in fresh waves when I studied a picture of Clough, having briefly broken a holiday in Majorca, arriving at Elland Road wearing shorts, carrying squash rackets and leading his son Nigel by the hand.

I didn't think that was showing great respect to the champions of England. The team had never been less than fully competitive for more than ten years, but of course that was merely by way of an opening insult. His introductory speech to Giles and his teammates, as most football followers now know well enough, was quite different from the one I had in mind. He said that they should throw all their medals in the rubbish bin for all they mattered to him. He thought they were cheats. He told Eddie Gray, a brilliant winger whose career had been bedevilled by injury, that had he been a horse he would have been shot long ago. It was not easy to believe he had uttered these crass remarks, and when I thought about what they would do to the morale of the team, and how gratuitously insulting they were, it was like spreading a ton of salt across my wounds.

It may be that there is no such thing as a perfect job in football, and certainly this is something you can easily read into the careers of even the most successful managers, but that knowledge didn't take away any of the pain. I knew the quality of Leeds very well. Clough said they were cheats but that came from some personal agenda that I just couldn't understand. Maybe Leeds had been too successful against his teams and had presented too many problems. They were hard and ruthless, but in their refusal to concede the possibility of defeat, they were surely a manager's dream.

I had no difficulty in admitting that the job had gone to a man of much greater experience and more solid achievement. He had lifted an excellent Derby County to the title. (Later, he would go on to perform brilliantly at Nottingham Forest, where he guided the club to two European Cups.) However, that was of little comfort when he waded so arrogantly towards the low point of his extraordinary career. With each new disaster for Leeds in the opening of the 1974–75 season, and each story of Clough's outrageous behaviour, my own sense of loss deepened.

Then, for me, the knife was twisted. In the time it took Clough to make an absolute mess of the job – just forty-four days – and the Leeds board to see that they had made a terrible mistake in picking a brilliant football man for the wrong place and the wrong time, I had ruled myself out of a second chance. Jimmy Armfield, then manager of Bolton Wanderers, was appointed as Clough's successor and, despite the sneers Leeds had suffered under their new management, Armfield found a team good enough to get to the final of the European Cup. They lost, largely because of some outrageous refereeing, to a Bayern Munich team containing the great Franz Beckenbauer and Gerd Muller.

I had disqualified myself by accepting an offer from a man who said he was going to revolutionise that fine old club, Portsmouth. He said he was going to put enough resources in my hands for me to do for Pompey what Revie had done for Leeds and Shankly for Liverpool. I believed him and since then I have rarely known a day when I haven't regretted it. It was the great disaster of my football life. In the great mistake, there was also the greatest of ironies. The man who put me in for the Portsmouth job was Bill Shankly.

'How would you like to go to Portsmouth?' Shankly called to ask. 'You know they're a club with a great tradition and, though they're in the Second Division now, they have fantastic potential. Their chairman has called me and told me about his plans – and the money he's going to put behind them. I've put your name in the frame.'

He went on to talk about the meaning of Portsmouth Football Club and how they carried a great name in English football. I've never doubted that he was sincere in what he said – indeed, it may have been that he saw this as some way of finally healing the rift that had developed between us – but he had ideas about Portsmouth that were rooted in the past.

The chairman of Portsmouth was John Deacon, a property developer. He arrived at our house in Motherwell with his wife Dolly, a very large woman, in a Rolls-Royce, which of course gave a good impression. He talked about the future of his football club and there was no doubt it was exciting talk. I would have an immediate budget of £400,000 to sign new men, which in 1974 meant that a lot of talented players would be within my reach. He also said there were plans, and the finance, for a new stadium on the edge of town, a modern stadium with plenty of car parking. I said to Betsy, 'This really is exciting – £400,000 to spend on new players and a new stadium.' In a different way, it was as exciting as the Leeds job. At Elland Road I would have inherited a football world created by another man. At Portsmouth, I could make my own.

After a brief talk with Betsy, I said yes. I also told the Deacons that they would not have to pay any compensation to Motherwell for my services. I explained that I had gone into this when the Leeds job was in the offing, and that the Motherwell chairman had confirmed that I was free to move to any English club, but Deacon insisted that he would pay Motherwell. Despite being told quite pointedly that this was not necessary, he gave the club the equivalent of the last two years of my contract – £10,000. This rang a small alarm bell. It was a little worrying that this man who said he was going to make such an impact on football was capable of such a poor business decision.

On the drive down to Portsmouth, Deacon stopped to show us the site for the new stadium. It was just a mile or so away from the famous old Fratton Park stadium – a perfect location with easy access from the motorway. I might have been perturbed by Deacon's generosity to my old club, but it did seem that the Portsmouth project was indeed in place. In fact, thirty years on, Pottsmouth fans still await their shining new stadium.

Earlier I had gone to see my new club perform at Nottingham Forest, and although it was true that my predecessor, John Mortimer, had spent quite a bit of money without obvious success, the team he had left me was good enough to beat Forest, which was an encouraging sign. Still another was our first sense, when Betsy and I started to look for a house, that this was an impressive town with a big catchment area. Although my new salary had fallen short of the Leeds proposal by £5,000 a year, it was still a good rise and I had the strong feeling that if the lost opportunity at Elland Road was a terrible blow, here might be some considerable compensation. At least, it was pretty to think so – but for such a little time.

The most sobering moment came when I reviewed my troops. Despite the victory at Forest, there was little cause for confidence. Plenty of well-known names were at the club but they belonged to players who had been good, or at least eye-catching, in the past. It seemed to me they didn't have too much to offer today.

A classic example was my old adversary from Coventry, Brian Lewis – the guy who grabbed me so painfully at the free kick. He was a talented player and outside of that old outrage I found him a likeable lad, but he was shot physically. I remember an early training session of Portsmouth when I grabbed him by his jersey and tried to get him running. I did everything to get him fit but I found it impossible. He hadn't looked after himself and I remember thinking that there would come a day when he just crumbled out on the field. He would pay the price for neglecting the basic fitness that is the first duty of a professional.

Norman Piper was a neat, clever midfielder but he was plainly past his best. Paul Went, a big defender, had built a strong reputation as a young player, but his instincts didn't seem to be truly professional. Peter Marinello had been described as the next

George Best, but he had misfired badly at Arsenal after coming down from Scotland as a big signing. Now it was clear he was never going to make it as a top player, which was something that unfortunately had never occurred to him. Up front, Ray Hiron wasn't good enough. He was partnered by Richie Reynolds, who had a fish and chip shop. I had a theory that he was eating most of the product. There was also a serious problem with the goalkeeper. His knee would go after he made a dive or two, and the big question was always whether he would get through the game.

The most conscientious member of the team was Kenny Foggo, a winger who had played for West Bromwich. At the end of my first season he said, 'Ian, I wish you had come here a bit earlier, but I just can't do it now.' I said I understood what he was saying, but that at least he had been trying.

All of this would have seemed hopeless without the chairman's assurance that when I deemed the moment right, when I had thoroughly examined my resources, I could make major moves into the market. In this, I had an additional advantage – a big network of scouts led by Tony Barton, who would later move to Aston Villa as an assistant to Ron Saunders, then take over to lead the team to victory in the European Cup.

After one early board meeting, when the directors had talked proudly of the club's network of scouts, Barton came to me with an enthusiastic report about Tony Woodcock, who was playing in the reserves at Forest. According to our scout, he represented an absolute steal at the asking price of £12,000. Given Woodcock's development as a fine striker at the top of the English game, in Germany and on the international stage, it would have proved to be an excellent call. I told Deacon about Woodcock and added that it was undoubtedly time to make our first move towards shaping a new team. 'I'm afraid there's a slight problem,' he said.

'My money is tied up at the moment in a business project. I'm trying to sell some land.'

I was sickened to my stomach and told him I couldn't believe what I was hearing. He had sat in my house in Scotland and, in front of his wife, had sworn that I would have £400,000 to spend on the team. It was the key reason why I had taken the job. I knew then, without any doubt, that I had made a terrible mistake. Later, when matters had got so much worse, I brought up his promise of the £400,000. Dolly, who had now been co-opted on to the board, was present and Deacon turned to her and said, 'I don't think I said that, did I, Dolly?' She said no. What I said is not repeatable here.

In my rage was the terrible awareness that I had been conned. This was the part that was so hard to take. I had warned Ronnie Yeats against the pitfalls that can be created by smooth-talking businessmen. I prided myself on a reasonable level of street smarts, but I had simply walked into this catastrophe, and it did no good to tell myself that I had acted on impulse after the terrible disappointment of losing the Leeds job. That was no excuse for taking Deacon's proposals at face value. I should have done a bit of investigating. I had made the big move of my football life and now I was trapped. I told the Deacons they were liars. It was the start of three years of desperate struggle, my worst days in football, days which for the first time made me question my place in the game. In my three years at Portsmouth I was able to make just one move into the market, and it came near the end of my time there, when all my hopes of building a new Liverpool or Leeds had been stretched to breaking point. I had been involved in a daily battle for survival, and over three years that can wear you down. Lawrie McMenemy, then the Southampton manager, told me that he was letting go his striker Paul Gilchrist, who had played in the club's FA Cup victory over Manchester United in 1976. I could have him for £5,000, and it could be paid in instalments. Such was the belated, pitiful launching of John Deacon's brave new football world.

I did what I could to strengthen the team, bringing in young John McLaughlin and Doug Livermore from Liverpool when it was clear that they would not make it at Liverpool. McLaughlin was a clever midfield player, but he never proved strong enough for the top of the game. I hoped he would have a bigger impact at a lower level, but he was dogged by a physical frailness that Shankly had identified when the boy was trying to make his way in the first rebuilding of the sixties team.

Portsmouth had become a skid-row football club. The phone was cut off. We managed to keep my line open for incoming calls but if I wanted to make one, I had to walk over to a public telephone box. Sometimes I had to queue. Sometimes the players had to do their own laundry. An elderly woman was brought in to do the washing because the laundry company said they would only continue if we paid a bill that had been accumulating over months. The coach company withdrew their services and we had to use our own cars on match days.

I used to rail against that Liverpool habit of handing out ten shillings for dinner, but now the practice seemed like part of a fantasy world. Before games we stopped at a Happy Eater for tea and toast. We were operating as an amateur team.

I refused to quit, however. I believed, maybe a little irrationally, that I might just turn things round if I fought hard enough. A shocking aspect of the situation was that the potential of the club remained high. We had a fine youth system led by Ray Crawford, the old Ipswich Town hero, who learned something about beating the odds when winning a league title under Sir Alf Ramsey. We were consistently doing well against the big London teams at the youth level and this fact produced still another edge of tension between the Deacons and me.

Directors of London clubs were expressing admiration for some of our best prospects and when this happened in the West Ham boardroom after one youth team game, Deacon came over to me and said, 'West Ham like the look of one of our boys and I think they're prepared to make an offer.' I said there was no way we could run down the lifeblood of the club. Everything else had been cut back but the boys did offer some promise. It was soon after this that I received a letter from Deacon (reproduced opposite). It said everything about the problem of trying to bring success to the club. I was bound to report to him any interest expressed in any of our players. He had to know of any approach because it was vital for the survival of the club to get some money in, even if it meant we were relegated.

It was inevitable that there would be interest in such a fine group of young players. We beat Tottenham at White Hart Lane, and more than held our own against an Arsenal team that included such prospects as David O'Leary and Graham Rix, hand-picked players tracked down by the scouting staff of one of the most powerful clubs in the country. Making such a foundation was the only satisfaction I had. I believed I might just be able to drag the club up out of the mire, and doing it without money would, I thought, be a feat that would help to develop my credentials as potentially the manager of one of the top clubs. It was, however, hard, grinding work. Sometimes I would go to pubs and social clubs for darts and bingo nights to grub up money to cover some of the incidental costs of running the football club. Quite often players' wages cheques bounced and when I told the chairman he would say, 'Oh just tell them to re-present.' You could wait several weeks for your wages.

One Saturday the club secretary Jimmy Dickinson, a stalwart Portsmouth player in his time and a former England interna-

PORTSMOUTH
FOOTBALL COMPANY LIMITED

Registered Office:
FRATTON PARK, PORTSMOUTH, HANTS. PO4 8RA

Tel: 31204-5

Our Ref: BJD/SMD.

PRIVATE AND CONFIDENTIAL.

Please reply to: "Marlborough House"
139, Bassett Avenue,
SOUTHAMPTON, SO1 7EP.

26th February, 1975.

I. St. John, Esq.,
Manager,
The Portsmouth Football Company Limited,
Fratton Park,
PORTSMOUTH,
Hants,
PO4 8RA.

Dear Ian,

I confirm my telephone conversation with you today, when I intimated it was absolutely necessary that we sell one or two players prior to the deadline date of the 14th March.

I did outline to you the serious financial position that the Club is in and told you I am constantly having to put my hand in my pocket to cover wages and other items, and whether or not the selling of any of our star players means the effecting of results, even to the event of relegation to the Third Division, it is imperative at this stage that we realise cash for some of our players.

I would be most grateful if you would kindly circularise the First and Second Divisions with the players that we talked about, Piper, Marinello and Went. I would also be grateful if you would kindly let me know the names of any Club that make enquiries and in fact keep me in the picture as much as you possibly can.

I am sorry to have to press this matter, but it is absolutely imperative for the continuance of the Club, to realise some cash immediately.

I do appreciate what you are doing. I hope you understand and appreciate my point of view. I am sure the wheel of fortune will eventually turn and put us in a better position financially, but at the moment for mere survival, we must realise some cash.

With best wishes.

Yours sincerely,

B.John Deacon.

CHAIRMAN: B. J. DEACON   VICE CHAIRMAN: D. J. SPARSHATT   DIRECTORS: G. C. SPRIGINGS
J. D. P. COLLETT   A. R. L. OLIVER   E. W. REEVES   F. P. FAULKNER   D. K. DEACON   J. P. N. BROGDEN
MANAGER: I. St. JOHN   EXECUTIVE MANAGER: R. TINDALL   SECRETARY: J. W. DICKINSON M.B.E.

Registered in England   Registered No 123480

tional, paid for the match ball after I told him the club didn't have the money. On another occasion, my friend Kenny Lynch, the entertainer who was working with Jimmy Tarbuck at nearby Hayling Island, paid for a ball.

In all of this disaster, I was at least spared the classic ordeal of a football manager fighting the odds. The crowd never barracked me, even when we were relegated to the Third Division in my second season in charge, 1975–76. This had a lot to do with the work of a local reporter, Mike Neasom, who saw clearly what was going on and, much to Deacon's anger, painted a true picture of the club's difficulties. I suppose Deacon would have preferred a rather different slant, one in which all the blame was heaped on me.

When I look back to those days, the one comfort is the quality of the young players who were nurtured into good careers despite a situation that so often seemed hopeless. One of them was goalkeeper Alan Knight. He spent thirty years of absolute devotion at Fratton Park and was eventually given an OBE for his services to the community. Other graduates from an embattled Portsmouth were the defenders Steve Foster, who played for England, and Graham Roberts, who signed for Tottenham, then Rangers. Chris Kamara, a powerful player and now something of a cult figure with his reports for Sky television, was signed straight from the navy. His fee was the price of buying him out of the service – £200.

That sort of enterprise and swap deals were my only means of strengthening the team. Another problem the Deacons hadn't told me about when they came to my house in Motherwell was that the club was operating under a transfer embargo. Even if the club had some liquid cash to move into the market, they couldn't do it until they paid off all their debts on previous transfer deals. Some of them, including one for £20,000 to Fulham after the signing of Went, were substantial.

Despite that restraint, I did make a few deals, and the best of them was when I got David Kemp from Crystal Palace in an exchange deal for my old friend George Graham. Kemp was a good professional and a good player – he had scored a lot of goals for Palace – and he brought exactly the right attitude to the club. George had arrived at the club in a less successful exchange for Ron Davies, the once formidable Welsh striker. I had originally earmarked George for the leadership role Kemp eventually filled so well.

Davies had been a tremendous front man but it didn't take me long to establish that he was running on near empty. He could no longer do the one thing that had made him so menacing. Once he terrified defenders with his ability to get above them. Now I doubted whether he could jump over a line on the carpet. He was an agreeable person, not an ounce of trouble, but he knew that his best days were long gone. I heard stories that he was spending quite a bit of time in the pub. Fortunately, these reports hadn't reached Manchester United manager Tommy Docherty and he fancied he could still get some service out of the big Welshman.

My old Scottish team-mate Paddy Crerand was working as Docherty's assistant and the three of us went over a lot of the old ground over drinks in the United boardroom. The deal was struck most amiably – Davies for Graham, with no money exchanged after we valued both players at around £40,000. Graham was pleased about the move. He had been edged out of the United first team and wanted a little more action on the field before he ended his playing days.

I brought George back to Fratton Park as a prize, telling the young players, 'Now look at this guy. He's a top professional, so very skilful – you'll learn a lot from him.' It was a nice theory but it fell apart the moment George looked around the club and saw the state we were in. Soon enough he voiced his misgivings to me. He said that he didn't like the mood of the dressing room and he felt that he had made a mistake in coming down.

'George, I brought you here as a leader,' I told him. 'Yes, I know there is poison in the dressing room, but we have some good kids in there and I want them to inherit a few good habits.'

I was terribly disappointed when George replied, quite coldly, 'No, Ian – leave me out.'

Ten years later, when George moved to Arsenal and started to build his championship-winning team, I speculated on what his reaction might have been if he had asked his captain Tony Adams to be strong in the dressing room, and the big lad had turned to him and said, 'Leave me out, Boss.'

George's departure was triggered by a dispute on the training field with Went. As training eruptions go, it wasn't anything exceptional. Went had gone clattering in, but I was still surprised at the way Graham had risen to the bait.

Went had a bullying streak and it surfaced most unpleasantly when he injured a young kid who, while not making much headway in the Football League, had been offered a deal in the North American Soccer League. I confronted Went, asked him if he realised that he had wrecked the boy's chances of making a little progress in the game. The conversation got intense to the point of becoming physical, but the big man walked away.

Went led a faction who plainly wanted to see me off but my mood was to make sure that the opposite happened. By the time I left, most of the malcontents had been moved on, Went going to Cardiff.

I also had some battles with the full-back, Phil Roberts. I called him a cheat for his habit of going down too easily and claiming to be injured. Later, when I'd just packed in the job in the most bizarre circumstances, Roberts asked Billy Hunter, who had joined me at Fratton Park in yet another reunion, about his Cup final tickets from the club's allocation. I told Billy to tell him that if he wanted to claim his tickets, he should come round to my house. He never showed up.

Eoin Hand, the Irish defender, was another problem but it had nothing to do with any malign attitude. Although he went on to become team manager of the Republic of Ireland, I have to say that he never struck me as a potential maestro of tactics. Before a game at Fulham, I did a lot of work in training on the threat presented by the strikers John Mitchell and Viv Busby, a very handy pair. Time and again I impressed on Eoin that he had to get in front of one of the Fulham strikers at the near post. Mitchell and Busby had developed a routine that was very difficult to defend against. One would get to the near post and back-flick across the goal, where the other would be waiting to knock in the ball. In training, Eoin repeatedly took up a position behind the striker, giving him the chance to produce the back-flick.

However, things seemed to be going well enough during the match. With just a few minutes to go we seemed certain to gain a valuable point. Then the nightmare scenario unfolded. Fulham won a corner, Hand stayed behind Mitchell, who got in his back-header, and Busby headed in what I thought was the winner. I stormed around the back of the stand to the Craven Cottage dressing room, rehearsing a very stiff dressing down for Hand, but when I got to the players I was astounded by the buzz in the room. As I was marching angrily to the dressing room, they had produced an equaliser. My lecture to Eoin lost a certain intensity.

By the time I finished, the job had finally reached the point where I considered it impossible. The breaking point was my decision to sell Peter Marinello to Motherwell. Peter was a pleasant lad with some talent, but he found it impossible to follow any kind of basic instruction. All week in training I would ask him to do certain things but then when the match arrived he proceeded to do precisely the opposite. A typical example would be if we had perceived a weakness in a rival full-back. In training, I would say now run, and keep running, at your marker, and often he would do it splendidly. 'Brilliant, Peter,' I would say by way of encouragement, 'you're skinning him.' However, in the match all that was forgotten. In one game, when he had been told to attack the left-back, he showed up on the other side of the field within minutes. At half-time I asked him what he had been doing. 'Oh, I just thought I'd test out the right-back,' he told me. It was at that point that I decided it would be as advantageous to start talking to the wall. Marinello had to go.

I told the Deacons that Motherwell had come in with a decent offer and I strongly recommended selling him. There were the three of us in the room. Dolly Deacon chipped in, saying, 'Oh no, John, we can't sell Peter – I like Peter.' The chairman nodded and then I made my second biggest mistake since agreeing to join Portsmouth.

'That's it,' I said. 'This is a joke. I'm finished.'

The cardinal rule in football management is that you don't resign. You wait for the axe to fall and take the compensation you are due. The following day, Deacon said to me, 'So you've resigned?' I told him that I had reconsidered and decided to carry on. I had put in a lot of hard work and I didn't want it to end in this way. He told me that it was too late. He had appointed Jimmy Dickinson as manager and I was suspended. I guessed immediately that he didn't have the money to pay off my contract if I insisted publicly that I had withdrawn my resignation, something he knew would be reported fully and honestly by my journalist ally Neasom. The suspension was his convenient solution. He could pay me the few weeks remaining on my contract.

It was not quite what I had imagined in those thrilling days that followed the phone call from Jock Stein, or when I looked over the still untouched site of the stadium where a new football power in the land was about to rise. Instead of such dreaming, I had lived through the reality of the worst side of football. I was not sure whether I would ever get back my appetite for being in the game.

17

ANOTHER CROSSROADS

T HE INSTINCT to walk away from football, so unthinkable at
any point over the previous twenty years of my life, received
encouragement from two sources. One was completely unex-
pected, the other had been the strongest influence in my life ever
since I first collided with it, romantically, in a Scottish dancehall.

Betsy had been appalled by my experiences at the hands of the
Deacons and she speculated on whether the game would ever be
a secure and appropriate place for a grown man to earn his living.
I didn't want to accept that view, but even as I argued that what
happened to us at Portsmouth was the result of a set of peculiar
circumstances – not least the killing disappointment of missing
out on the Leeds job, which would have been such a sensational
development in my career – I wasn't sure I was convincing
myself. To encourage any doubts I had, I had only to look
around at the fate of many of the great managers after so many
years of superb success. Even the great Jock Stein was feeling a
chill at Celtic Park and soon enough he would receive the
derisory offer of a job in the club's pools development office. Bill
Shankly was a lost soul after breaking away from Anfield. If this
was what happened to the legends of the game, what could those
scuffling in the foothills truly expect?

This debate was raging in my head when, in the spring of 1977,
I received a call from Paul Doherty, the son of the great Irish
player Peter, and now head of sports at Granada Television. He

asked me if I would like to appear on a Friday football show. I said, with what I liked to think was casual irony, that I would check my diary but off the top of my head I didn't see any reason why not. It was not as though I was being besieged with offers for my services. I drove up to Manchester from Portsmouth with no great expectations. The fee wasn't great but it would eke out my pay from Portsmouth, and it might be worth reminding football of my continued existence.

The show went well enough and Doherty asked me to come back the following week. I did the spot for those last few weeks of the season and, after the last one, Doherty offered me a contract to cover the following season. I was in no position to refuse. Soon my role began to expand. I asked Betsy how she fancied being married to a star of the silver screen.

My basic duties were to continue with the Friday preview slot and to cover a game with Granada's number-one commentator, Gerald Sinstadt. I would add what was known as 'colour' to the commentary and pick the man of the match.

It was a difficult time domestically. Elaine had left school but Ian was still in the middle of it and, for me, the travelling was becoming quite arduous. We had to make some decisions and, given that my work was now based in Manchester and Betsy's mother was happily settled in Liverpool, we decided to move back to the north west. Initially, we stayed with Betsy's mother, then bought a house in Liverpool. I was back in football's heartland in a new and quite challenging role, but one that didn't tear at your guts on a daily basis. There was also some encouragement that I might indeed make a new career for myself.

On the strength of the shows, at the end of the 1977–78 season I was selected for the ITV team covering the 1978 World Cup in Argentina. Jack Charlton was also part of the TV squad. Jack, with whom I had always had an easy relationship, was then manager of Sheffield Wednesday and during the course of the World Cup he invited me to join him and his faithful assistant Maurice Setters at Hillsborough. He said I could continue with my television work; he could see a role for me as a special coach, someone to go into the details of developing the players in the way he wanted.

It was a stimulating time in South America, and a good time. It was tremendous to be around the game, and able to use some of my knowledge, without all the pressure that comes with trying to run a professional club with limited resources. The trip was also significant in that I met again, and forged a great relationship with, John Bromley, a former journalist who was head of ITV sports. He was a tremendously relaxed character and towards the end of the assignment he suggested that Jack and I might like to take a little rest and recuperation in Rio de Janeiro on the way home. Neither of us required our arms to be twisted and the break in Rio was superb. I have a lasting image of lying on Copacabana beach in the hazy sunshine, watching Jack's head and long neck poking out of the ocean swell as though he was some old seahorse. Each time he thought he had made dry land, the rip tide tugged him back, and any chance I had of helping him out was hindered by the fact that I couldn't stop shaking with laughter. Fortunately, eventually he struggled out of the sea under his own power.

Betsy noticed the difference in me when I returned home. I was infinitely more relaxed than when the bells of Pompey were tolling for me just a few months earlier, and I was also, I liked to think, rather fetchingly suntanned.

There was no doubt in Betsy's mind. Football, or at least being tied to a certain club, living at the mercy of the whims of directors, should no longer be part of our future. She put it in her usual forthright fashion. 'If you go back to football, Ian,' she said, 'that's it for our marriage as far as I'm concerned.' It was the heaviest of ultimatums and I could only be grateful that my infant television career appeared to be thriving.

If Betsy's position was a hard one, I could understand it well enough. I had been aware of what the struggles of Portsmouth had done to me. I realised how strongly the tension had built itself into my daily life. There had simply been no respite. The job was all-consuming. I thought about it, talked about it, every minute of the day, and then I dragged all of it back home in the evening. Night-time was the worst. Some nights I just thrashed and turned, and abandoned the hope of slipping into oblivion. Often, I would get up, make myself a cup of tea, and then start the whole churning process all over again.

The TV work was not without its pressures, however. Some of them came from my sponsor, the man who got my TV career off the ground, Paul Doherty. Paul was a bright guy who, in many respects, was ahead of his time. He saw the value of bringing former professional players into his game and irrigating the coverage with real insight. What he wasn't so good at, though, was guiding a new boy through the potential ambushes of his business. There was no element of training. You went out there and did it, and if you didn't do it well, you would soon be history. Another part of the problem was that Paul was quick to criticise and he rarely reflected on the fact that this was new ground, which could only be smoothly negotiated with help from a professional.

One flashpoint came early. I had gone out with a crew to do a feature on Stockport County. It was a basic job. County were having a run in the Cup — another one — and I did a few interviews with the manager and players. Back in the studio we were working on the editing and Doherty said we had to do some 'cutaways'. When I asked him what he meant, he said that I should know, and started lambasting me. I said that I would do whatever was necessary for the job, but I couldn't do something that I didn't know about. I had a strong sense that part of his operation, for reasons he best knew, was to demean the professional football men he had recruited for the best of reasons.

He seemed very keen to establish who was boss – although that was never an issue with me – and he didn't seem to realise that his style was completely opposed to the way of thinking in football. In the game, one of the greatest themes is repetition, of moves and training and even basic skills. You tell a young player everything you can, and you are ready to do this for a reasonable time. The huge problem comes when a player, however talented he may be, is clearly not absorbing the message. It is only when the player has failed to do his job after being adequately prepared that the criticism starts to flow in the way that was routine in Doherty's production offices and studios.

When the Friday night show was over, people sat around tearing it to pieces. Everyone was expected to have a go. If a reporter had been out on a job and picked the wrong angle, or asked a stupid question, he was supposed to be roasted. I thought it was a terrible way of going about things and said so. In the circumstances of my situation, though, I thought it best to express my view as mildly as possible.

Often it seemed to me that Paul was a frustrated football manager. Certainly, he hated it when anyone referred to him as Peter Doherty's son. Once he was introduced in that way in my company and I could see the anger flooding his face. 'Don't call me Peter Doherty's son,' he ordered. I said I would be very disappointed if my own son reacted in that way if he was ever associated with me.

'Paul,' I added, 'what has got into you? As Bill Shankly never stopped telling me and the rest of football, your father was one of the truly great players. You should be proud of what he did – it takes nothing away from your achievements.'

Despite his sometimes illogical approach, Paul helped foster my career in a crucial way and for most of the time I deeply enjoyed my new existence. The most wonderful aspect for me was that I could talk about the game. I could be pleased with it or angered by it, but none of it any longer tore at the lining of my stomach. I put it firmly in the category of 'non-stressful' and, to be honest, I was never impressed by the argument of the TV men that they operated under the terrible pressure of going live and being instantly judged by a vast audience. Possibly that was a failure of perception on my part, but that aspect of the job never really touched me. I knew my subject, I said what I thought and if it didn't work, that was just too bad. I wasn't going to improve by worrying about how I was seen and heard. I suppose I was conditioned by all the years in football, going out to play in big matches knowing that I would be judged up close, and often ferociously, every time I touched the ball. A television miscue did not, at least not at that time, seem like the end of the world.

My starting money at Granada was £100 a week for the Friday show, and I received a decent rise when I signed a contract, reflecting my new and wider duties. The most irksome part of the job was dictated by the ruling technology of the day. Compared with the modern operation, TV production was quite primitive back in the seventies. Saturday nights were spent editing film, but we had to wait for the film to be processed. Eventually, the process would become quite streamlined, but back then it was the nearest point to hard labour that the TV business ever came.

My first taste of television had come in 1970 when I was invited to join the BBC's studio panel for the World Cup in Mexico. We had a big cast that included Brian Clough, Johnny Haynes, Ray Wilson, Noel Cantwell, Bob Wilson and the referee Jim Finney. Although we were strong in numbers, ITV had signed some of the more flamboyant hitters – Malcolm Allison, Bob McNab, Derek Dougan and Paddy Crerand. I didn't take myself too seriously, but I thought I did all right, not least in picking Brazil as the winners. That wasn't as automatic before the tournament as it was in the wake of the glorious triumph of Pele, Tostao, Gerson and Jairzinho, who were part of what was possibly the greatest international team ever to take the field.

In off duty hours I would go over to see the ITV panel, where the social life and conversation was a little livelier than at the BBC. One night, some of us were watching an ITV preview show and one of the BBC's top executives, Bryan Cowgill, came storming in to say that he didn't approve. He wanted to switch off the television. 'I don't want you watching the opposition – it might taint your opinions,' he said. I was quite indignant. I demanded to know what he meant, which was a difficulty for him.

'Look, we have our own opinions,' I told him. 'We've been in the game long enough to know what we think. What those guys on ITV say is up to them. If I should say something similar, it's not because I've heard them say it. It's because I'm big enough, and I know enough, to have my own opinions.'

That incident seemed to define the difference that existed at that time between the BBC and ITV. It seemed to me that the Beeb was still locked in the past, stuffy and proprietorial about everything they broadcast, while the ITV lads were trying to stretch the boundaries on what could be done by way of fresh presentation and bold, controversial comment.

Ironically, I had come close to making a bit of an impact on television with the BBC even earlier, and that I didn't was by a margin as close as the one that lost me the job at Leeds United. Following some work for the BBC on a European Cup final in the company of Jock Stein, I was invited to enter a commentary competition. I finished in a deadlock for the prize. It was settled, against me, by Sir Alf Ramsey. Naturally, I have to believe it was the fruit of pure English prejudice against the Scottish. As the adjudicating judge, Ramsey ruled in favour of a Welshman. He probably thought it was the better of two evils.

I had entered the competition on the suggestion of Gerry Harrison, a former journalist with the *Daily Express* who had made his way in television commentary. When he was a young lad fresh from university, Gerry had got me involved in some local radio work while I was still a Liverpool player, including a brief, ill-fated stab at becoming a part-time disc jockey. Now Gerry said that the BBC were looking for a new name and an immediate reward would be to join their commentary team for the 1970 World Cup finals. There was apparently quite a big entry – local broadcasters, young guys pushing for the big time, schoolteachers, a lot of people who thought they should be sitting in the seats of David Coleman and Barry Davies, and an up-and-coming boy called John Motson. One entrant was Clive Tyldesley, one of today's top TV commentators but back then he was working for Nottingham radio.

Clive didn't make it to the final six, and he reminded me of it many years later with what I thought was a tone of deep resentment in his voice. 'You know I entered that competition in which you reached the final,' he said, as though it was one of the most astounding, incomprehensible facts he had ever encountered. No doubt he had talent but it seemed to me that, in the way of many people in television, he had mistaken himself a little for Mr Big-Time.

Some stiffness accompanied most of our encounters after that. One I remember particularly was at a match in Germany. After the broadcast, he dismissed the point of criticising referees. For me, that was a rather sore subject and I found myself asking him what he was going on about. My point was that referees were part of the game and, as such, not above criticism – especially when their incompetence had done something to mis-shape a game.

Gerry helped me prepare for the competition with some script work and I did a tape to determine whether I had the required quality of voice. The bulk of the contenders were apparently eliminated at this point. The BBC whittled us down to twelve finalists, and the survivors included Ed Stewart, the disc jockey, and Idwal Robling, a Welsh schoolteacher. Six of us, sitting in separate booths, worked the first half of an England–Ireland international at Wembley, with the other half dozen making their run for glory in the second half.

When the judging panel totted up their points, Robling shared the lead with me on 20 points. When Ramsey pronounced Robling the winner, I couldn't resist a touch of sarcasm. Ramsey, a wonderful football man, was not without his airs and graces and sometimes he worked a little hard on refining, with professional help, what was once apparently a fairly broad London accent. 'Well, it just shows you,' I said. 'Maybe I should have had elocution lessons.'

I was nettled at that moment, but there it was and it didn't matter too much to me back then when I couldn't really imagine operating outside the professional game. In the end, it turned out that I didn't lose too much. Idwal never landed one of the big jobs and a few months later I was sitting on the World Cup panel. We were obliged to discuss Ramsey's handling of substitutes when England, who had played so well, surrendered a 2–0 lead and lost to Germany in the quarter-final after withdrawing Bobby Charlton, who had been in majestic form. I like to think my comments were a shining example of objective analysis.

As the years went by, the world of sports television increasingly struck me as a desperate battle of egos. You needed plenty of self-belief to get somewhere, I understood that easily enough, but where did you draw the line? It seemed from my perspective that the greatest trick was to do your work, have good strong opinions balanced by knowledge, but to remember that after you had made it to a good position, it was a lot easier to make enemies than friends.

Elton Welsby was another ambitious youngster who came marching in at that time of dramatic expansion in TV football coverage. After he did a test at Granada, Paul Doherty showed me the tape and invited my opinion, saying, 'He's good, don't you think?' It was a leading question but I had no difficulty in agreeing. He was a very polished performer and was making a lot of progress until, I suspect, he suffered a common ailment among upwardly mobile sports presenters. He assumed he had become a permanent fixture and that the stars would never fade. Now I understand he works in local radio and Betsy reported to me not so long ago that she saw him sitting alone on the balcony of a golf club with a rather wistful look on his face.

Perhaps my view of the TV world was shaped, as I imagine it might have been for some other former players, by the fact that celebrity status came early. By the time I was twenty I was used to seeing my picture in the Scottish newspapers. I knew how it was to be at the centre of quite a bit of attention, not least when clocking on at the old steelworks after playing well – or badly – for Motherwell or Scotland. For some of the TV boys, fame comes in a late and disorientating rush.

For me, TV was a new and largely enjoyable world. It gave me the chance to look from a new angle at the game I had lived with for so long. Best of all were the opportunities to work on World Cup football, which never came my way as a player. Of all my memories of covering World Cups, one of the warmest is of a time in 1978 when I managed to squeeze my way into an Argentina training session a few days before the start of their winning campaign. These days media access is strictly limited with blanket security. Back then it wasn't quite so difficult but there could be problems. We went out to the little stadium in Buenos Aires shortly after getting off the plane from London. One of the producers had said, 'Let's go and see the Argy-bargeys train,' which seemed like a good idea until we ran into a wall of officials, police and security men. Somehow I managed to get myself through the gates by chatting and patting people and generally trying to give the impression I was somebody who should have been there. Who knows, I might also have affected a wee swagger. Whatever the reason, I found myself in the stadium while the rest of the boys, and most crucially the cameramen, were locked out.

My instincts as a TV operator were soon overtaken by those of a football man. I was dazzled by what I saw in that training match. The work was marvellously sharp. Ossie Ardiles, Daniel Passarella and Mario Kempes would play huge roles in the triumph, but this night they were just members of a wonderfully impressive cast. I remember saying to myself, 'Jesus Christ, this is some team. Whoever beats them wins the Cup.' There were, of course, other formidable contenders. The Dutch were deeply impressive, hard and capable of beautiful football. You could not discount Brazil on their own continent. The Italians, defensively sound, might spring something, but sometimes in football you see what you believe is a flash of certainty and that was what I had that night in Buenos Aires.

I backed Argentina on my first broadcast and I never wavered throughout the competition. Most significant for me was the pace of their game. Cesar Menotti had produced a team that played with skill and a sense of adventure but most of all he had come to exploit the value of genuine speed about the field. Never

Right Coventry City manager Noel Cantwell was a good friend.

Below A goal for me against the mighty Leeds United, and a high five with my clever Coventry team-mate Willie Carr. The grounded Gary Sprake didn't have a chance.

Above Ron Yeats, Tranmere manager in 1973, is another good friend. We made our last stands together.

Above 'My boy' Willie Pettigrew of Motherwell joins forces with Joe Jordan for Scotland in 1976.

Below Back to my roots – my Motherwell squad for the 1974–75 season.

Above left Paul Gilchrist of Portsmouth was one of the players I hoped would help me make my name as a manager.

Above right John Deacon, the Portsmouth chairman, promised me the football world but delivered rather less.

Right David Kemp on the ball for Portsmouth against Millwall in 1977 – a good player and a good lad.

Above left A famous golf victory for 007 and 09 – the day Sean Connery and I beat Lee Trevino and Sandy Lyle.

Above right Winning the green jacket – of the Variety Club, that is. Bernard Gallacher, Ryder Cup captain, awards me the prize after my victory in the golf celebrity event in 1991. Impresario Bernard Delfont looks on.

Below Teaching the game – a pleasure that never fades.

Above A working shift with commentator Clive Tyldesley, covering Rangers against Ajax in 1996.

Below Liverpool captain Steve Gerrard raises the Champions League trophy in Istanbul on the night that brought back the past.

Left The St John line — son Ian, grandson Iain and the old boy.

Below I always say Elaine favours her dad and here's the evidence.

Below Proud grandparents, Betsy and I spend some of our best times with granddaughter Abigail and the likeliest of lads, Iain, Alex and, on my knee, Jamie.

before had I seen a team display so much subtle movement at such a high tempo. All their instincts were to attack. I concluded that you just couldn't see work like that and not believe the team producing it weren't going to win.

When it came to the final, Jack Charlton and I were sitting in little wooden seats by the running track at the edge of the pitch. We had been doing an 'atmosphere' piece to camera before the kick-off. We settled down for what we knew would be an awesome occasion. Thunder rolled down from the great terraces when the Argentinians came on the field and, to be honest, I elected myself a home fan that night.

This had nothing to do with any lack of respect for the Dutch. Despite the misadventure against Scotland in that extraordinary group game, they had once again confirmed themselves to be one of the world's top teams – they should have won the elusive prize four years earlier in Germany – but Argentina were on fire and it was impossible not to identify with their hopes. When the Falklands War broke out a few years later, I found it sickening. I liked the Argentine people very much; I found them warm, hospitable and passionate, and it grieved me that politics had set two nations at war in that way. Of course one great problem was the leadership of Argentina. In an earlier afternoon game, the leader of the junta, General Galtieri, walked just a few feet away from me in the stadium tunnel. I found myself saying, 'You waddling little shit,' and reflecting that had it been night-time, and with some reasonable chance of escape, I might well have whacked him on his head.

After the victory, the streets of Buenos Aires were choked. There was no chance of getting a cab back to our hotel, so we had to walk miles through the streets, and I remember thinking it was one of the greatest experiences of my life.

I had escaped what was potentially one of my life's worst

experiences a few weeks earlier when I was partnering Hugh Johns for the Scotland–Peru game, which plunged Scotland into a sea of humiliation. Hugh had the nightmare experience of talking into a void for the entire first half. A technical hitch had cut off the link with home. Ten minutes into the second half a producer told Hugh, 'Sorry, we're still not getting it.' Johns had had enough. He pulled off his headphones and stormed out of the booth. I was sitting with mine on in front of the microphone with an engineer on one side and Hugh's empty seat on the other, so I turned to the engineer and said, 'Well, I might as well do the commentary . . .' It was a spoof and the most perilous I had ever pulled in my life. I said, 'So-and-so's on the ball now, the lazy bastard, and now he's playing it to another useless bastard.' There were quite a few more expletives, and most of them were reserved for the team manager, Ally MacLeod.

After the game I was told that the disaster of the failed link could easily have been rectified at any moment. The engineers had been working on it through the game and if two wires had been put together, my tide of purple language would have flowed into millions of British households. I would have been the Ron Atkinson of my time, saying things I wouldn't have done had I known I was working with a potentially live microphone. I would never have worked in television again.

As it was, I didn't get off completely unscathed. John Bromley took me on one side and gave me a tremendous bollocking. He said I'd behaved very irresponsibly and he just didn't see the funny side of it. I didn't think it wise to say that the engineer had been laughing his head off. It had been, I realised as I sipped a cold beer later that night, another crossroads for me, although this one had been negotiated without too much devastation to my career prospects. From that moment on, I treated a microphone with as much respect as I would a live hand grenade.

Other lessons were to be learned in Argentina. One was always to make sure you were in the right place at the right time. I nearly missed the opening game of the tournament when my taxi driver took me miles away from the airport. Eventually, I got out my passport and shouted 'aeropuerto', and he said dryly, 'Oh, the airport.' When I got to the desk, I was told the flight was closed. I told them it was a matter of life and death which, professionally speaking, it might well have been, and after a few more desperate appeals I was told to jump in a jeep. They raced me out to the plane and I got there just as they were about to take the steps away.

Later in the tournament, I was flying back to Buenos Aires when the stewardess told me that the pilot had Scottish ancestry and would be delighted to entertain me on the flight deck. This was a hair-raising honour. He told me to sit in a little jump seat beside him, then he put his feet up, lit a cigarette and proceeded to paint a warm profile of his Scottish grandfather. This was very uplifting, but not so much as the fine three-point landing he performed what seemed like an eternity later.

When the work was done, I was exhausted but happy enough that overall I had earned my money. I had learned a lot and benefited from working beside experienced men, not least Bob Gardem, who would later be a big influence when my television career moved on to a higher level. In Argentina he was already proving himself to be one of the most innovative of TV sports broadcasters. He was the first producer to put a camera behind the goal.

Another lesson I learned was that in television not much is achieved without careful planning, and a lot of discipline. You always have to be in position to seize the moment. The consequences of a breakdown in organisation were highlighted four years later at the World Cup of Spain when a potentially brilliant feature was lost simply because a camera crew were late on the assignment.

Paul Doherty had sent Gerry Harrison and me up to the USSR team camp in the hills outside Barcelona. The Soviet players were in a hotel behind a wire and we were not allowed to enter. There was not a lot we could do, anyway, until the crew arrived, and it was while we waited that the beautiful, made-for-television scenario unfolded. Johan Cruyff, who happened to have an apartment in a nearby complex, came walking by, in a very relaxed mood. We chatted with him and, suddenly, the place was flooded with Soviet players. They had seen Cruyff talking to us quite amiably and had come rushing out to mob him, led by Oleg Blokhin. After a few minutes, the great forward of Dinamo Kiev went back to his quarters, saying he had a present for Cruyff. He returned with a balalaika, which he formally presented to the man he said was one of his great heroes. Cruyff and Blokhin embraced and the other players applauded.

On such occasions an old footballer is reminded that nothing in his life will perhaps ever compare with the thrill of playing, with the companionship and respect that grows among team-mates and opponents alike. Always you know you are fortunate to play football for a living, but where it becomes more than a mere game is in the achieving of certain levels of performance, when you win from your peers the kind of respect that can produce the scene enacted that day in the hills of Barcelona. It didn't make it to the camera but I will have a picture of it always.

I will also remember the charity game I played in during the Argentina tournament, more vividly than any of the television production dramas. I played for the European press against the South Americas. It may not have been the most eloquent gathering of wordsmiths, but looking around the dressing room brought prickles to my skin. Our team included Alfredo di

Stefano, Raymond Kopa, the Charlton brothers, the great Italian full-back Giacinto Facchetti and Billy Wright. The brilliant Omar Sivori came into the dressing room with his overcoat over his shoulders. It was a gathering of champions.

The score was 5–5 and di Stefano scored after playing a one-two with me. When I was a young Motherwell player watching Real Madrid prepare for their epic performance against Eintracht Frankfurt in the 1960 European Cup final, I could never have imagined writing such a sentence. The goal was all sweet simplicity. Di Stefano came charging through the middle in his unique style. I was facing him on the edge of the box. He played it to me and, naturally, I laid it back into his path. A great roar shook the stadium, which was jammed with around 10,000 fans. I can hear it now.

I can also hear the rage of Jack Charlton when Kopa, the imperious Frenchman, blasted two free kicks over the bar. On each occasion Jack had come racing upfield drawling, 'Hold on, man, hold on.' Kopa, unaware of Jack's reputation for the plundering of set-pieces, twice ignored him.

When a third free kick was awarded, Kopa again stepped up to the ball. On this occasion I feared a major eruption from Jack if the same thing happened again. So I stood in front of the Frenchman to prevent him from taking the kick until Jack was in position, but as I did so I heard someone else's pounding footsteps. They were Bobby Charlton's. He too sent the ball flying over the bar. Jack's cry of, 'Don't let that French bastard take it,' was presumably not heard, but then maybe it was. The puckish grin on Bobby's face said it might just have been.

It made me think that however experienced, or even successful, I became as a television man, I would always be a footballer — and footballers never grow old.

18

KEEP SMILING

HOWEVER intense Jack Charlton became on or around a football field when the action was unfolding, he always had a sense of the wider world. Where he discovered it I don't know, maybe on the side of some Irish fishing stream or Northumbrian shooting moor. It doesn't matter. He had it. He understood how the game worked, how it could destroy men as easily as it extended their youth, and his understanding of my situation was the perfect example of this.

We worked well together in Sheffield Wednesday's preparations for the 1978–79 campaign after our brilliant pause in Rio and I was enjoying a return to football that was, to Betsy's satisfaction, underpinned by my progress in television. It seemed quite possible that I might enjoy the best of two worlds, and this was quickly confirmed when John Bromley arrived at Hillsborough to take me to lunch. The top man at ITV sport had clearly forgiven me for my dangerous behaviour in possession of a microphone that could suddenly have come to life.

John told me that the voice and face of ITV football, Brian Moore, wanted to cut back on his commitments. He came quickly to the point. Would I would be interested in taking over the flagship Saturday preview show, 'On the Ball'? It was a great opportunity for me, a chance to build a national image while Brian concentrated on the Sunday show, 'The Big Match'. I didn't know it, of course, but it also meant I was taking the first steps towards my second marriage – the one with Jimmy Greaves. The job would take up Fridays and Saturdays – Friday for preparation and editing of features, Saturday for presentation. Fridays and Saturdays are key days on the football calendar but when I told Jack about the offer his response was exactly as I had hoped.

'That's no problem,' he said. 'You can work here through Thursday, then go off and do your stuff for the telly. If there's a game that needs looking at in London on Saturday, you can take that in before coming home.' It was a sweetheart deal and I would always be grateful for that time I spent with Jack and Maurice Setters. It was good to work with a hard but generous professional.

John Bromley was offering me a superb chance to develop my television career but it was also a major challenge. With Granada I had been doing bits and pieces and learning the business on a trial and error basis, with hardly a hint of formal training, but now the stakes had been raised quite sharply. I had to face the nation at a prime viewing time with a lot of new responsibility. I was in charge of the smooth running of the show and filling the dead air that comes so suddenly when something goes wrong. I had to purvey the general sense that the show was aptly entitled 'On the Ball' and was a much sharper version of the BBC rival, 'Football Focus'. 'Brommers' must have had quite a bit of faith in my ability to pull it off. I was sent into action with a fairly basic set of instructions – I was told to make sure I always wore a collar and tie, and a smile.

Today's presenters, I'm told, have to submit to hours of grooming and detailed instructions. In 1978 I had a simple imperative. I just had to go out in front of the cameras and do it. There were twin nightmares. One was that the film would fail to appear on cue. The other was that the autocue would stick. One day Dickie Davies, the superbly slick presenter of our parent show 'World of Sport', asked me, 'Do you have standby for when the video goes down?' No, I told him, I had a ragbag of lines such as, 'a few gremlins have got into the works' and a desperate determination to try to keep the panic out of my eyes. Davies suggested I developed a deeper strategy than merely flying by the seat of my pants. It was going well enough, however. We had a corps of bright young men working the features; Jim Rosenthal, Martin Tyler and Alan Parry would all go on to enjoy long and successful careers, and if I was grateful for Davies's good advice, it was also true I didn't go into work with any great sense of dread.

Mark Sharman was the producer in those days and he ran the show without any theatricals. He would say, 'Okay, boys, this is what we're going to do.' We had a clear outline and we worked with the pressures that cannot be avoided in any form of live television. I felt I had certain natural attributes to bring to this new business. I didn't panic easily, and it was no doubt a great help dealing with a subject in which I'd been schooled for most of my life. Another advantage was that I didn't have a problem with laughing at both the game and myself.

Looking at today's television, I have to salute the tremendous work of Jeff Sterling on Sky's Saturday afternoon football show. His grasp of detail, and general sharpness, makes a great success of a concept that was considered impossible to pull off by ITV executives when it was suggested by Bob Patience. Bob was a brilliant producer who eventually took over 'On the Ball' and played a key part in the television careers of both Greavsie and me. Bob, groomed in newspaper journalism, came up with the idea of monitoring the entire Saturday afternoon action with a panel of football men, long before Sky launched their programme. The ITV men told Bob that there were too many problems. 'It just will not work,' he was told.

'On the Ball' prospered for four years, and so did I. Then a little gold dust was sprinkled on our show and my career. It was brought by Jimmy Greaves. We became a small and popular item and then we grew. Before that, however, my own sense of expanding horizons had become ever stronger. The 1982 World Cup in Spain was a brilliant centrepiece to one of the happiest phases of my time in television. It was wonderful to go to the great games and talk about them without any of the old tension that comes with the need to win. The experience of watching Argentina train behind closed doors four years earlier had whetted my appetite for that probing side of the business. I wanted to see what was happening around the game and, maybe, be the first to recognise new trends, new forces.

For a little while, my world seemed rounded, complete. I could go my own way confidently. The lost, bitter years marooned on the south coast of England were a fading memory. I had a good living and respect. I was, perhaps finally, my own man. I was wrong in one respect. It turned out I was awaiting one last dimension – Jimmy Greaves, the legend of Spurs and England, the man who was bravely, chirpily emerging from the long road of rehabilitation required by any serious brush with alcoholism.

'On the Ball' was now in the hands of Bob Patience, who arrived in London after doing a big job turning around the sports coverage of ITV in Scotland. Like his predecessor, who was also brought up in newspaper journalism, Bob had a sharp news instinct and he had developed the big edge we had over the BBC's 'Football Focus'. Sam Leitch, a veteran sportswriter, had fronted 'Football Focus' and he was succeeded by Bob Wilson. First Sharman, then Patience insisted we took a bolder, fresher approach than our rivals. We went farther behind the football scenes. We looked for the new angle.

We had an advantage and it was one that neither Patience nor Bromley had any intention of surrendering. Bromley had spotted Greavsie when he was brought onto a World Cup panel by Central Television. Until then, Jimmy's TV work had been concentrated on the successful kids' show 'Tiswas' put out by Central. He had been a comic element in the programme that also made the name of Chris Tarrant, the host of 'Who Wants to be a Millionaire?' Bromley liked the light and quirky approach Greavsie brought to his work on the World Cup panel. He said Bob should look at some tapes and see if he could find a role for him in 'On the Ball'. Bob was impressed by what he saw and decided he would try a link-up between Greavsie and me as a potentially regular segment of our show.

There were a few technical problems at first. The unions were very strong at that time and there was some question about staffing requirements to set up Jimmy's contribution from a little room off the 'Tiswas' studio. However, Gary Newbon, the head of Central Television sport, managed to work a compromise in which Jimmy would race down a corridor from the 'Tiswas' set and do his slot before a single camera. On one occasion, he had to do this in a full suit of armour he had worn for a 'Tiswas' item. Patience suggested that the hilarious footage of him clanking down the corridor should be buried.

Initially, it was just a three-minute slot but Bob saw immediately that the two old football pros had a little chemistry. Very soon the reaction was so good that Bromley and Patience agreed that the Greavsie segment should become a more central part of the show. Up to then it had consisted of me asking something along the lines of, 'Now Jimmy, what did you make of Tommy Docherty's statement this week?' Greavsie would preface some dry reaction with the line, 'Well, Saint,' and we would knock the subject around for three or four minutes.

After the 1982–83 season, and with the item well established, Bromley went to see Jimmy with a proposition. He would buy him out of the 'Tiswas' contract and bring him down to London to sit with me in the studio. There would be no more armour-clad charges down the corridor. Greavsie agreed and the new billing was 'On the Ball – with Ian St John and Jimmy Greaves'. Our audience had another spurt on its way to a stunning lunch-time figure of five and a half million and Jimmy and I had acquired the dubious distinction of becoming household names.

Our strength in the market was so established that we survived the breakdown of negotiations with the Football League that resulted in football action disappearing from the television screen for a while. That was the signal for the BBC to close down the unequal battle with our show – satisfyingly, if I am very honest, quite soon after Bob Wilson had written an article for *Woman's Own* in which he had announced sniffily that the BBC would never resort to the kind of personality style ITV had built around Greavsie and me. In fact, at the following Wimbledon they adopted a similar format with Des Lynam and the tennis man Gerry Williams.

Another test of our strength in the market came when, suddenly, 'World of Sport' was cancelled. That was a crushing blow to Dickie Davies, but it appeared that not only had Jimmy and I survived, we were going to get more time and projection under a bold new title – 'The Saint and Greavsie'.

Bob had come up with the title and Bromley was very taken with it. Jimmy and I were far from sure. We thought the reaction in football would be quite negative, and it would be seen as turning the programme into a showcase for ourselves rather than football. We made our reservations very plain when we went to John's office overlooking the Thames. Bob was present as we discussed details and terms for the next season's run. Everything went well until the subject of the title came up again.

'Look, John,' I said, 'we're just not happy about this – it doesn't feel right.' John had always been Mr Amiable. There had never been a problem so intractable that it couldn't be settled easily over a glass of gin, but this was the exception. Suddenly, he was ramming his fist into the table, much to the amazement of the rest of us.

'Bloody hell,' he said, 'here we are offering you a new show, a good deal, and you're quibbling over the title. I like it. It's a natural – and I want it.'

I turned to Greavsie and said, 'Well, what do you think about that?'

'It doesn't look like we have a lot of choice, Saint,' Jimmy replied. Our future was fixed – for more than ten brilliant years.

They were brilliant years in the effect they had on the television audience, and for what they did for the rest of our lives after football, but I cannot say they were always easy years. I loved Jimmy and his oddball demeanour, and I loved what he meant as a footballer – he was one of the truly special players, an original, a scoring genius – but he could be very difficult. Part of the problem was that he was still deeply into the battle of fighting the drink.

He did it bravely and well with the help of pills he gulped down at regular intervals, but his head certainly, and given his circumstances, maybe inevitably, wasn't always on the progamme. He never came in on Fridays. He would roll in on Saturday mornings without the offer of too much input. Bob and I might be going through the scripts while Jimmy sat at another table reading the racing form. Quite often, Bob and I had our patience tested to the limit. Bob had an easygoing style, but you could tell when he was beginning to boil. He would say something like, 'Jim, if you have a minute, maybe we could talk a little about what we're going to do.'

On such mornings you had a strong sense that Jimmy just didn't want to be there. The temptation I had – and I knew Bob also suffered from it – was to get hold of him and say, 'Look, we're not just doing this for our own good, you know. If you don't want to play, why don't you push off.' Mostly, though, we kept on the kid gloves and as the years wore on I was glad of it. Increasingly, Jimmy and I would attend social events together and the more we did, the more I saw what a strain he was under. He couldn't socialise naturally. He couldn't unwind in the bar. Being around drinkers while he sipped a Perrier was not a feasible possibility. On our journeys together he told me about his past, about how it was coming through the wasteland years, and when he described the depths of the battle, I was grateful that Bob and I and the programme editor Richard Worth had been able to suppress our irritation at some of his behaviour. He had been on a different journey, a long and tough one, and you could only respect him deeply for the way he had come through it.

One memory is of a golf day at the RAC club and the pleasant anticipation of a relaxing drink and reflection in the club bar. Jimmy threw his clubs in the boot of his car and sped away. I can't forget the look on his face. He had a hard, grim expression. Our pleasure was his no-go area, and he knew that it would have to be for always.

Both of us had been to the mountain tops of football, and we had had our disappointments. The worst of those for Jimmy, no doubt, was his omission from England's World Cup final team in 1966, and although he never spoke of it, there was also a sharp pain when Bill Nicholson traded him to West Ham in a deal for one of England's Wembley heroes, Martin Peters. Between us, we had a working knowledge of how far football can lift you up and take you down, and I think this was an important ingredient of our talk on the game — because of our experiences, we were never in danger of taking ourselves too seriously.

One of the highpoints was a tour we did in America as a preview to the 1994 World Cup. We did one piece against the Manhattan skyline and a gust of wind carried away a hat Jimmy had been given by a friend in England and had come to prize very much. His look of distress was so memorable it was for some time included in television out-take shows.

Getting Jimmy to make the tour was a major achievement. He had never enjoyed flying and the problem had intensified with the days of abstinence. In his playing days with Tottenham and England, he was able to tranquilise himself with a few beers and brandies. Now it was a white-knuckle operation, but the effort to persuade him to make the American trip proved well worth it. We were able to do some lively features and even managed to persuade the celebrity entrepreneur Donald Trump to make the draw for an early round of the League Cup in his Trump Tower headquarters. He had to be reassured that clubs such as Scunthorpe, Rochdale and Exeter were 'big league teams', but he was happy enough to appear on English television. When we presented him with the usual reward for our guests, a Saint and Greavsie mug, he accepted it graciously and said he would give it to his English secretary, a confirmed 'soccer' fan.

Jimmy's face was the key to his success. He was better on camera than on the microphone. However, this did not prevent him developing a fixation on the idea that he should be doing commentary. He pushed for this with both John Bromley and Bob Patience and he didn't understand their reluctance. The fact was that Jimmy's talent for improvisation and drollery didn't transfer to the commentary box. His style wasn't urgent enough. Instead of a snap comment, he tended to ramble on when the subject was exhausted and the action had shifted. Soon enough, even Jimmy realised he had made a mistake.

What neither of us could know was that, in the end, the success of our show would be caught up in the changing times in television. When Sky made their big push to own English football, and most major sport, we were among the victims. Sky went to the contract negotiations with the new Premier League with a simple and well-financed ambition. The instruction was quite explicit. Their negotiators were told from on high to 'blow the opposition out of the water'. You could understand football's willingness to grab at the big money. For so long the BBC and ITV had operated a cosy cartel. They were getting football on the cheap.

The word was out that Sky were about to take over and you could sense a changed atmosphere when Jimmy and I went out to the European Championship in Sweden in 1992. No one said anything to us outright – they rarely do in television until the moment the axe falls without any kind of ceremony – but we sensed that maybe we were no longer the kings of our part of the television universe. At the end of the tournament, we shot a piece from a theme park with Jimmy and I sharing a tandem bicycle. Quite prophetically, we sang, 'This could be the last time . . .' as we rode out of camera. It was. 'The Saint and Greavsie' was pulled.

Bob Patience, who rightly had a great sense of proprietorial pride in the show, fought as hard as he could to keep us on the air. He had nurtured the programme to great success, had been the first to see the potential in getting Jimmy and me together, and now all his drive and imagination was being cast aside. It didn't help, either, that John Bromley, who had worked so closely with Bob, had been lured away to Sky. Suddenly, with Bob deciding to return to Scotland as a freelance producer, we were without either allies or a show.

Unlike Jimmy, who always had people around him, I didn't have an agent and so I had to return to my home in Liverpool, hoping that the rich years of high-profile television would draw some benefit now that my career had been so harshly interrupted. I had to go through the ordeal suffered at some time or other by almost all those who enter some form of the entertainment business. I had to wait for the phone to ring. It did eventually, but only after a drama involving one of the biggest names in British television – Michael Parkinson.

Bob had set up a show in Scotland, which was going very well. Entitled 'Sport in Question', it was a version of David Dimbleby's topical panel show. He had ambitions for an ITV network run and sent a tape to the newly established Carlton ITV franchise. They liked the look of it and, thus encouraged, Bob set about looking for a big-name chairman of the panel. He settled on Parkinson – and this would prove extremely ironic – partly at my suggestion. I put the two of them together. I was playing golf with Parkinson and Jimmy Tarbuck on the Algarve at the time, and I raised the subject as we walked down the fairway. Parkinson was doing an antiques TV show at the time but was otherwise being lightly used in a medium in which he had once been such a dominant figure. Parkinson, Patience agreed, had perfect credentials. He was a big name and had a good background in sports and a fine sense of humour. It was also true he was popular among the ladies.

Bob wined and dined Mike at Langan's Brasserie and made a deal. He was delighted about his coup as he prepared to go on holiday to Florida. Then he got a call from Carlton saying that they didn't see Parkinson as their man. Bob was stunned and angry. He knew his business and had negotiated in the certainty that he had picked the right man. It meant that he had two immediate priorities. He had to extricate himself from the embarrassment of having to back out of the deal he had struck with Parkinson, a man he admired and liked a lot, and then he had to come up with a new candidate.

Parkinson sent Bob a note saying that he knew how these things happened in television and that no doubt somewhere along the line they would again share a good bottle of wine. Bob then sent a list of new candidates to Carlton. He put down various names, including Jim Rosenthal, who had been such a promising young prospect in the early days of 'On the Ball', and Frank Bough of the BBC, as well as several other established broadcasters. Then, almost as an afterthought, he pointed out that Greavsie and I were out of work, despite fronting one of the most successful sports shows in the history of British television. He said we were big names who had proven how well we could communicate with a mass audience.

While Bob was in Florida, his secretary called to say that the choice was Saint and Greavsie. We were back in business, bruised but pleased and relieved that the impact of our work was not just going to ebb away. A sour note was struck by Mike Parkinson, though, someone I had always regarded as a good friend. It was all the more surprising, and hurtful, to pick up a newspaper and read a column by Parkinson that criticised the use of old footballers by television, particularly on panel shows that demanded a wide range of sports knowledge and professional interviewing technique. It was a general attack on the trend of former sportsmen making their way into televison, but there were specific shots at Jimmy and me. Betsy, knowing the background of my involvement in the original move for Parkinson, was incensed. She vowed never to speak to Parkinson again, which was rather embarrassing when we found ourselves in Singapore at the same time as Mike and his wife, Mary. Parkinson, who had been conscious of Betsy's coldness in previous meetings, invited us to dinner. Betsy said we should do a runner but on this occasion I couldn't bring myself to take her advice. We went to dinner and healed the wounds, at least to a certain degree.

For Jimmy and me there were a few more good years. The show went well, climbed up the ratings and one official report on Carlton, which at the time was being criticised for its lack of original feature material, said that 'Sport in Question' was exactly the kind of show it should be developing on a wider front. That made extremely reassuring reading but in television, we knew well enough by now, nothing could really be taken for granted. A new set of executives moved into Carlton and one of their first decisions was to revamp our show. They thought it needed a new title and a new presenter. Richard Littlejohn, the newspaper columnist, got the job and the show was called, 'Do we not like that?' The audience didn't. It had one season.

Naturally, I was disgusted and more than a little bitter. Our show had been successful, the audience figures showed that, but we had fallen to executive whim. No one, not even an indignant and knowing Bob Patience, established quite who had put the knife in. Bob called to say how sorry he felt for Jimmy and me. He said that twice now we had been shot off the air for no good reason. We had connected with the public but not the executive suite. No one explained the decision. No one, apart from Bob, even said thanks for some good work. It was the way of television, and perhaps it was as well that no one approached me with an explanation. I would have had an overwhelming desire to tell them what I thought of their understanding of their own profession.

It took me a while to get the whole business out of my system. At first I was angry at being out of work while these people who were supposed to know what the public wanted were still picking up their salaries. Eventually, I became a little more philosophical, grateful to the good men who helped me make a second career – Paul Doherty, John Bromley, Bob Patience, Mark Sharman and Richard Worth. I remembered the excitement created by working, and playing, with Bob Gardam, one of the most innovative of all television sports directors. Bob was a character to the point of eccentricity, and generally he was equal to any challenge – except, I still remember vividly, the one that came to him in a Buenos Aires nightclub during the 1978 World Cup. He was being pursued by a striking young lady who, it became clear, was in fact a young man. Bob retreated to the hotel in some confusion. Mostly, though, he was a cool, enterprising head in the most challenging of situations.

These people gave me twenty good years and made me a celebrity at a time when, in the normal experience of an old footballer, people who remember you at all are wondering who you played for.

Jimmy and I found ourselves featured on 'Spitting Image' and we said that we were the only ones who looked better on that show than in real life. You could laugh at that, and celebrate it, because it was reassuring that we were having a little impact. In one of the more memorable moments, 'Jimmy' had hold of a puppet of Colin Moynihan, the diminutive sports minister of the time. We had criticised his plan to institute 'pass laws' with football ID cards, and 'Jimmy' had a card he was trying to insert into a certain part of the puppet's anatomy. You gave some criticism so it wasn't hard to receive it from time to time and, well, a little mockery never hurt.

Once on the balcony of the bar at London Weekend Television, when Jimmy made a rare appearance, I noticed that a group at a nearby table were studying us very closely. They were guys from an impressionist show starring Bobby Davro and Alan Stewart, and they were clearly checking our mannerisms. It was on that show that my character said, 'You kill me, Greavsie' and received the response, 'It's a funny old game, Saint.' It worked well and we incorporated it in our act.

What we didn't realise was that our show would stimulate a trend towards a less affectionate look at the game by people who, I will always believe, gauged its popularity, the hold it had on so many people, and decided they could exploit its high profile. At the time of the European Championship in 2004 Jimmy and I, against our better judgement, went on the show in which stand-up comedians Frank Skinner and David Baddiel had in the past used former players including Jeff Astle as fodder for what I thought was the worst of mockery. It was an uncomfortable time and I think both of us regretted the experience.

Neither Skinner nor Baddiel came to us before the show to say hello and give us some idea of what they were doing. It would have been pointless, anyway. The show had very little to do with us. We were simply the vehicles for what could only be described as an elaborate effort to put us down. Neither Jimmy nor I were prepared to be the butt of their version of humour, and after they admitted pinching ideas from our show, Baddiel asked me if I had seen what they had done with our material. I wasn't biting and said, 'No, I didn't see it – what time of night did the show go out?' Greavsie got so irritated he uttered a few expletives. At the end, they wheeled on Ron 'Chopper' Harris, dressed up as a Greek orthodox priest – presumably to mark the success of the Greek team – and the cameras faded on him singing, rather badly I have to say, a hymn of celebration. That slot of just a few seconds made me very angry. It was a complete mickey-take of a former player for the benefit of these guys who had latched on to football as some profitable gig of cheap laughs – and the audience howled. Jimmy sloped away from the studio while I went into the Green Room and had a drink with some of the young production lads. There was no sign of Skinner or Baddiel.

Nobby Stiles had a similar experience when he went on the show that pours more hard-core ridicule on football than any other, 'They Think It's All Over'. Nobby, one of the folk heroes of the nation, was promoting his autobiography. When he left the stage after his brief appearance, Jonathan Ross had one observation – 'He looked like the guy on the "George and Mildred Show".' Big, cheap laugh. The self-regarding Ross, who is seen fawning on celebrities from the worlds of cinema and showbiz in his other television outlets, didn't see fit to have a word with Nobby. Why would he? He was just another piece of fodder.

It seems that a lot of people have latched on to football as an easy hit, an easy way of making a living. On 'The Saint and Greavsie' there was no doubt quite a bit of fun and mickey-taking, but it was done with tongues in cheeks. Our show was maybe a catalyst for this new crowd of entertainers. For the first time someone was having a laugh about the game and the people in it, but I always thought it was acceptable because we played at the highest level, and in that basic sense were part of the game. It meant we were also laughing at ourselves. You have to wonder where the humour is in getting Jeff Astle to make a fool of himself or dressing up Ron Harris. You wonder about the point, and the right of Skinner or Ross to sneer at men who have got to the top of the national game by their talent and their effort. I remember Ross as a young, pushy guy at London Weekend Television. He had a brother who read bits of news. Now he has his own shows. It always struck me that a lot of television was about the formation of tight, incestuous little circles.

Perhaps it is inevitable that I now look at television sport with a somewhat jaundiced eye. What offends me most is the lack of true comment, the unwillingness of so many to say what their professional experience insists that they should. There is also the relentless selling of the product, which is performed nowhere more openly than on Sky TV. They own football and they don't so much cover it as merchandise it. Andy Gray, a fine player, has become the archpriest of this process. He wants to be everybody's pal but if you are doing the job right, it cannot be so. If a player or a manager has made a mistake you are obliged to say so. It is your duty to the viewer. I gather that Andy wields great clout in Sky football, gets a lot of say in who gets on to the programmes, who gets to make their points or not.

Alan Hansen has had great success in recent years, and for this he owes, as I did, a debt to Bob Patience. Bob knew Alan as a young player at Partick Thistle and followed his career closely. When Hansen elected himself to the world of TV analysis, Patience gave him the most vital advice. He said, 'Always comment strongly, always say what you feel. That's what you're being employed for, not pussyfooting around an issue.' I don't always agree with Alan, but he has good knowledge and something to say, and that's what underpins his success on television, although sometimes I wonder if he is maintaining the strength of his opinions. It is easy to slip into the bromides of easy comment. When you mix with the top men in football, there is sometimes a temptation to consider their reaction to what you might have to say.

For this reason, I would make it a rule that working managers stay off the box at all times, except before or after a game when they are obliged to discuss their own teams. Graeme Souness, when struggling at Blackburn, made the mistake of commenting on other teams on television. I recall thinking, 'Graeme, your team is playing rubbish, why are you discussing other clubs? You are leaving yourself so open to criticism.' I saw Martin Jol, the Tottenham manager, laying into Iain Dowie and John Gregory.

He pointed out that Gregory had lost his job and said that Dowie didn't know what he was talking about. He said they had no right to comment on his team. I could see his point.

My own time in front of the camera, except for casual appearances, is in the past now, along with football, but it is something I will always value. It was a chance that came along and I was glad I was able to take it. By today's standards, it didn't provide a great fortune but it helped to make my life, give me a sense of myself at a critical time when the cheers to which I had become so accustomed were dying in my ears. A few years ago I was walking along a Florida beach, paddling in the sea with the sun on my back. The beach was quite deserted but for a guy about a hundred yards away. Suddenly, he shouted, 'Where's Greavsie then?' Jimmy's reaction might have been, 'It's a funny old life, Saint,' but a good one, too.

19
A FINE, COMPETITIVE EDGE

S o what does an old burned-out footballer and time-expired television star do with the rest of his life when he isn't musing about days gone by on some deserted beach? If he is of my vintage, he walks the dogs and keeps body and soul together with some corporate work and after-dinner speaking. He does a little bit of radio, the odd television spot and writes a column for the *Sunday Post* in Scotland. He helps out his son with a long-established football coaching school. In all of this, though, he never forgets to be grateful for all that football has brought him.

For over twenty years I did the summer football school across the country, and with a great cast of helpers. In Northern Ireland, Harry Gregg and Gerry Armstrong came along. In Wales, Neville Southall, the hero goalkeeper and Evertonian, was a helper. Once I even persuaded Denis Law to come to the school we put on in his native Aberdeen. Denis, the most spontaneous of talents, never put much store on coaching, but after a few days he told me how much pleasure he felt working with the boys.

Martin Buchan was another who re-kindled the camaraderie of playing days. In Yorkshire, Eddie Gray taught, and then mesmerised the lads with some of his skills. Sometimes I wonder if the culture of today's game would permit such an easy mingling of old team-mates and rivals.

In Scotland, the Ryder Cup captain Tony Jacklin visited our school and made the presentation to the medal-winners at the end of the session. They were happy days when I could maintain my link with the game at grassroots level, and although I knew the football camps would never make a fortune for me, or the old pros who received a few hundred pounds a week for their help, I never regarded a minute of the time I spent among the boys and my old colleagues as wasted.

My debt to the game that opened so many doors to me has stretched down through all my days. There have been so many rewards. I've done after dinner-speaking in Cairo and after-breakfast speaking on the oil rigs of the North Sea. That latter experience was particularly rewarding because, on the rigs, drinking is banned and so I had to deal with a 'cold' audience who had showered after coming in off the night shift. They were attentive and appreciative, and they also laughed at the jokes of my travelling companion, the late Scottish comic Gary Dennis.

One of my gigs was for the Ministry of Defence in Kosovo and Bosnia, talking to the troops and feeling again the strength of feeling that ordinary lads have for the game of football. The celebrity that the game gave to me has brought so many rewards – and at least one tragically haunting story. I heard about this when I received a letter from an Australian television producer, who told me about the sad fate of a young aboriginal man who was killed in a racist murder by some skinheads. His name was Louis St John. He had been adopted by a Liverpool immigrant, Bill Johnson. He was a fine young man, working hard at college when he suffered his appalling fate. Early in 2005, when Betsy and I stopped off in Australia during a world tour we had always promised ourselves, I played a 'pick-up' game with an expatriate, who said he was from Liverpool. I said he might know my name. I was Ian St John. He was astounded. Yes, he knew my name well enough. He was Bill Johnson's brother, the uncle of Louis St John.

When the old pro is lucky, he plays golf, sometimes villainously, off a 14 handicap, all over the world and at Wallasey Golf Club.

If he gets even luckier, he makes sure his audience is sitting at full attention, pours himself a wee dram of single malt, and tells the story of how he made an eagle against Faldo's birdie on the last at Gleneagles. It happened in the pro-am before the Scottish Open. On such occasions, it can rarely be said that the great Faldo — I describe him in this way without a breath of sarcasm because he is undoubtedly one of the most phenomenal sportsmen these islands have ever produced — is the bubbling life of the group. He doesn't naturally reach out to touch his admirers. A few years ago, it seemed he hadn't considered for a flickering moment Walter Hagen's declaration that all professional golfers should take time to smell the flowers. Now Faldo seems a little hurt when the world steps back from him in memory of those days when he was so fiercely committed, when he lived, utterly alone, in the tunnel of competition. It brought him the greatest haul of major trophy wins for any Briton, and back then when I had my moment of glory he was at his most intense.

You understand that a pro-am can be something of an ordeal for the professional. He is going about his work, re-acquainting himself with the course and trying to get into a groove — the Open was just a week away — and he is obliged to be at least reasonably civil to the amateurs who are often hacking away in his company. That was one duty Faldo never embraced.

A complication this day was that one of our number, an Irish sportswriter, was having a nightmare round. At one point I said to Faldo's famous coach, David Leadbetter, 'Never mind your man, what are you going to do for this guy?' While Faldo glowered, Leadbetter amiably gave the Irishman some basic pointers as we waited to drive. After Faldo, the other member of the group and I drove off, the Irishman stepped up to the tee. There was a small bush nearby. Unfortunately, the embattled sportswriter duck-hooked straight into the bush. Leadbeater attempted to cut the embarrassment by saying, 'Yes, but he did it with style.'

As far as Faldo was concerned, this was all happening on another, lesser planet. Not a peep was heard from him all the way to the 18th tee. There were no murmurs of 'good shot' or 'hard luck' or any other hint that he was aware of our presence. I had driven decently but my second shot had drifted into a little rough, not too far from the green. I was quite confident I would make the green for a birdie chance on the par-five hole. A big stand overlooking the last green was occupied by quite a number of spectators. It was wonderful to hear a smattering of applause as my ball rolled on to the putting surface and towards the flag — and then a roar as it went into the hole. Of all my golf days, that was my truest Walter Mitty moment. Naturally, I waved to the crowd when I fished my ball out of the hole. Faldo solemnly made a birdie.

A little later someone came into the clubhouse bar and asked what the cheering and roaring had been about. 'Ian St John made an eagle,' he was told, and Faldo broke his silence with more than a mutter.

'Yes,' he said, 'and he's a lucky bastard.'

I could only imagine what my old Motherwell team-mate Alex Bain would have given for such a moment. Like quite a number of the team, Alex had been drawn to the game when, after a good run of form, the club rewarded us with a trip to Turnberry. None of the boys had clubs but we hired some and I have an old picture of us charging on to the fairways of the great, wind-blown course, dragging our trolleys behind us. Alex, a striker, was the most affected. When the play had moved into our half he could often be seen practising his golf swing. Once I saw him doing it in the centre circle, oblivious of the course of the game. He had been captured by golf.

Bill Shankly, anti-golfist, would have been appalled had he known any of this when he signed Bain for Huddersfield. He said the game should be ignored for various reasons, not least that it made your legs tired. It was because of this that I avoided golf when the Scottish managers Andy Beattie and Ian McColl allowed the team to play a round on the Fridays before inter- nationals in Northern Ireland and Wales. When my playing days were over, I took special pleasure in playing the great courses in Porthcawl and County Down.

When we moved back to Liverpool at the start of my television career, both Betsy and I began to play as often as we could. We joined Lee Park, a Jewish club, which had a fine course. Betsy did particularly well, getting her handicap down to seven. That is good golf for a man or a woman and her enthusiasm and talent for the game is another valuable bond between us. Over the years, we have managed to play in most parts of the world. They say that the family who prays together, stays together, and in our case it has also proved true of playing golf – well, at least, most of the time. The exception that almost broke the rule was when we followed a suggestion of Ronnie Corbett's that we should spend some time at the new Tunisian golf resort of El Cantoui. The hotel sparkled beside a marina and the course was well laid out but now, when I sometimes see an advert for El Cantoui in a golf magazine, I cannot stop myself shuddering.

On the way from the airport the driver fell asleep and crashed off the road and into the trees. I threw myself across Betsy. Somehow, in the dark, we managed to get the minibus back on to the road. Ronnie had called ahead to ensure a warm welcome from the resort manager and his staff but they had to greet some surly guests. In the crash Betsy had lost the bag that contained all our money and credit cards. Within twenty-four hours she was struck down with a stomach bug. Then, when I eventually went on the course, a ball narrowly missed my head as I went to make a putt. The place had been invaded by French tourists who knew little of golf. It was a nightmare relieved only by the fact that eventually Betsy's bag, and its untouched contents, were recovered. No doubt El Cantoui has matured into an excellent golf resort – it had all the potential to do so. However, it was hard to express any enthusiasm when Ronnie Corbett, one of the most charming of men, brightly asked how much we had enjoyed our trip. My reply was as liverish as one of the script lines of his comedy partner Ronnie Barker.

That was a rare time when the magical healing properties of golf had gone missing. Another such occasion was when I again encountered Nick Faldo, this time in the company of Johnny Miller. The American had always impressed me as both a great player and a superb golf commentator, but on the course he was no less dour than Faldo. Jimmy Tarbuck and I were grouped with them in a BBC celebrity event at Turnberry. As we went on to the first tee, Jimmy and I were laughing – no doubt nervously as we prepared to play in the company of such great performers – and Miller was quick to complain.

'Too much laughing on the tee,' snapped the man who had walked away from professional golf the moment he felt he had passed his professional peak. Tarbuck, being Tarbuck, couldn't resist some kind of response.

'It's what happens when you have a sense of humour,' he said. The temperature dropped several degrees.

If it wasn't a great social occasion, playing alongside a man of the highest talent is still a superb memory. On a par-three hole I happened to have found the green while Miller was resting in a sand-trap. He said to me, 'You go for it, I've got the three,' and so he had. I went for the putt and missed. Miller tied the hole as if he was doing something no more challenging than folding a newspaper. It was a small flash of revelation of what it is to be in charge of your game, knowing absolutely what can be taken for granted.

Seve Ballesteros once had that, and it is one of the most painful developments in the game that I have come to love so much to see the level of suffering he appears to be enduring these days. No one played the game more thrillingly, and then it seemed that all of his wonderful facility disappeared. I cannot pass on any personal insights because I denied myself an opportunity to meet him one morning in the breakfast room of Royal Liverpool. Seve came in and sat at a nearby table, alone. All my instincts were to go over and say hello, express my admiration for him, but I resisted the urge.

I had done the same when I found myself in exactly the same situation with Pele, a football player whom I admired, like most of my breed, more than any other. This was in 1978 during the Argentina World Cup, when his playing days were passed and he had become a monument to all that was best in the game. I just wanted to say that I too had played football, and that no one had ever been a greater inspiration. In both cases I kept my thoughts and my admiration to myself. The great men were having a break from the constant attention that washed against them. I left them to their thoughts, their brief pockets of space.

I have one more scorecard of note, and sheer immodesty insists that I mention the details. The occasion was the victory I shared with Sir Sean Connery over Lee Trevino and Sandy Lyle at that Turnberry event. Normally, Connery and I would have partnered the professionals but the organisers announced that the format had been changed. Lyle was the agreeable lad who never seemed to lose his good nature despite the disappointments that followed his victories in the Open and the US Masters, and Trevino was everything I might have expected. He joked with Connery and me and the crowd. He talked about our game, made little suggestions.

In the evening, Betsy and I found ourselves on a table with Gareth Edwards, Jimmy Tarbuck – and Nick Faldo. For a while we talked about football and rugby and South Africa. Everything seemed to be going along amiably enough until Faldo interjected. He said, very baldly, 'Can't we change the subject?' The point was unmissable. It was time to talk about golf – and Nick Faldo.

Now I often read of Faldo's regrets that he didn't learn to relax at an earlier stage of his life. It is sad in a way. For all his brilliant success on the course, he has obviously paid a high price in failed marriages and periods when he was plainly not a happy man. Faldo made a pact with himself early in his life. He said he wanted to be a golf machine, he wanted to win the big prizes and nothing would ever get in the way of that. In human terms, that's a harsh deal to broker with yourself, although many have made it without gaining the results that made Faldo the most successful British golfer. He has to accept that being loved wasn't part of the contract.

Betsy and I made our deal, too. After the hard years at Portsmouth, we agreed that I wouldn't pursue success in football to the detriment of our life together and the attention we could pay our children. In some ways this was a sacrifice for me. Football had been the great passion for all those years, and I was young to say that I would no longer climb the greasy pole of football management. But if I had my yearnings, if sometimes I wondered if I should have persisted in the game, put into practice all my feelings about how football players should be handled and organised, I certainly had my compensations. Golf has not been the least of them.

The beauty of golf for various sportsmen who have operated at the highest level in fast tempo, contact sports, is that they can play with a fine competitive edge right down to the last of their physical resources. Golf doesn't have magic, it doesn't, as some people say, heal the mind. You cannot forget everything when you walk on to a golf course, your worries don't go away, but you can put them on one side for a few hours. You can enter another world and concentrate entirely on that old urge to win.

An ageing footballer cannot say, 'I played Hampden or High-bury, San Siro or Anfield the other day and I did rather well,' but when he takes up golf he can say he played St Andrews or Wentworth or Turnberry or Carnoustie. I played Carnoustie in a pro-celebrity event on the 150th anniversary of the wild and forbidding course. My partner was the American former PGA player, Gene Autry – he had the same name as the famous old Hollywood cowboy, and that day he must have felt as though he had wandered into the 'High Chaparral'. The wind blew so hard that if it had stopped suddenly, we would surely have fallen down. It was the most terrible ordeal on the most horrendous of Scottish days. Later, I was asked what I thought of Carnoustie. I said I didn't know, I never saw it. I could only see my feet as I buried my head in the wind. A few years later, though, I played it on a lovely sunlit day and it was an extraordinary pleasure, one strong enough to remind me of the line that a golf course can be as beautiful or as ugly as a woman, depending on her mood. On that first time I was tempted to tear up my card. It was almost impossible to make a score. Even the old pro Autry could hardly hit the ball. The wind came straight through you.

I've played golf in many parts of the world and had my triumphs and failures. Into the first category, I suppose, goes a tournament to which the European media were invited in Mendoza during the 1978 World Cup in Argentina. I was given some clubs and a partner, a young Argentine, and we played a nice course, decently. Afterwards, at dinner, the MC announced the prizes. He said the winner of the media section of the tournament was Ian St John of ITV. Naturally, I was quite pleased with myself and made a gracious victory speech. When I returned to the table I wanted to know from one of the tournament organisers how many of my peers I had beaten to the prize. He seemed reluctant to answer. Finally I prised it out of him. I was the only entrant from the media.

Four years later in the Spanish World Cup I played a beautifully green and mellow course in La Coruna – the favourite playground of the late Spanish dictator, General Franco.

In the second half of our lives, golf has been a recurring gift for Betsy and me. One of our best trips was to the Great Smoky Mountains in America. Then we went down to North Carolina, where the scenery was beautiful. You could throw your voice across empty, sunlit valleys. We were staying in a condo complex and in the evening looked forward to a glass of wine, only to be told that we had to drive to a little town thirty miles away to find a liquor store. We were sold our wine in brown bags, and on the journey home we laughingly speculated that we were becoming alcoholics. We gave ourselves reassuring answers and toasted our good luck on the terrace of the condo.

I still have a few golfing ambitions. Jimmy Tarbuck tells me I must play Dornoch in the Highlands before I'm through. He says the beauty of the course as it runs down to the sea is breathtaking. Tom Watson, the most brilliant American player of British links courses, has been up to Dornoch several times and he rates it among his favourites.

Some friends have contacts in America, who have enabled them to play at Augusta, and that too is a dream. I know the feeling I would have because I have had it before at so many other great courses. I have woken up on a sharp morning in St Andrews and gone down to the course that made Jack Nicklaus weep tears of joy and pride. Standing on the first tee, I have been reminded that I am privileged to be alive.

20
THE LOST AND FOUND

W HEN I made my compromise and elected to take at least one step back from the compulsion and pressure of being involved at the heart of football, I never surrendered an ounce of my feeling for the game that had given me so much. Indeed, I like to think that at a little distance I have been able to see a clearer picture of how it has been developing. At times, this has made me an angry witness.

Maybe inevitably, Liverpool Football Club have always been the touchstone of my analysis. The lowest point in my relationship with the club undoubtedly came in the days of Gerard Houllier and I have made clear my disgust at what he did to Anfield over his years in charge; how he squeezed away so much of its life and its meaning, and how, ultimately, he missed the whole point of it. It is also true that in the thirty-four years or so since I officially belonged to Liverpool, other ruptures have occurred.

My relationship with Bill Shankly gradually healed, partly because I developed a better understanding of the problems he faced when he had to break up his first Liverpool team. I suppose too much passion had gone into our relationship for any easy rapprochement after it first went wrong. There were, however, other points of dispute with my old club and one of the worst of them came at the time of the Heysel tragedy in 1985. Then, I fell out quite severely with the man who had had such an important role in the administration of Liverpool since the day poor, overwhelmed Jimmy McInnes took his own life in the shadow of the Kop – Peter Robinson, the chief executive. Our row had nothing to do with my reaction, as a working journalist, to the trouble in Brussels. I was very critical of the behaviour of some of the Liverpool fans, but that wasn't the issue that smouldered between Robinson and me – and burst into public in the wake of those desperate, shocking hours at the Heysel in 1985.

The trouble came from the fact that, as Liverpool approached their European Cup final with Juventus, strong rumours were circulating that Joe Fagan was about to follow Bob Paisley into retirement. Liverpool, it was widely believed, were looking for a new manager. The days before the final were busy ones for me. Before my Saturday stint with 'On the Ball' I had to attend the Manager of the Year awards in Glasgow, go to Iceland with the Scotland team and then get to Brussels for the final on the Wednesday night. In Glasgow, I saw the Anfield scout Tom Saunders and asked him if Fagan was indeed packing in as Liverpool manager.

'Between you and me,' said Tom, 'yes.' Tom was off the record, and I didn't turn the story in to ITV, nor did I think any more of it until after the final, which I covered for local radio.

It was a worrying scene in Brussels. On a hot day, the strong Belgian beer had clearly been having an effect on some of the Liverpool supporters. Drunken fans were everywhere. At the ground, I watched grimly the pushing and shoving, particularly in that part of the crowd where the Liverpool and Juventus fans were separated by a strip of wire fencing. You could see the horrible scenario unfolding as though in slow motion.

The fence came down and then there was a bit of a surge from the Liverpool fans. As it would be reported from Hillsborough four years later, I was telling the radio audience in Liverpool that the police appeared to be doing nothing. Eventually, mounted police appeared and then there was pushing against a wall that turned out to be rotten and finally, fatally, the collapse of the wall. Later, there was talk of Italians attacking Liverpool fans but I saw no evidence of that. They were being pushed against the wall by the Liverpool supporters. Clive Tyldesley was reporting, I was making some comments and a runner, a kid from the radio station, was coming back with progress reports. At one point I could see that he had tears in his eyes.

When the deadline work was done, and we all sat in the press bus shocked into a terrible numbness, Robinson walked in and said something that I will always consider quite extraordinary. Looking in my direction, he said, 'No thanks to some people that we've lost.' I leapt from my seat and demanded to know what he was talking about. He said he meant the rumours going around about the future of Joe Fagan. He suggested they had destabilised the team and that I was to blame. In all those dreadful circumstances, I was very much on edge, like everyone else, and when Robinson made his charge I had to be restrained from having a go at him.

For many years after that no words passed between us. We passed on the Anfield stairs and in the corridors. He didn't look at me. I didn't look at him. Then, just a few years ago, we again passed on the stairs and suddenly he turned and said, 'Will you accept my apology?' For a moment all of those angry feelings I had in the Brussels press bus welled up again, but then, just as quickly, they went away, and I said, 'Aye, I accept your apology.' In itself the episode was not so important, but it had helped to create a little more distance between me and the club I had served, and then cared about deeply for so long.

A lot of controversy surrounded my stance on the Heysel affair. On the following night's radio show many of the callers got stuck into me, and I replied strongly. I said I was there and I had seen what happened. I wasn't castigating all Liverpool fans. They were my people, they had supported me down the years, but no doubt some of them had misbehaved in Brussels. This wasn't a question of tribal loyalty, it was about facts and truth and we had to remember that a lot of people had died.

I wasn't at Hillsborough. I had worked my television shift and was taking the train home to Liverpool. Someone said that he had heard people had died. When I got into my car at Lime Street I turned on the radio and got all the gut-wrenching details. Everybody knows how the police fell down on the job, how they so absurdly, fatally, opened the gates and allowed the pressure to build so cruelly on the people at the front of the Leppings Lane end of the ground – and how scandalous it is that there has been no accountability, that no member of the South Yorkshire police force has stepped up to take ultimate responsibility. It is sickening that various home secretaries have slammed the file back shut without anything like an admission that those people who died in Sheffield lost their lives because of official incompetence.

None of this is to say that there wasn't any unruly behaviour by some Liverpool fans, but to over-emphasise that is to miss the main issue completely. If the people who were paid to look after the interests of the public, all the public, had done their jobs, properly, nobody need have died.

It was terrible that no one in the police held their hands up. I found that very hard to deal with. I drove over to the hospital on the Monday. Brian Clough and others from Forest were there at the same time as I was. I saw kids in comas, fighting for life. A year or so later I was tending my front garden when a car pulled up. Some young lads got out and asked me how I was doing. I said, 'Very well, boys, and what about you?' They said they had brought one of their friends to see me. He had been in the

Sheffield hospital that I had visited and he remembered the meeting very well. They were taking him to a game at Anfield. He had had tubes in his throat and various life supports for a long time, but he was making his way now, and this would be his first match since the disaster. It was good to see a survivor, but I couldn't help thinking of all those who hadn't made it.

Kenny Dalglish took a tremendous battering at the time of Hillsborough. He went to the funerals, he became a lightning rod of the grief and, inevitably, it took its toll. He saw a lot of suffering and it took his head out of football for a while and maybe it never came back, not fully. He had success both at Anfield, where he launched himself with the double, and at Blackurn, where he won the Premiership title before promptly kicking himself upstairs. Maybe, deep down, Hillsborough took away some of his appetite for the game. Maybe he couldn't dissociate himself and football from the pain that came that spring day.

The greatest benefit of Dalglish's appointment as player-manager after Joe Fagan's retirement was his retention as a player. He was so integral to the success of Liverpool under Paisley and Fagan that I just didn't think any other player out there at the time could have adequately replaced him. I admired him hugely as a player, but as a man I have to say he was hard to fathom.

There was a bit of tension in our relationship for reasons that I think went no deeper than the fact that Kenny kept a lot of himself back and, unlike Shankly, Paisley or Fagan, had to play everything very close to his chest. Once I was presiding over an ITV awards show and Kenny had won manager of the year. I made the small crack that while I wouldn't say Kenny was secretive, he wouldn't give you the team until five minutes past three. I was surprised that he took such umbrage at what was meant to be a lighthearted remark.

'Whenever I picked a team you wouldn't be in it,' he said. It seemed like a harsh piece of over-reaction, but I laughed it off.

'Well, that's okay, Kenny, my knee's not great at the moment,' I responded.

In fact, there was a little history to the flare-up. One Saturday, I was standing in the lobby at Stamford Bridge with Brian Moore. Brian was doing his notes for his match commentary and was anxious to know the Liverpool team. As the Liverpool party came in, I got hold of Roy Evans, who was then assistant manager, and asked him if Gary Gillespie was playing. Roy confirmed that he was. The next thing I knew, Roy was telling me, 'Saint, you got me into a load of trouble. Kenny went mad that I was giving the team before it was necessary.'

I understood easily enough when Kenny walked away from Anfield early in 1991. He left the team in excellent shape and in a good position to maintain their domination – they were top of the League and had just drawn 4–4 in the FA Cup at Goodison Park when he made his decision. The Anfield empire wasn't exactly crumbling. Hillsborough bit into him so deeply, it affected everything and you could feel only sympathy when he decided he had had enough of the pressures of the job.

Some Liverpool fans were very critical when he left and then, quite soon afterwards, was lured to Blackburn by the big money of Sir Jack Walker. I couldn't join in that criticism. It seemed to me that some of the fans hadn't quite grasped what he had gone through. It is also true that a football man can leave the game battered, even broken, and yet in a few months all his fears can be washed away. Kenny looked at Blackburn and saw great resources and a lot of reward – it has to be said that the appeal of money was never lost on him – and he no doubt said to himself, 'Hey, wait a minute, I have a bit of a chance here.' He went there and he did the job.

He signed quality players, as his Liverpool predecessors had, and with Alan Shearer leading his team there was always a guarantee of outstanding effort – and goals. His successors at Liverpool, Graeme Souness and, supremely, Houllier, might have profitably learned that lesson. Souness had been close to Dalglish and I was more than a little surprised when he came out with the view that his old team-mate and friend had left him with an old team. It was a team that was still plainly capable of winning, and Souness's challenge wasn't so daunting. He had resources and he could re-seed the team without any hint of panic, but Souness failed the Dalglish quality test. Souness is an intelligent man, he learned a lot in Italy, and I admired him hugely as a player but some of his signings left me dismayed. He took a diametrically opposite position to the one I would have adopted had I been lucky enough to inherit the ageing but still great Leeds United team.

My media work for Radio City in Liverpool and ITV in London meant that my opinion on the team's progress would be sought. I was in a position to question Souness's policy and I had to ask publicly, 'Why is he signing these guys?' They were simply not of the required standard. Torben Piechnik, a Danish centre-half, was terribly vulnerable to strength and pace. Souness picked up a Hungarian – Istvan Kozma – from Dunfermline for £300,000. He scarcely played. The breaking point, for me, was when Julian Dicks was signed. When he announced the move, Souness said, 'I'm looking for winners.' I had to ask how many medals Dicks had won and since when did being a hatchet man automatically equate with being a winner.

That mistake had not been made in all the years of Liverpool glory. Of course, Tommy Smith and no one more than Souness knew how to make their presence felt. They were relentlessly hard. Graeme was particularly cynical at times, making tackles that took your breath away because they threatened to wreck careers, but Souness was also a magnificently rounded footballer. He could play the game at the highest level with power, skill and imagination. What Souness was bringing in now, it seemed to me, was football of a much lower order. Neil 'Razor' Ruddock was another recruit who offended my idea of what a Liverpool player should be. No doubt Ruddock would go flying into the tackles, just as Dicks was happy to clatter someone over the touchline, but championship football demanded more than that.

Souness should have been upgrading the team in a gradual, measured way, but instead he swept through Anfield. He changed the training pattern quite profoundly and he didn't seem to grasp that he was ransacking a winning formula, one that had been in place for thirty years. When I said so, he didn't like it, and what I thought was a good personal relationship was put into the deep freeze. This was before his ultimately killing folly of selling his personal story to the *Sun*, the most reviled newspaper on Merseyside after its coverage of the Hillsborough disaster. When he suffered a heart-attack that required surgery, he should have had just one clear course of action. He should have told the club and dealt with the problem privately. He was wealthy and it was hard to imagine he had any pressing need to sell his story to the *Sun* so soon after the Hillsborough tragedy. It meant that he was dead as far as the Liverpool football public were concerned,

The perilous reign of Roy Evans, before his brief, misbegotten partnership with Gerard Houllier, was an attempt to return Liverpool to their old, solid foundations. Dalglish's style had been different but he hadn't stepped away from the principle of continuity, of methods and values that created the great tradition. Souness did. Souness wanted revolution rather than the seamless evolution that had served the club so well, and when

Evans, a kind, decent man, took up office, he faced a massive rebuilding operation.

Roy first came to Anfield filled with ambition. He had played for England Schoolboys at full-back and had a lovely left foot, but Shankly soon recognised a critical deficiency – he had no pace. Roy spent almost all his time in the reserves. He could have earned a living in the lower divisions but when he reached the point when it was clear he wasn't going to progress beyond the Liverpool second team, Shankly, who was very fond of him, said, 'Look, Roy, I can let you go to Bury or Stockport, but why don't you pack it in as a player and work on the training staff?' In the Boot Room, Roy was a gentle but knowing voice, and although the club turned to Ronnie Moran, briefly, as stand-in manager when Dalglish left, the quieter, more reflective style of Evans was more attractive to the directors when they came to replace Souness.

Roy Evans inherited a team that just wasn't good enough and had a few problem players, but when he comes to look at his downfall, he can hardly avoid the harsh conclusion that no one did more to damage his chances than himself. He wrecked his managership when he paid £7 million for Stan Collymore.

Collymore had sensational talent and a genius for destruction, his own and the team around him. For all the disasters of Collymore's career and life, the explanation was that he suffered from depression. Well, I'm not a medical expert and I wouldn't presume to pass judgement on Collymore's mental health. Evans was not an expert in such matters, either. What was clear, though – and Evans didn't act upon it quickly enough – was that Collymore, for whatever reason, was sheer poison to the manager's attempt to build a new team spirit at Anfield. Even Roy Evans knew it was hopeless, however, when he asked Collymore to take a run out in the reserves after injury.

Collymore refused, got into his car and drove home to Staffordshire.

The problem of the Spice Boys was another that Evans had to face. Reports came in that some of the younger players, including Robbie Fowler, Steve McManaman and Jamie Redknapp, were putting at least as much into their social lives as their football. Plainly the team needed sorting out and some of the old values restoring. That was underlined when they appeared at Wembley in white suits, looking rather like a bunch of ice-cream salesmen, and strolled around the field before the match with mobile phones pinned to their ears. It simply wasn't the Liverpool way.

The terrible compromise reached by the Liverpool board was of no help. Instead of taking the honest course, saying that much as they respected Evans, the club needed new leadership, new direction, they brought in Gerard Houllier as joint manager with Evans. Whatever you thought of the Frenchman – and my view of him became more negative with every season he was in charge – you knew that the idea of sharing control of a football team was absurd. It simply couldn't work. Players need one voice, one leader, one man making decisions about their futures. Roy Evans was finally convinced of this during the build-up to a game with Spurs at White Hart Lane. Houllier said that he wanted to drop Michael Owen – in his view, the young player was showing signs of tiredness. Evans said that he couldn't agree and if Owen was dropped, it would be against his better judgement. Houllier won the day, Owen was left out and Liverpool lost.

One of my initial reservations about Houllier was that he took a job that wasn't feasible and, I believe, on the understanding that when it became obvious to everyone it wouldn't work, he would stay and Evans would go. I come from a background where you don't take another man's job and it's never a case of first in, first out. To my mind, Houllier had only one honourable option when he was offered the job on the original terms and that was to say, no, this is not possible – you sort it out, create a genuine vacancy, and then I will consider the possibilities.

When the experiment failed, there was only one position to take as a critic – both Evans and Houllier had to go. The Frenchman rode through the situation, however, and quickly identified me as his leading accuser among the old Liverpool players. He ridiculed my managerial record without knowing any of the background. He talked about my stint at Portsmouth as though the two challenges, his at Anfield, mine at Portsmouth, could be reasonably compared. He spent around £120 million – I spent £5,000. None of this would have mattered to me if I'd seen any value in Houllier's work, or any progress in the team. Instead, I saw them slipping away from the old Liverpool principles of balanced, attacking football built on a sound defence, a real integration of the two basic elements of any team.

Houllier bought time – a lot of time – with three trophies in 2000–01, the League Cup, the FA Cup and the Uefa Cup, but I wasn't convinced by that surge of success, and I don't think any serious judge of the game could have been. He left Michael Owen, the most effective striker in the country, out of the League Cup final against Birmingham City, a team from a lower league but a better team on the day – and won on penalties. A few months later Owen won the FA Cup for Liverpool with a couple of flashes of scoring brilliance, after Arsenal had utterly dominated the game. The Uefa Cup win over the Spanish team Alave was exciting, but it represented a travesty of defence at that level of the game.

The first player Houllier signed was Jean-Michel Ferri, a young French player of such mediocrity he played a few games and then disappeared. I was told that his chief value to the manager was the eyes and ears he provided in the dressing room. As I said at the time, it might have been cheaper to hire the services of the Pinkerton detective agency. Soon Houllier was pronouncing the need to destroy the Spice Boy image, and then asked the Liverpool public a question that was deeply insulting to all those who helped lay down the Liverpool tradition. He said, 'Do you want to go back to the drink culture of the sixties?' Did they want to go back to the roaring passion – and the roaring football – of Bill Shankly? If they had such an option, you had to believe they might just have taken it.

Houllier's strategy of tightening up the defence would have been a laudable ambition if it had been coupled with genuine development of the team's play – but it wasn't. He tightened defence at a terrible cost, turning Liverpool's midfield into a wasteland. He took away all the traditional craft. Owen and Robbie Fowler, two great striking talents, were obliged to live on scraps. There is no easier task in football than tightening defence at the cost of all other aspects of the team. You get bodies behind the ball. You play in a tight band across the middle of the field. You don't have shape or rhythm. You don't break out of defence, building quickly to strike at the heart of the opposition.

Liverpool always had width and penetration and then, suddenly, it was gone. The one great chance of sustained creativity, provided by one of the best players in Europe, ended when Houllier decided to sell Jari Litmanen. Houllier was apparently upset when he heard that the Finnish star, who amazingly couldn't command a first-team place, had been trying to bring a little sophistication to the game of Emile Heskey.

As an example of waste, the treatment of Litmanen was rivalled only by that meted out to Fowler. Undoubtedly, Fowler had a bit of Liverpool 'scally' in him, but some encouragement from Houllier, an occasional arm around the shoulder, would almost certainly have done much to bring out more of the boy's superb natural talent. I was standing in the foyer at Anfield one day before a match when Fowler was handing tickets to friends. Houllier came to the entrance of the corridor leading down to the dressing rooms and bellowed, 'Robbie . . . Robbie . . . it's two'clock,' then marched off, every inch the schoolmaster he once was. Fowler no doubt felt like a schoolboy who had just been ticked off. He walked off to the dressing room, head down and not looking anyone in the eye.

Fowler didn't need the schoolteacher's approach. He needed Houllier, or his assistant manager Phil Thompson, to take hold of him and say, 'Look, son, you have enormous talent, you have a great future. Maybe you're running with the wrong crowd. Maybe you have to take a bit more time over your game.' They could have done it so as not to drive the boy into a corner – Thompson, as a former captain of the club, was ideally placed but maybe that would have involved taking too much power and influence away from the headmaster's study.

Michael Owen, who threatened to break every scoring record at Anfield, is another story of Houllier waste. As the Houllier years wore on, Owen's chances were getting fewer and fewer simply because of the decline in the team's approach play. As he proved at Real Madrid with limited opportunities Owen will always score, although it is also true that a serious hamstring injury did take away a vital edge.

Houllier stockpiled mediocrity. He paid £11 million for Heskey, who was never worth that kind of money. It was amusing, in a sour sort of way, when, after a brief outburst of scoring from the big lad, Houllier revealed that he had been giving him special coaching. When the goals dried up again, I had to wonder what had happened to the special coaching.

The stream of poor signings was relentless. El-Hadji Diouf

looked good in the World Cup of 2002, but how much time did Houllier spending assessing his character and the place he would occupy in the team? However long he spent on that, it was a disaster. Eirik Meijer played a few games and disappeared. Vladimir Smicer? He flies so high in the tackle he could have been a high-jump champion. Bernard Diomede? That French-man played two games for Liverpool in three seasons. Titi Camara was said to be a star signing but he disappeared after a few rave reports.

Eventually, with the team 30 points adrift of the leaders of the Premiership at the end of the 2003–04 season, Liverpool found the nerve to fire Houllier. It was the day of liberation for the football tradition of my old club, and quite how profoundly that would be so with the appointment of Rafael Benitez we could not know until the European Cup was lifted in Istanbul in his first spring as a successor to Bill Shankly.

Benitez was the first to say that there was much work still to do, but he had already given his passionate audience – and an old player – a great gift. He had awoken an old love, an old optimism, for the team who had been lost – and then was found.

EPILOGUE

I CANNOT apologise for my dismay at the forces of greed that are so rampant in football today, or for my fears that the influence of such avarice, and its companion urge to cheat at every level, is eating away at the foundations of the world's most popular game.

An honest account has to flow from your instincts and your experience. When I read that Manchester United's Rio Ferdinand, after an indifferent season, was demanding £120,000 a week, I could only recall all the failed attempts of my own generation of players to win earnings just a little more in line with the mass appeal of their work. I thought, too, of the story Jimmy Greaves once told me of his brilliant Tottenham team-mate Cliff Jones, a winger of such pace and skill his value in the world football market today would be astronomical.

Jones came home from a tour of South America with Wales bathed in rave notices. In a time of great players including the Brazilian Garrincha and the Spaniard Gento, one headline had proclaimed 'Jones − the best winger in the world'. When Jones considered such acclaim, it gnawed at him that he was earning less than his team-mates Greaves, Dave Mackay and Danny Blanchflower, and that the disparity might be as huge as £10 a week. He voiced his dissatisfaction over a few drinks with his team-mates in the pub they frequented just around the corner from White Hart Lane. Naturally, they egged him on. 'Go in there and tell the manager how you feel,' they urged. 'You're right — you *are* the best winger in the world, so be a man — demand your rights.'

They rehearsed Jones. They took up the arguments that the manager Bill Nicholson would adopt. They gave their team-mate the counter-argument. Finally, Jones agreed that it was the moment to act. He went to Nicholson's office to make his case. Nicholson looked up from his desk and said, 'Yes?' Cliff said he should be on the same wages as the rest of the top players at the club because 'I'm the best winger in the world.'

'That's your opinion,' Nicholson said. 'Shut the door on your way out.'

That was Jones's story, but it could have come from any of his generation. Johnny Haynes was the first £100-a-week player, but he never had freedom. When the Italians wanted him, as they had Sir Tom Finney, they were turned down and Haynes, no more than Finney, did not have a say. It is history now and bitterness cannot be cultivated over the years. It doesn't do anybody any good. Still, you can sound a warning when you see that the values of the game have never been under greater siege.

I can also report from ground level. I can say that in twenty-five years of running a football school I cannot but notice the dwindling of natural talent. There are still diamonds to polish, a Wayne Rooney can still emerge, but the circumstances surrounding such a prodigy have never been more hostile to a sure march to greatness. Maybe you have to draw comfort and encouragement where you can. Maybe you have to dwell on the triumph of a Jamie Carragher, and note that the achievements of such a modest young man cry out in support of some of the values of the past.

For someone like me, it was a case of the best of days and the worst of terms. You have to take what is delivered and, as I hope I have made clear, there is never a day when I don't count the blessings of my life and the strength of my memories. I celebrate my wife and family and all the good men, in and out of football, who have enhanced my days. Even now, I cannot leave without one last image of the man who stood so high among them all.

Bill Shankly came along to a session of my football school long after he had detached himself from his Anfield fortress. Ronnie Yeats and I were organising a session of penalty kicks. Shankly loved nothing more than taking a penalty. A nine-year-old was keeping goal. Shankly tore in and blasted home his kick. If it had hit the boy on the head, it could have decapitated him. Shankly glowed and said to the youngster, 'Don't worry, son, Ray Clemence wouldn't have stopped that.'

By then, Bill Shankly was an old and rather saddened man but something inside him still blazed. Like Liverpool Football Club, I guess I still feel the benefit.

INDEX